Memoirs of Rear-Admiral

PAUL JONES

A Da Capo Press Reprint Series

THE ERA OF THE AMERICAN REVOLUTION

GENERAL EDITOR: LEONARD W. LEVY
Claremont Graduate School

Memoirs of Rear-Admiral PAUL JONES

Compiled from His Original Journals and Correspondence.

Two Volumes in One

DA CAPO PRESS · NEW YORK · 1972

Library of Congress Cataloging in Publication Data
Jones, John Paul, 1747-1792.
Memoirs of Rear-Admiral Paul Jones.
(The Era of the American Revolution)
Reprint of the 1830 ed.
1. U. S.–History–Revolution–Naval operations.
E207.J7A3 1972 973.35'0924 [B] 77-166333
ISBN 0-306-70247-9

A Da Capo Press Reprint Edition

This Da Capo Press edition of the
Memoirs of Rear-Admiral Paul Jones
is an unabridged republication in
one volume of the two-volume first
edition published in Edinburgh and
London in 1830.

Library of Congress Catalog Card Number 77-166333

ISBN 0-306-70247-9
Published by Da Capo Press, Inc.
A Subsidiary of Plenum Publishing Corporation
227 West 17th Street, New York, New York 10011

Manufactured in the United States of America

MEMOIRS

OF

REAR-ADMIRAL PAUL JONES.

C. J. Notte, pinx.

PAUL JONES.

Printed for R. Wilkinson, at No. 58 Cornhill.

MEMOIRS

OF

REAR-ADMIRAL PAUL JONES,

CHEVALIER OF THE MILITARY ORDER OF MERIT, AND OF THE RUSSIAN ORDER OF ST ANNE, &c. &c.

NOW FIRST COMPILED FROM HIS ORIGINAL JOURNALS AND CORRESPONDENCE: INCLUDING AN ACCOUNT OF HIS SERVICES UNDER PRINCE POTEMKIN, PREPARED FOR PUBLICATION BY HIMSELF.

VOL. I.

PUBLISHED BY OLIVER & BOYD, EDINBURGH;
AND SIMPKIN & MARSHALL, LONDON.

MDCCCXXX.

PREFACE.

SEVERAL years since a work purporting to be a "Life of Paul Jones" appeared in America, compiled by Mr Sherburne, Register of the Navy of the United States. An abridgment of the same work was reprinted in London by Mr Murray. The Life of Paul Jones still, however, remained to be written, for this good reason, that Mr Sherburne possessed no adequate materials for his work. The official correspondence of Paul Jones, while in the service of the United States, a few fragments of papers left by him in America, and discovered in a baker's shop of New York, and his letters to Mr Jefferson, though all probably quite authentic, afford but scanty materials for the memoirs of a life so varied and full of adventure as was that of Paul Jones.

While Mr Sherburne was arranging these memoirs, the really private papers of their subject remained in the custody of his relatives in Dumfries. Mr Sherburne, and other individuals, aware of their existence, endeavoured to obtain these documents, but were refused, as there was a view to the present publication.

The history of the private papers on which Mr Sherburne rests his narrative is briefly this :—When at the end of the war, in 1783, Paul Jones was appointed by Congress agent for prize-money in Europe, he deposited, among other effects, certain account-books, log-books, and copies of letters, in the custody of his friend, Mr Ross of Philadelphia. His private correspondence, and whatever he thought most interesting, he brought with him to France. On his death, his sisters in Scotland, who were his heirs, removed those books and papers left in America, from Mr Ross to the custody of Mr Robert Hyslop, merchant, New York. This gentleman died soon afterwards of the yellow-fever, and the papers left in America by Paul Jones were transferred to the custody of Mr John Hyslop, baker, the cousin and executor of Mr Robert Hyslop. There they remained, the heirs of Paul Jones not thinking it worth while to reclaim them. Mr John Hyslop, baker, also died, and left his affairs in great disorder; and soon after, or probably before his death, it was mentioned in a New York paper, that a letter "of that distinguished hero, Paul Jones," had been discovered in a baker's shop in the city. This led to inquiry, and Mr Ward obtained the wreck of these loose papers, which have been scattered far and wide; one original log-book, that of the Ranger, being now in the possession of a gentleman in Greenock, while that of the Bon Homme Richard belongs to Mr George Napier, advocate in this city. The circumstances under which those fragments were obtained by Mr Ward obviates all charge of impropriety on the part of that gentleman. By Mr Ward they were sold, or given, to Mr Sherburne; and on such slender and mutilated materials, of which he has perhaps made the most that was possible, together with the letters filed in the public offices, that writer has raised the structure entitled "The Life of Paul Jones."

The papers from which the present work is compiled may now be enumerated:—it is, however, in the first place, worthy of notice, that though Paul Jones acted a prominent part in the American war, a very small portion of his public life was spent in America. His field of enterprise was Europe. Though he had made two visits to the United States between the years

1780 and 1792, when he died in Paris, he spent but a short time in America, and that in comparative inactivity.

By his will, dated at Paris on the day of his death, Paul Jones left his property and effects of all kinds to his sisters in Scotland and their children. Immediately on his decease a regular, or rather an official inventory was made of his voluminous papers, which were sealed up with his other effects, till brought to Scotland by his eldest sister, Mrs Taylor, a few months after his death. They have ever since remained in the custody of his family; and are now, by inheritance, become the property of his niece, Miss Taylor of Dumfries. They consist of several bound folio volumes of letters and documents, which are officially authenticated, so far as they are public papers; numerous scrolls and copies of letters; and many private communications, originating in his widely-diffused correspondence in France, Holland, America, and other quarters. There is, in addition to these, a collection of writings of the miscellaneous kind likely to be accumulated by a man of active habits, who had for many years mingled both in the political and fashionable circles, wherever he chanced to be thrown.

The Journal of the Campaign of 1788 against the Turks, forms of itself a thick MS. bound volume. This Journal was drawn up by Paul Jones for the perusal of the Empress Catharine II.; and was intended for publication if the Russian government failed to do him justice. He felt that it totally failed; but death anticipated his long-contemplated purpose. To this Journal, Mr Eton, in his Survey of the Turkish Empire, refers, as having been seen by him. It was, however, only the official report, transmitted by Paul Jones to the Admiralty of the Black Sea, that this gentleman could have seen. This singular narrative, which so confidently gives the lie to all the Russian statements of that momentous campaign, is written in French. In the following work the language of the original is as closely adhered to as is admissible even in the most literal translation. Several passages have been omitted, and others curtailed, as they refer merely to technical details, which might have unduly swelled this work, without adding much to its interest. Much of the voluminous official correspondence which passed between Paul Jones and the other commanders during the campaign is also omitted. These *pièces justificatives* were only intended to corroborate, or elucidate, the narrative; they are, save in a few instances which are cited, not particularly interesting.

Besides the above papers and documents, the Editor has been furnished with the letters written by Paul Jones to his relations in Scotland, from the time that he was a ship-boy at Whitehaven till he died an Admiral in the Russian service, and the wearer of several Orders. From these materials an attempt has been made to exhibit, for the first time, the real character of this remarkable and distinguished individual, fairly, but liberally,—keeping clear of Trans-atlantic hyperbole and exaggeration on the one hand, and of English prejudice and misrepresentation on the other. Of each of these, the reputation, and true character of Paul Jones, have long been the alternate sport or victim.

MEMOIRS OF PAUL JONES.

CHAPTER I.

JOHN PAUL JONES was born on the 6th of July, 1747, at Arbigland, in the parish of Kirkbean, and stewartry of Kirkcudbright, in Scotland.

The family of the Pauls was originally from Fife; but the grandfather of John Paul,—the name of Jones being long afterwards assumed,—kept a public, or, as it was then called, a mail-garden in Leith, on a spot long since covered with buildings. His son, the father of John Paul Jones, followed the same profession; and, on finishing his apprenticeship, entered into the employment of Mr Craik of Arbigland, in which he remained till his death, in 1767.

A gardener at that period was understood to

be a person of better education than a common operative mechanic in ordinary handicrafts. The father of Paul Jones must have been a man both of intelligence and worth. The garden of Arbigland was laid out by him; and he planted the trees that now embellish the mansion. The period of his service, and the interest which his employer took in his orphan family, establish the general worth and respectability of his character.

Shortly after entering into the employment of Mr Craik, John Paul married Jean Macduff, the daughter of a small farmer in the neighbouring parish of New-Abbey. The Macduffs were a respectable rural race in their own district; and some of them had been small landed proprietors in the parish of Kirkbean, for an immemorial period. Of this marriage there were seven children, of whom John—afterwards known as John Paul Jones—was the fifth: he may indeed be called the youngest, as two children born after him died in infancy.* The first-born of the family, Wil-

---

* Among the many calumnies by which the memory of Admiral Paul Jones has been loaded, and the nume-

liam Paul, went abroad early in life, and finally settled and married in Fredericksburgh, in Virginia. He appears to have been a man of enterprise and judgment. Beyond his early education and virtuous habits he could have derived no advantage from his family; and, in 1772 or 1773, when he died, still a young man, he left a considerable fortune. Of the daughters, the eldest, Elizabeth, died unmarried,—Janet, the second, married Mr Taylor, a watchmaker in Dumfries,—and the third, Mary Ann, was twice married, first to a Mr Young, and afterwards to Mr Louden. Of the relations of Admiral Jones, several nieces,

---

rous vulgar traditions that hang about his reputation, and conceal his genuine character, is an absurd story of his having been the son of either Mr Craik, his father's employer, of one of the Earls of Selkirk, or of some other great personage, name unknown; as if it were impossible that a man so distinguished by gallantry and enterprise, could be, in very deed, merely the fifth child of Mr John Paul the gardener. His correspondence in the farther progress of this narrative will sufficiently refute an obsolete slander which was perhaps scarcely worth notice.

and a grand-nephew, now in the United States, still survive.

The residence of his father, near the shores of the Solway, in one of the most beautiful points of the Frith, must have been favourable to the genius of one who was destined to play the part of John Paul Jones—to have,—

> " His march upon the mountain wave,
> " His home upon the deep."

In the traditions of his family, young Paul is described as launching, while a mere child, his mimic-ship, hoisting his flag, and issuing his mandates to his imaginary crew, with all the firmness and dignity of one born to lead and to command his fellows.

Among the numerous unfounded slanders and rumours of which this brave and misrepresented man has been the object, is the assertion, that he ran off to sea against the will of his relations. Even this transgression might have been atoned by his after life; but it was not committed. His inclination for the bold and hardy mode of life which he adopted, appears, as it often does in boyhood, to have been a strong passion, fostered by his childish pastimes, and encouraged by much that he saw and heard in his daily intercourse with ships and seamen. Man or boy, Paul Jones was not moulded in the stamp of character which shrinks from facing out what is once firmly resolved. A sailor's life was his decided choice; and at the age of twelve he was sent across the Solway by his relations, and bound apprentice to Mr Younger of Whitehaven. This gentleman, who was then a respectable merchant in the American trade, he found a kind and liberal master.

Though Paul Jones was thus early estranged from his family, and was afterwards prevented from much personal intercourse with them, this narrative will afford abundant evidence that, like almost every other young Scottish adventurer—to the national honour be it told—he continued a most affectionate son and brother, even when at the highest elevation of his fortune, giving constant proof, not merely of his readiness to minister to the comforts of his relations, but of his anxiety for the union, respectability, and prosperity of his sisters and their families.—To them he at last bequeathed the whole of his fortune.

The education which young Paul received at the parish-school of Kirkbean, must have terminated when he went to sea. His after acquirements—and they were considerable—were the fruits of private study, and of such casual opportunities as in boyhood he had the forethought and good sense to improve as often as his ship came into port. His first voyage was made to America, the country of his after adoption. He sailed in the Friendship of Whitehaven; and, before he was thirteen, landed on the shores of Rappahannock. While the Friendship remained in port, young Paul lived in the house of his brother William, and assiduously studied navigation and other branches of learning, either connected with his profession or of general utility.

In the course of a short time, his good conduct, intelligence, and knowledge of his profession, procured him the confidence and friendship of his master, who promised him his future protection and favour. From the subsequent embarrassment of his own affairs, Mr Younger was unable to fulfil this promise; but, in giving the young seaman up his indentures, he did all he could then perform. Thus honourably released from his early engagements, Paul Jones, while still a mere boy, obtained the appointment of third mate of the King George of Whitehaven, a vessel engaged in the slave-trade. From this ship he went about the year 1766, being now nineteen years of age, into the brigantine Two Friends, of Kingston, Jamaica, as chief mate. This ship was engaged in the same nefarious traffic. It is stated by his relatives, the only source of information on the early period of his life that is either accessible or to be relied on, that he quitted this abominable trade in disgust at its enormities; and, in consequence of abandoning it, returned to Scotland in 1768, as a passenger in the brigantine John of Kirkcudbright, Captain Macadam, commander. On this voyage the captain and mate both died of fever; and there being no one on board so capable of navigating the ship, Paul assumed the command, and brought her safe into port. For this well-timed piece of service he was appointed by the owners, Currie, Beck, & Co., master and supercargo. This was almost the last time that young Paul had an opportunity of seeing his relations. He only met them once again, about the middle of the year 1771.

While Paul Jones was on board this vessel, a circumstance occurred which afterwards, in times of violent prejudice and party-feeling, was eagerly laid hold of to traduce and blacken his character, and to represent him as a cruel and lawless brigand, eager for plunder and thirsting for blood,* guilty of a thousand enormities, though of what precise kind no one could specify. It was confidently stated—and is still indeed very generally believed—that while in the command of the John he punished a man named Mungo Maxwell, the carpenter of that vessel, so severely, that he died in consequence of the stripes he received. The

* It is not a little remarkable, that many of his own intelligent countrymen do to this day know of Paul Jones only as a wild reckless adventurer, a sort of modern buccaneer, possessed of no redeeming quality save great personal courage and intrepidity,—or as the subject of vulgar ballads and marvellous legends, daring impossible and acting horrible deeds, among which was the one above alluded to.

affidavits* given below clearly refute this calumny, which probably originated among those of his contemporaries who envied the place and influ-

---

"*Tobago.*

* "Before the Honourable Lieutenant-Governor, William Young, Esq. of the island aforesaid, personally appeared James Simpson, Esq. who, being duly sworn upon the Holy Evangelists of Almighty God, deposeth and saith, That some time about the beginning of May, in the year of our Lord one thousand seven hundred and seventy, a person in the habit of a sailor came to this deponent (who was at that time Judge Surrogate of the Court of Vice-Admiralty for the island aforesaid) with a complaint against John Paul, (commander of a brigantine then lying in Rockley Bay of the said island,) for having beat the then complainant, (who belonged to the said John Paul's vessel,) at the same time showing this deponent his shoulders, which had thereon the marks of several stripes, but none that were either mortal or dangerous, to the best of this deponent's opinion and belief. And this deponent further saith, that he did summon the said John Paul before him, who, in his vindication, alleged that the said complainant had on all occasions proved very ill qualified for, as well as very negligent in, his duty; and also, that he was very lazy and inactive in the

ence his superior intelligence and energy had so early acquired for him. So tenacious of life is

---

execution of his (the said John Paul's) lawful commands, at the same time declaring his sorrow for having corrected the complainant. And this deponent further saith, that having dismissed the complaint as frivolous, the complainant, as this deponent believes, returned to his duty. And this deponent further saith, that he has since understood that the said complainant died afterwards on board of a different vessel, on her passage to some of the Leeward Islands, and that the said John Paul (as this deponent is informed) has been accused in Great Britain as the immediate author of the said complainant's death, by means of the said stripes herein before mentioned, which accusation this deponent, for the sake of justice and humanity, in the most solemn manner declares, and believes to be, in his judgment, without any just foundation, so far as relates to the stripes before mentioned, which this deponent very particularly examined. And further this deponent saith not.

"James Simpson.

"Sworn before me, this 30th day of
June, 1772, William Young."

"James Eastment, mariner, and late master of the

slander, however false and groundless, that twenty years afterwards, when Paul Jones was a rear-

---

Barcelona packet, maketh oath, and saith, That Mungo Maxwell, carpenter, formerly on board the John, Captain John Paul, master, came in good health on board his, this deponent's said vessel, then laying in Great Rockley Bay, in the island of Tobago, about the middle of the month of June, in the year one thousand seven hundred and seventy, in the capacity of a carpenter, aforesaid; that he acted as such in every respect in perfect health for some days after he came on board this deponent's said vessel, the Barcelona packet; after which he was taken ill of a fever and lowness of spirits, which continued for four or five days, when he died on board the said vessel, during her passage from Tobago to Antigua. And this deponent further saith, that he never heard the said Mungo Maxwell complain of having received any ill usage from the said Captain John Paul; but that he, this deponent, verily believes the said Mungo Maxwell's death was occasioned by a fever and lowness of spirits, as aforesaid, and not by or through any other cause or causes whatsoever.

"James Eastment.

"Sworn at the Mansion House, London,
this 30th of January, 1773, before me,
James Townsend, Mayor."

admiral in the Russian service, the same calumnious story was revived, though Maxwell the carpenter was then transformed into Jones's own nephew. This was done to injure him with the Empress Catherine, and when, instead of his ancient school-fellows of Kirkbean, or ship-mates of Kirkcudbright, his rivals were the Princes Potemkin and de Nassau.

One of the earliest letters of Jones now extant relates to this unfortunate affair, which was calculated to make a deep impression on a young and ingenuous mind, and gave much uneasiness and pain to him. The letter is addressed to his mother and sisters, and gives a better and fairer

---

"These do certify to whom it may concern, that the bearer, Captain John Paul, was two voyages master of a vessel called the John, in our employ in the West India trade, during which time he approved himself every way qualified both as a navigator and supercargo; but as our present firm is dissolved, the vessel was sold, and of course he is out of our employ, all accounts between him and the owners being amicably adjusted. Certified at Kirkcudbright this 1st April, 1771.

"Currie, Beck, & Co."

view of his youthful character than could be given by the most laboured panegyric of a biographer:—

"London, 24th September, 1772.

"My dear Mother and Sisters,

"I only arrived here last night from the Grenadas. I have had but poor health during the voyage; and my success in it not having equalled my first sanguine expectations, has added very much to the asperity of my misfortunes, and, I am well assured, was the cause of my loss of health. I am now, however, better, and I trust Providence will soon put me in a way to get bread, and (which is by far my greatest happiness) be serviceable to my poor but much-valued friends. I am able to give you no account of my future proceedings, as they depend upon circumstances which are not fully determined.

"I have enclosed you a copy of an affidavit made before Governor Young by the Judge of the Court of Vice-Admiralty of Tobago, by which you will see with how little reason my life has been thirsted after, and, which is much dearer to me, my honour, by maliciously loading my fair character with obloquy and vile aspersions. I believe there are few who are hard-hearted enough to think I have not long since given the world every satisfaction in my power, being conscious of my innocence before Heaven, who will one day judge even my judges. I staked my honour, life, and fortune for six long months on the verdict of a British jury, notwithstanding I was sensible of the general prejudices which ran against me; but, after all, none of my accusers had the courage to confront me. Yet I am willing to convince the world, if reason and facts will do it, that they have had no foundation for their harsh treatment. I mean to send Mr Craik a copy properly proved, as his nice feelings will not perhaps be otherways satisfied;* in the mean time, if you please, you may show him that enclosed. His ungracious conduct to me before I left Scotland I have not yet been able to get the better of. Every person of feeling must think meanly of adding to the load

* Mr Craik was perfectly convinced of his innocence, but they never either met or corresponded afterwards.

of the afflicted. It is true I bore it with seeming unconcern, but Heaven can witness for me that I suffered the more on that very account. But enough of this. And now a word or two in the family-way, and I have done."

* * * * * * *

As the employer and patron of his deceased father, young Paul naturally looked to Mr Craik for advice and countenance to himself, and for protection and kindness to his helpless female relatives. The following letter illustrates the true nature of his connexion with that gentleman, the fetters of whose cautious kindness do not appear to have sat very easily upon him. It also throws an incidental light on his energetic and self-depending character, even at this early period of his life :—

"St George's, Grenada, 5th Aug. 1770.

"Sir,

"Common report here says that my owners are going to finish their connexions in the West Indies as fast as possible. How far this is true I shall not pretend to judge; but should that really prove the case, you know the disadvantages I must of course labour under.

"These, however, would not have been so great had I been acquainted with the matter sooner, as in that case I believe I could have made interest with some gentlemen here to have been concerned with me in a large ship out of London; and as these gentlemen have estates in this and the adjacent islands, I should have been able to make two voyages every year, and always had a full ship out and home, &c. &c. &c.

* * * * * * *

"However, I by no means repine, as it is a maxim with me to do my best, and leave the rest to Providence. I shall take no step whatever without your knowledge and approbation.

"I have had several very severe fevers lately, which have reduced me a good deal, though I am now perfectly recovered.

"I must beg you to supply my mother should she want any thing, as I well know your readiness.

"I hope yourself and family enjoy health and happiness. I am, most sincerely,

"Sir, yours always,

"JOHN PAUL."

It has been alleged, that about this time young Paul was engaged in the contraband trade, then very generally practised among the self-named *fair-dealers* of the towns along both shores of the Solway. Without entering into the question of how far at that period the act of smuggling might otherwise affect a man's moral character or estimation in society, it is certain that Jones long afterwards decidedly and indignantly repelled this degrading charge, and that the first entry of goods from England to the Isle of Man, after that nest of smugglers and centre of the contraband trade had been annexed to the crown, stands in his name in the Custom-house books of Douglas.

Soon after this period Paul obtained command of the Betsy of London, a West India ship, and remained for a time in the islands engaged in commercial speculations, to which his subsequent letters refer. He appears to have left considerable funds in Tobago; and in 1773 we find him in Virginia arranging the affairs of his brother William, who had died intestate, and without leaving children. About this time he assumed the name of Jones.

The American Revolution, of the progress of which Paul Jones could not have been an indifferent spectator, found him living in deep retirement, unoccupied, and for the time in a state of great privation, occasioned by the dilatoriness or misconduct of his agents. At this time he had subsisted for twenty months on the sum of fifty pounds. It is to this period that Jones refers in his celebrated letter to the Countess of Selkirk, when he says, "Before this war began I had at the early time of life withdrawn from the sea-service, in favour of 'calm contemplation and poetic ease.' I have sacrificed not only my favourite scheme of life, but the softer affections of the heart, and my prospects of domestic happiness, and am ready to sacrifice my life also with cheerfulness, if that forfeiture could restore peace and good-will among mankind."

CHAPTER II.

But Jones, whatever he might think, was not of the temperament to which the cultivation of maize and tobacco—which in America about that period must have comprehended "the rural life in all its joy and elegance"—could long remain the favourite scheme. He was now twenty-eight—the very prime of active existence—full of talent and enterprise, ardent and ambitious, and quite of the mind in which he seems to have held through life, that though it might be shame to be on any side but one, it was greater shame to lie idle when blows were going. Many causes combined to make him believe the cause of the colonies the right one—the cause of liberty, justice, and humanity. A man who from the age of twelve had been a wanderer on the deep, must have been as much at home in America as in Britain. Both countries must have appeared integral portions of the same state; and in its civil dissensions, circumstances determined the part he should take. Thus right or wrong as to the side he took, Jones stood clear in his motives to his own conscience. To him indeed the cause of America—the country, as he afterwards terms it, of his "fond election"—was the elevating source of his most brilliant actions. It is but fair to allow him to be the interpreter of his own motives:—of his deeds every man is at liberty to judge. Four years after he had volunteered in the cause of America, it is thus he addresses the Baron Vander Capellan, having, it must be owned, a favourite object to carry at Amsterdam:—

"I was indeed born in Britain; but I do not inherit the degenerate spirit of that fallen nation, which I at once lament and despise. It is far beneath me to reply to their hireling invectives. They are strangers to the inward approbation that greatly animates and rewards the man who draws his sword only in support of the dignity of freedom. America has been the country of my fond election from the age of thirteen, when I first saw it. I had the honour to hoist with my own hands the flag of freedom, the first time it was displayed, on the Delaware; and I have attended it with veneration ever since on the ocean."

Though in the heat of a struggle, which, from its very nature, was, like the feuds of the nearest relatives, singularly rancorous and bitter, Jones was branded as a traitor and a felon, and after his most brilliant action, his capture of the Serapis, formally denounced by the British ambassador at the Hague as a rebel and a pirate according to the laws of war,* it must be remembered that he bore this stigma in common with the best and greatest of his contemporaries—with Franklin and Washington; which last had actually borne arms in the service of the King of England. The memory of Paul Jones now needs little vindication for this important step. After the peace he enjoyed the esteem and private friendship of Englishmen who might have forgiven the most imbittered political hostility, but never could have overlooked a taint on personal

* Memorial of Sir Joseph York to the States-General, dated the Hague, 8th October, 1779.

honour. Of this number was the Earl of Wemyss, who after the peace endeavoured to promote the views of Jones on various occasions. He himself, however, discovers a lurking consciousness of having incurred, if not of meriting, suspicion on this delicate ground. This is chiefly displayed by his eloquent though rather frequent assertions of purity of motive, superiority to objects of sordid interest, and disinterested zeal for the cause, now of America, now of human nature, as was best adapted to the supposed inclinations of his correspondents. In ordinary circumstances much of this might have appeared uncalled for; but the situation of Jones was in many respects peculiar both as a native-born Briton, and as a man of obscure origin, jealous—and pardonably so—of his independence and dignity of character. Somewhat of the heroic vaunting which marks other parts of his correspondence appears incident to the enthusiastic temperament of many great naval commanders. How would Nelson's tone of confident prediction, and boasts of prowess, have sounded from the lips of an inferior man?—In any other than himself the customary language of Drake would have been reckoned that of an insolent braggart.

Besides the public spirit and love of liberty which in Jones were both warm and sincere; other motives of that mixed nature, by which every human being, how disinterested and devoted soever, must at times be influenced, were not wanting to enlist him on the side of the colonies. He was living at the most active period of life in penury and neglect. His friendships, his interests, his gratitude, all inclined him to the part of America. In a letter addressed to Mr Stuart Mawey of Tobago, written immediately before he went to Europe in open hostility as an officer of the United States, a letter which does as much honour to the clearness of his head as to the integrity and filial kindness of his heart, these circumstances are distinctly explained.

"Boston, 4th May, 1777.

"Dear Sir,

"After an unprofitable suspense of twenty months, (having subsisted on *fifty pounds only* during that time,) when my hopes of relief were entirely cut off, and there remained no possibility of my receiving wherewithal to subsist upon from my effects in your island, or in England, I at last had recourse to strangers for that aid and comfort which was denied me by those friends whom I had intrusted with my all. The good offices which are rendered to persons in their extreme need, ought to make deep impressions on grateful minds; in my case I feel the truth of that sentiment, and am bound by gratitude, as well as honour, to follow the fortunes of my late benefactors.

"I have lately seen Mr Sicaton, (late manager on the estates of Arch. Stuart, Esq.) who informed me that Mr Ferguson had quitted Orange Valley, on being charged with the unjust application of the property of his employers. I have been, and am extremely concerned at this account; I wish to disbelieve it, although it seems too much of a piece with the unfair advantage which, *to all appearance*, he took of me, when he left me in exile for twenty months, a prey to melancholy and want, and withheld my property, without writing a word in excuse for his conduct.

Thus circumstanced, I have taken the liberty of sending you a letter of attorney by Captain Cleaveland, who undertakes to deliver it himself, as he goes for Tobago *via* Martinico. You have enclosed a copy of a list of debts acknowledged, which I received from Mr Ferguson when I saw you last at Orange Valley. You have also a list of debts contracted with me, together with Ferguson's receipt. And there remained a considerable property unsold, besides some best Madeira wine which he had shipped for London. By the state of accounts which I sent to England on my arrival on this continent, there was a balance due to me from the ship Betsy of £909, 15s. 3d. sterling; and in my account with Robert Young, Esq., 29th January, 1773, there appeared a balance in my favour of £281, 1s. 8d. sterling. These sums exceed my drafts and just debts together; so that, if I am fairly dealt with, I ought to receive a considerable remittance from that quarter. You will please to observe, that there were nine pieces of coarse camblets shipped at Cork, *over and above the quantity expressed in the bill of lading.* It seems the shippers, finding their mistake, applied for the goods; and, as I have been informed from Grenada, Mr Ferguson laid hold of this opportunity to propagate a report that all the goods which I put into his hands were the property of that house in Cork. If this base suggestion hath gained belief, it accounts for all the neglect which I have experienced. But however my connexions are changed, my principles as an honest man of candour and integrity are the same; therefore, should there not be a sufficiency of my property in England to answer my just debts, I declare that it is my first wish to make up such deficiency from my property in Tobago; and were even that also to fall short, I am ready and willing to make full and ample remittances from hence upon hearing from you the true state of my affairs. As I hope my dear mother is still alive, I must inform you that I wish my property in Tobago, or in England, after paying my just debts, to be applied for her support. Your own feelings, my dear sir, make it unnecessary for me to use arguments to prevail with you on this tender point. Any remittances which you may be enabled to make, through the hands of my good friend Captain John Plainer of Cork, will be faithfully put into her hands; she hath several orphan grandchildren to provide for. I have made no apology for giving you this trouble: My situation will, I trust, obtain your free pardon.

I am always, with perfect esteem,

Dear Sir,

Your very obliged, very obedient,

And most humble servant,

" J. PAUL JONES.

" STUART MAWEY, Esquire,
Tobago."

Among the friends whose fortunes Jones conceived himself bound to follow by gratitude as well as honour, was probably Mr Joseph Hewes of the Marine Committee of the infant Republic. Under the united influence of so many powerful motives he entered the American service.

Though Paul Jones had not received his maritime education in ships of war, he had frequently sailed in armed vessels, and had been early trained into an excellent practical seaman, completely realizing the merchant sailor's adage, "Aft the more honour—forward the better man." His nautical skill, as well as his boldness and capacity, were thus of incalculable value to the infant navy of America; and in 1775, when the combustibles of revolution, so long smouldering, burst into an open irrepressible flame, his services were as readily accepted as they were heartily tendered. From this date Paul Jones owned no country save America.

In organizing the maritime service of the young republic, three classes of lieutenants were appointed by Congress; and of the first class Jones was appointed senior lieutenant. The first commission he received from Congress bears date the 7th of December, 1775. He was appointed to the ALFRED, a name of good omen to an infant state sprung from England; and on board of that vessel, then lying before Philadelphia, he, in a few days afterwards, first hoisted that starry flag which he so bravely followed in many seas.

The American navy at this time consisted of only two ships, two brigantines, and one sloop. Even these it was not easy to officer with persons properly qualified. Thirteen frigates were, however, about the same time ordered to be built.

Of this first period of his service three different accounts, drawn up by himself, remain among the papers of Captain Jones,—one contained in a *refreshing* memorial addressed to Congress while he lay in the Texel, dated December, 1779,—another addressed to Robert Morris, the minister of the marine, in 1783, when Jones had just reason to think his former services neglected, if not forgotten,—and a third in a journal of his campaigns drawn up for the private information of the King of France, and read by that unfortunate prince while a close prisoner. This last document contains the following clear and succinct account of his early operations, written in the third person:—

"When Congress thought fit to equip a naval force towards the conclusion of the year 1775, '*for the defence of American liberty, and for repelling every hostile invasion thereof*,' it was a very difficult matter to find men fitly qualified for officers, and willing to embark in the ships and vessels that were then put into commission.

The American navy at first was no more than the ships Alfred and Columbus, the brigantines Andrew Doria, and Cabot, and the sloop Providence. A commander-in-chief of the fleet was appointed; and the Captains Saltonstall, Whipple, Biddle, and Hopkins, were named for the ships and brigantines. A captain's commission for the Providence, (bought, or to be bought, about the time, from Captain Whipple,) which Mr Joseph Hewes of the Marine Committee offered to his friend Mr John Paul Jones, was not accepted, because Mr Jones had never sailed in a sloop, and had then no idea of the declaration of independence that took place the next year. It was his early wish to do his best for the cause of America, which he considered as the cause of human nature. He could have no object of self-interest; and having then no prospect that the American navy would soon become an established service, that *rank* was the most acceptable to him by which he could be the most useful in that moment of public calamity. There were three classes of lieutenants appointed, and Mr Jones was appointed the first of the first-lieutenants, which placed him next in command to the four captains already mentioned. This commission is dated the 7th day of December, 1775, as first lieutenant of the Alfred. On board of that ship, before Philadelphia, Mr Jones hoisted the flag of America with his own hands, the first time it was ever displayed. All the commissions for the Alfred were dated before the commissions for the Columbus, &c. All the time this little squadron was fitting and manning, Mr Jones superintended the affairs of the Alfred; and as Captain Saltonstall did not appear at Philadelphia, the Commander-in-chief told Mr Jones he should command that ship. A day or two before the squadron sailed from Philadelphia, manned and fit for sea, Captain Saltonstall appeared, and took command of the Alfred. The object of the first expedition was against Lord Duncan in Virginia. But instead of proceeding immediately on that service, the squadron was hauled to the wharfs at Reedy Island, and lay there for six weeks frozen up. Here Mr Jones and the other lieutenants stood the deck, watch and watch, night and day, to prevent desertion; and they lost no man from the

Alfred. On the 17th of February, 1776, the squadron sailed from the Bay of Delaware. On the 1st of March the squadron anchored at Abaco, one of the Bahama Islands, and carried in there two sloops belonging to New Providence. Some persons on board the sloops, informed that a quantity of powder and warlike stores might be taken in the forts of New Providence. An expedition was determined on against that island. It was resolved to embark the marines on board the two sloops. They were to remain below deck until the sloops had anchored in the harbour close to the forts, and they were then to land and take possession. There was not a single soldier in the island to oppose them; therefore the plan would have succeeded, and not only the public stores might have been secured, but a considerable contribution might have been obtained as a ransom for the town and island, had not the whole squadron appeared off the harbour in the morning, instead of remaining out of sight till after the sloops had entered and the marines secured the forts. On the appearance of the squadron the signal of alarm was fired, so that it was impossible to think of crossing the bar. The Commander-in-chief proposed to go round the west end of the island, and endeavour to march the marines up and get behind the town; but this could never have been effected. The islanders would have had time to collect; there was no fit anchorage for the squadron, nor road from that part of the island to the town. Mr Jones finding by the Providence pilots that the squadron might anchor under a key three leagues to windward of the harbour, gave this account to the Commander-in-chief, who objecting to the dependence on the pilots, Mr Jones undertook to carry the Alfred safe in. He took the pilot with him to the foretopmast-head, from whence they could clearly see every danger, and the squadron anchored safe. The marines, with two vessels to cover their landing, were immediately sent in by the east passage. The Commander-in-chief promised to touch no private property. The inhabitants abandoned the forts, and the governor, finding he must surrender the island, embarked all the powder in two vessels, and sent them away in the night. This was foreseen, and might have been prevented, by sending the two brigantines to lie off the bar. The squadron entered the harbour of New Providence, and sailed from thence the 17th of March, having embarked the cannon, &c. that was found in the fort. In the night of the 9th of April, on the return of the squadron from the Providence expedition, the American arms by sea were first tried in the affair with the Glasgow off Block Island. Both the Alfred and Columbus mounted two batteries. The Alfred mounted 30, the Columbus 28 guns. The first battery was so near the water as to be fit for nothing except in a harbour or a very smooth sea. The sea was at the time perfectly smooth. Mr Jones was stationed below deck to command the Alfred's first battery, which was well served whenever the guns could be brought to bear on the enemy, as appears by the official letter of the Commander-in-chief giving an account of that action. Mr Jones therefore did his duty; and as he had no direction whatever, either of the general disposition of the squadron, or the sails and helm of the Alfred, he can stand charged with no part of the disgrace of that night. The squadron steered directly for New London, and entered that port two days after the action. Here General Washington lent the squadron 200 men, as was thought, for some enterprise. The squadron, however, stole quietly round to Rhode Island, and up the river to Providence. Here a court-martial was held for the trial of Captain Whipple, for not assisting in the action with the Glasgow. Another court-martial was held for the trial of Captain Hazard, who had been appointed captain of the sloop Providence at Philadelphia, some time after Mr Jones had refused that command. Captain Hazard was broke, and rendered incapable of serving in the navy. The next day, the 10th of May, 1776, Mr Jones was ordered by the Commander-in-chief to take command '*as captain of the Providence*.' This proves that Mr Jones did his duty on the Providence expedition. As the Commander-in-chief had in his hands no blank-commission, he had this appointment written on the back of the commission that Mr Jones had received at Philadelphia the 7th of December, 1775. Captain Jones had orders to receive on board the Providence the soldiers that had been borrowed from General Washington, and carry them to New York,—there enlist as many seamen as he could, and then return to New London, to take in from the hospital all the seamen that had been left there by the squadron, and were recovered, and carry them to Providence. Captain Jones soon performed these services; and having hove down the sloop and partly fitted her for war at Providence, he received orders from the Commander-in-chief, dated Rhode Island, June 10th, 1776, to come immediately down to take a sloop then in sight, armed for war, belonging to the enemy's navy. Captain Jones obeyed orders with alacrity; but the enemy had disappeared before he reached Newport. On the 13th of June, 1776, Captain Jones received orders, dated that day at Newport, Rhode Island, from the Commander-in-chief, to proceed to Newbury Port to take under convoy some vessels bound for Philadelphia; but first to convoy Lieutenant Hacker in the Fly, with a cargo of cannon, into the sound for New York, and to convoy some vessels back from Stonington to the entrance of Newport. In performing these last services, Captain Jones found great difficulty from the enemy's frigates, then cruising round Block Island, with which he had several rencontres; in one of which he saved a brigantine that was a stranger, from Hispaniola, closely pursued by the Cerberus, and laden with public stores. That brigantine was afterwards purchased by the Continent, and called the Hampden. Captain Jones received orders from the Commander-in-chief to proceed for Boston instead of Newbury Port. At Boston he was detained a considerable time by the backwardness of the agent. He arrived with his convoy from Boston, safe in the Delaware, the 1st of August, 1776. This service was performed while the enemy were arriving at Sandy Hook from Halifax and England, and Captain Jones saw several of their ships of war. Captain Jones received a captain's commission from the president of Congress the 8th of August. It was proposed to Captain Jones by the Marine Committee to go to Connecticutt, to command the brigantine Hampden; but he choosing rather to remain in the sloop Providence, had orders to go out on a cruise against the enemy 'for six weeks, [or] two or three months.' He was not limited to any particular station or service. He left the Delaware the 21st of August, and arrived at Rhode Island on the 7th of October, 1776. Captain Jones had only seventy men when he sailed from the Delaware, and the Providence mounted only 12 four-pounders. Near the latitude of Bermudas he had a very narrow escape from the enemy's frigate the Solebay, after a chase of six hours within cannon-shot, and part of that time within pistol-shot. Afterwards, near the Isle of Sable, Captain Jones had an affair with the enemy's frigate the Milford; and the firing between them lasted from ten in the morning till after sunset. The day after this rencontre, Captain Jones entered the harbour of Canso, where he recruited several men, took the Tories' flags, destroyed the fishing, &c., and sailed again the next morning on an expedition against the Island of Madame. He made two descents at the principal ports of that island at the same time; surprised all their shipping, though the place abounded with men, and they had arms. All this, from the Delaware to Rhode Island, was performed in six weeks and five days; in which time Captain Jones made sixteen prizes, besides small craft. He manned eight of them, and sunk, burnt, or destroyed the rest. The Commander-in-chief was at Rhode Island, who, in consequence of the information given him by Captain Jones, adopted an expedition against the coal-fleet of Cape Breton and the fishery, as well as to relieve a number of Americans from the coal-mines, where they were compelled to labour by the enemy. The Alfred had remained idle ever since the Providence expedition, and was without men. It was proposed to employ that ship, the brigantine Hampden, and sloop Providence, on this expedition, under the command of Captain Jones, who had orders given him for that purpose on the 22d October, 1776, and then removed from the sloop Providence to the ship Alfred. Finding he could not enlist a sufficient number of men for the three sail before the season would be lost, Captain Jones determined to leave the sloop Providence behind; but Captain Hacker ran the Hampden upon a ledge of rocks on the 27th, and knocked off her keel, which obliged Captain Jones to remove him into the sloop Providence. The Alfred and Providence sailed on this expedition the 2d of November, Captain Jones having only 140 men on his muster-roll for the Alfred, though that ship had 235 men when she left the Delaware. Captain Jones anchored for the night at Tarpawling Cove, near Nantucket, and, finding there a privateer schooner belonging to Rhode Island inward-bound, he sent his boat to search for deserters from the navy, and finding four deserters carefully concealed on board, they were taken on board the Alfred, with a few other seamen, agreeably to *orders from the Commander-in-chief.* The concerned in the privateer brought an action against Captain Jones for £10,000 damages, and the Commander-in-chief had the politeness not to support him. Captain Jones proceeded on his expedition. Off Louisbourg he took a brig with a rich cargo of dry goods, a snow with a cargo of fish, and a ship called the Mellish, bound for Canada, armed for war, and laden with soldiers' clothing. The day after taking these prizes (the 18th) the snow fell, and the wind blew fresh off Cape Breton. To prevent separation, and not from the violence of the weather, Captain Jones made the signal to lay to, which was obeyed; but as soon as the night began, Captain Hacker bore away. He made shift to arrive at Rhode Island a day or two before the place was taken by the enemy. Captain Jones ordered the brigantine and snow to steer for our ports; but determined not to lose sight of the Mellish, unless in case of necessity. Captain Jones, after that little gale and contrary winds, fell in with Canso, and sent his boats in to destroy a fine transport that lay aground in the entrance, laden with Irish provision. The party burnt also the oil-warehouse, and destroyed the materials for the fishery. Off Louisbourg, on the 24th, he took three fine ships out of five, the coal-fleet, then bound for New York, under the command of the Flora, that would have been in sight had the fog been dispersed. Two days after this, Captain Jones took a letter-of-marque ship from Liverpool. He had now an hundred and fifty prisoners on board the Alfred, and a great part of his water and provision was consumed. He found the harbour at the coal-mines was frozen up, and necessity obliged him to seek a hospitable port with the five prize-ships under convoy. No separation took place till the 7th of December, on the edge of St George's Bank, where Captain Jones again fell in with the Milford frigate. Captain Jones had the address to save all his prizes except one, (the letter-of-marque from Liverpool,) and that one would not have been taken, had not the prize-master foolishly run down under the Milford's lee, from being three leagues to windward. The Mellish arrived safe with the clothing at Dartmouth, and Captain Jones arrived at Boston the 15th December, 1776, having only two days' water and provision left. The news of the clothing reached General Washington's army just before he re-crossed the Delaware. By a letter from the Commander-in-chief, on board the Warren, at Providence, January the 14th, 1777, Captain Jones was superseded in the command of the Alfred, in favour of Captain Hinman, who said he brought a commission from Congress to supersede that of Captain Jones. The 21st of January, 1777, this drew from Captain Jones a letter to the Marine

Committee, stating his hopes that Congress would not so far overlook his early and faithful services as to supersede him by any man who was at first his junior officer, far less by any man who declined to serve in the Alfred, &c., at the beginning. Captain Jones paid off the crews of the Alfred and Providence, for which he has never been reimbursed. On the 18th of February, Captain Jones received an appointment by order of Congress from the Vice-President of the Marine Committee, dated Philadelphia, February the 5th, 1777, to command private expeditions against Pensacola and other places, with the Alfred, Columbus, Cabot, Hampden, and sloop Providence. Many important schemes were pointed out; but Captain Jones was left at free liberty to adopt whatever he thought best. This appointment fell to nothing; for the Commander-in-chief would not assist Captain Jones, but affected to disbelieve his appointment. Captain Jones undertook a journey from Boston to Philadelphia, in order to explain matters to Congress in person."

This attempt to supersede him was the first

occasion on which Jones decidedly showed the firmness and tenacity of his character, and his determination to assert his rights. Even then, unknown and unfriended, he was quite equal to their protection.

The remainder of this statement is more copiously and energetically given in the letter referred to in the prefixed extract, as addressed by him to the Marine Board, Philadelphia. It will show the neglect and heart-burning to which this brave man was exposed from the first hour of his entering the American navy. Three-fourths of his subsequent life was a struggle to overcome the prejudices, defeat the cabals, or quicken the tardy justice of his temporary official superiors.

"I am now to inform you, that by a letter from Commodore Hopkins, dated on board the Warren, January 14th, 1777, which came to my hands a day or two ago, I am superseded in the command of the Alfred, in favour of Captain Hinman, and ordered back to the sloop in Providence River. Whether this order doth or doth not supersede also your orders to me of the 10th ult., you can best determine; however, as I undertook the late expedition at his (Commodore Hopkins's) request, from a principle of humanity, I mean not now to make a difficulty about trifles, especially when the good of the service is to be consulted. As I am unconscious of any neglect of duty, or misconduct, since my appointment at the first as eldest lieutenant of the navy, I cannot suppose that you can have intended to set me aside in favour of any man who did not at that time bear a captain's commission, unless indeed that man, by exerting his superior abilities, hath rendered or can render more important services to America. Those who stepped forth at the first, in ships altogether unfit for war, were generally considered rather as frantic than as wise men; for it must be remembered, that almost every thing then made against them. And although the success in the affair with the Glasgow was not equal to what it might have been, yet the blame ought not to be general. The principal or principals in command alone are culpable; and the other officers, while they stand unimpeached, have their full merit. There were, it is true, divers persons, from misrepresentation, put into commission at the beginning, without fit qualification, and perhaps the number may have been increased by later appointments; but it follows not that the gentleman or man of merit should be neglected or overlooked on their account. None other than a gentleman, as well as a seaman both in theory and practice, is qualified to support the character of a commission officer in the navy; nor is any man fit to command a ship of war who is not also capable of communicating his ideas on paper, in language that becomes his rank. If this be admitted, the foregoing operations will be sufficiently clear; but if further proof is required, it can easily be produced.

" When I entered into the service, I was not actuated by motives of self-interest. I stept forth as a free citizen of the world, in defence of the violated rights of mankind, and not in search of riches, whereof, I thank God, I inherit a sufficiency; but I should prove my degeneracy were I not in the highest degree tenacious of my rank and seniority. As a gentleman, I can yield this point up only to persons of superior abilities and superior merit; and under such persons it would be my highest ambition to learn. As this is the first time of my having expressed the least anxiety on my own account, I must entreat your patience until I account to you for the reason which hath given me this freedom of sentiment. It seems that Captain Hinman's commission is N° 1, and that, in consequence, he who was at first my junior officer by eight, hath *expressed himself as my senior officer* in a manner which doth himself no honour, and which doth me signal injury. There are also in the navy, persons who have not shown me fair play after the service I have rendered them. I have even been blamed for the civilities which I have shown to my prisoners; at the request of one of whom I herein enclose an appeal, which I must beg leave to lay before Congress. Could you see the appellant's accomplished lady, and the innocents their children, arguments in their behalf would be unnecessary. As the base-minded only are capable of inconsistencies, you will not blame my free soul, which can never stoop where I cannot also esteem. Could I, which I never can, bear to be superseded, I should indeed deserve your contempt and total neglect. I am therefore to entreat you to employ me in the most enterprising and active service,—accountable to your Honourable Board only, for my conduct, and connected as much as possible with gentlemen and men of good sense."

"My conduct hitherto," he says, in the memorial addressed to Congress from the Texel, "was so much approved of by Congress, that on the 5th February, 1777, I was appointed, with unlimited orders, to command a little squadron of the Alfred, Columbus, Cabot, Hampden, and sloop Providence. Various important services were pointed out, but I was left at free liberty to make my election. That service, however, did not take place; for the Commodore, who had three of the squadron blocked in at Providence, affected to disbelieve my appointment, and would not at last give me the necessary assistance. Finding that he trifled with my applications as well as the orders of Congress, I undertook a journey from Boston to Philadelphia, in order to explain matters to Congress in person. I took this step also because Captain Hinman had succeeded me in the command of the Alfred, and, of course, the service could not suffer through my absence. I arrived at Philadelphia in the beginning of April. But what was my surprise to find that, by a new line of navy-rank, which had taken place on the 10th day of October, 1776, all the officers that had stepped forth at the beginning were superseded! I was myself superseded by thirteen men, not one of whom did (and perhaps some of them durst not) take the sea against the British flag at the first; for several of them who were then applied to refused to venture,—and none of them have since been very happy in proving their superior abilities. Among these thirteen there are individuals who can neither pretend to parts nor education, and with whom, as a private gentleman, I would disdain to associate.

"I leave your Excellency and the Congress to judge how this must affect a man of honour and sensibility."

In the organization of the navy Jones took a paramount interest. He had himself been trained in a good school. He knew the importance of proper subordination, and of the strict enforcement of a rigid system of discipline, which, however unpleasant to the turbulent, fierce spirit of republicans, is especially indispensable in the sea-service. His views of maritime policy discover much soundness, and, considering that he was still a young man, and a very young officer, very great ripeness of understanding. "As the regulations of the navy," he says, "are of the utmost consequence, you will not think it presumptive if, with the utmost diffidence, I venture to communicate to you such hints as, in my judgment, will promote its honour and good government. I could heartily wish that every commissioned officer were to be previously examined; for, to my certain knowledge, there are persons who have already crept into commission without abilities or fit qualifications:—I am myself far from desiring to be excused." In other letters on this subject, he eloquently recommends a liberal policy towards the private seamen, and a general system worthy of a great and enlightened nation.

"It is," he says, "to the last degree distressing

to contemplate the state and establishment of our navy. The common class of mankind are actuated by no nobler principle than that of self-interest. This, and this only, determines all adventures in privateers,—the owners, as well as those they employ; and while this is the case, unless the private emolument of individuals in our navy is made superior to that in privateers, it never can become respectable,—it never will become formidable; and, without a respectable navy, alas America!—In the present critical situation of human affairs, wisdom can suggest no more than one infallible expedient,—enlist the seamen during pleasure, and give them all the prizes. What is the paltry emolument of two-thirds of prizes to the finances of this vast continent? If so poor a resource is essential to its independency, in sober sadness we are involved in a woful predicament, and our ruin is fast approaching. The situation of America is new in the annals of mankind: her affairs cry *haste!* and speed must answer them. Trifles, therefore, ought to be wholly disregarded, as being, in the old vulgar proverb, 'penny wise and pound foolish.' If our enemies, with the best-established and most formidable navy in the universe, have found it expedient to assign all prizes to the captors, how much more is such policy essential to our infant fleet? But I need use no arguments to convince you of the necessity of making the emoluments of our navy equal, if not superior, to theirs. We have had proof, that a navy may be officered almost upon any terms, but we are not so sure that these officers are equal to their commissions; nor will the Congress ever obtain such certainty until they, in their wisdom, see proper to appoint a Board of Admiralty, competent to determine impartially the respective merits and abilities of their officers, and to superintend, regulate, and point out all the motions and operations of the navy."

The appearance of Jones at Congress at this time, his appeals to their justice, his animated remonstrances, and the capacity displayed in the hints and projects he threw out, had a good effect. They inspired esteem for his character, and gave confidence in his ability. This became apparent in the immediate proceedings of that body.

" Congress," he says, " saw fit to drop the expedition that had been proposed; and the Marine Committee appeared very sorry that there was not then vacant a good ship for my command. Three ships were ordered to be purchased in the eastern department, and by a *resolve* of Congress, which did me great honour, I was authorized to take my choice of these three ships, ' until Congress could provide for me a better command.' I returned to Boston; and before this last plan was carried into execution, I received a new and honourable proof of the good opinion of Congress, by being ordered, on the 9th day of May, 1777, to proceed to France from Portsmouth, in the Amphitrite, with a positive order to the Commissioners at Paris ' to invest me with the command of a fine ship,'—' as a reward of my zeal and the signal services I had performed in vessels of little force.' This was generous indeed! and I shall feel the whole force of the obligation to the last moment of my life."

The letter he brought to Europe, addressed to the Commissioners in Paris, confirms the sincerity of the purpose of Congress. It also puts to rest—were such refutation necessary—the charge of Jones being nothing more than the commander of a privateer, winked at, or perhaps secretly aided by Congress, but never recognised as a regularly-appointed commander in the American service during his cruises on the British coasts.

"Philadelphia, 9th May, 1777.

"Honourable Gentlemen,

"This letter is intended to be delivered to you by John Paul Jones, Esq., an active and brave commander in our navy, who has already performed signal services in vessels of little force; and in reward for his zeal we have directed him to go on board the Amphitrite, a French ship of twenty guns, that brought in a valuable cargo of stores from Mons. Hostalez & Co., and with her to repair to France. He takes with him his commission, some officers and men, so that we hope he will, under that sanction, make some good prizes with the Amphitrite; but our design of sending him is, (with the approbation of Congress) that you may purchase one of those fine frigates that Mr Deane writes us you can get, and invest him with the command thereof as soon as possible. We hope you may not delay this business one moment, but purchase, in such port or place in Europe as it can be done with most convenience and despatch, a fine fast-sailing frigate or larger ship. Direct Captain Jones where he must repair to, and he will take with him his officers and men towards manning her. You will assign him some good house or agent to supply him with every thing necessary to get the ship speedily and well equipped and manned,—somebody that will bestir themselves vigorously in the business, and never quit it until it is accomplished.

"If you have any plan or service to be performed in Europe by such a ship, that you think will be more for the interest and honour of the States than sending her out directly, Captain Jones is instructed to obey your orders; and, to save repetition, let him lay before you the instructions we have given him, and furnish you with a copy thereof. You can then judge what will be necessary for you to direct him in,—and whatever you do will be approved, as it will undoubtedly tend to promote the public service of this country.

"You see by this step how much dependence Congress place in your advices; and you must make it a point not to disappoint Captain Jones's wishes and expectations on this occasion.

"We are, &c.

(Signed) "ROBERT MORRIS.
"RICHARD HENRY LEE.
"WM. WHIPPLE.
"PHIL. LIVINGSTON.

"The Honourable
"BENJAMIN FRANKLIN,
"SILAS DEANE, and
"ARTHUR LEE, Esquires,
Commissioners," &c.

In Marine Committee.

"Philadelphia, May 9th, 1777.

"JOHN PAUL JONES, Esq.

"SIR,

"Congress have thought proper to authorize the Secret Committee to employ you on a voyage in the Amphitrite, from Portsmouth to Carolina and France, where it is expected you will be provided with a fine frigate; and as your present commission is for the command of a particular ship, we now send you a new one, whereby you are appointed a captain in our navy, and of course may command any ship in the service to which you are particularly ordered. You are to obey the orders of the Secret Committee, and we are, Sir, &c.

(Signed) "JOHN HANCOCK.
"ROB. MORRIS.
"WM. WHIPPLE."

In Marine Committee.

"Philadelphia, September 6th, 1777.

"SIR,

"As soon as these instructions get to hand, you are to make immediate application to the proper persons to get your vessel victualled and fitted for sea with all expedition. When this is done, you are to proceed on a voyage to some convenient port in France; on your arrival there, apply to the agent, if any, in or near said port, for such supplies as you may stand in need of. You are at the same time to give immediate notice, by letter, to the Honourable Benjamin Franklin, Silas Deane, and Arthur Lee, Esquires, or any of them at Paris, of your arrival, requesting their instructions as to your further destination; which instructions you are to obey as far as it shall be in your power.

"You are to take particular notice, that whilst on the coast of France, or in a French port, you are, as much as you conveniently can, to keep your guns covered and concealed, and to make as little warlike appearance as possible. Wishing you," &c. &c.

With these credentials and instructions, Jones sailed for Europe in command of the Ranger, in high spirits, expecting to be the first messenger of what he calls "the joyful and important news of Burgoyne's surrender." He reached Nantes early in December, having captured two brigantines on the voyage, laden with fruit and wine.

CHAPTER III.

It must be owned that Captain Jones at no time slipped any opportunity of bringing himself forward, and placing his services in a fair light. Though he indeed claimed no more than was his due, he never, through false delicacy, withdrew his merits into the shade. "It is civil cowardice," says the Spectator's modest friend, Captain Sentry, "to be backward in asserting what you ought to expect, as it is military fear to be slow in attacking when it is your duty." His first act, on reaching France, was to write to the Commissioners, to whom he was now to look for orders, and also for patronage. "I yesterday," he says, "enclosed you copies of two letters which I wrote you previous to my departure from Portsmouth, together with a plan which I drew up at Philadelphia, on the regulation and equipment of our infant navy. It is my first and favourite wish to be employed in active and enterprising services, when there is a prospect of rendering acceptable services to America. The singular honour which Congress have done me by their generous acknowledgment of my past services, hath inspired me with sentiments of gratitude which I shall carry with me to my grave; and if a life of services devoted to America can be made instrumental in securing its independence, I shall regard the continuance of such approbation as an honour far superior to what kings even could bestow."

Captain Jones was immediately summoned to Paris by the Commissioners of Congress, Franklin, Silas Deane, and Arthur Lee. They had not yet assumed the name of plenipotentiaries, nor was war declared between Great Britain and France; for though these countries were in a state of understood, if not avowed, hostility, in his private orders from the Marine Committee of Congress, Jones was directed to keep his guns covered and concealed as much as possible while on the coasts or in the ports of France, and as much as possible to avoid a warlike appearance. The object of summoning him to Paris was to concert, in conjunction with the Commissioners, a plan of operations for the powerful maritime force under the command of the Count d'Estaing, which—a treaty being now concluded between France and the new States—was destined to harass the British, and support the cause of the Republic on the shores of America.

The bold and sagacious plan of that campaign, which, if carried into effect as projected, must in all probability at once have ended the war, Jones repeatedly and openly claims the merit of having formed;* and there can be no doubt that his knowledge of the actual state of the British land and naval force then acting in America, and his practical nautical acquaintance with the scene of

---

* In the memorial to the King of France, Jones states that the plan adopted for D'Estaing's expedition was sent *by him* to the Commissioners from Nantes, on the 10th February, 1778, after he had returned from Paris, and immediately on hearing some agreeable news from America.

operation, enabled him to give most important advice. Those delays, and the baffling circumstances to which naval armaments are ever exposed, together, as has been alleged, with the timidity or irresolution of the French Commander, the promptitude and courage displayed by Lord Howe, and the excellent spirit of the whole British fleet on that memorable occasion, disconcerted this well-imagined scheme. In claiming the plan of that expedition, Jones says, in a letter addressed to the French Minister of Marine, M. de Sartine,—"Had Count d'Estaing arrived in the Delaware a few days sooner, he might have made a most glorious and easy conquest. Many successful projects may be adopted from the hints which I had the honour to draw up; and if I can still furnish more, or execute any of these already furnished, so as to distress and humble the common enemy, it will afford me the truest pleasure." Before d'Estaing appeared, however, Lord Howe, as has been noticed, had been able to place the fleet and the transports in safety; and the plan on which the American Commissioners justly prided themselves of blocking up the British ships, transports, and victuallers, in the Delaware, thus fell to the ground.

When Jones went to Paris to attend the Commissioners, he left the Ranger, which had been damaged in her voyage, refitting at Nantes. To the Commissioners he imparted plans of various enterprises to be undertaken in the bold predatory spirit of the private instructions of Morris, and he induced them to hold out to his crew, in the name of Congress, the hope or promise of some particular gratuity in reward of the "good, gallant behaviour and punctual obedience," so essential to the furtherance of his daring projects. In coming to Europe he expected to obtain command of the *Indien*, a large frigate, then building at Amsterdam, for the service of the United States. This vessel the Commissioners thought fit to present to the King of France. Jones felt the disappointment, and even complained of it to Congress, making it an argument for obtaining at least an equivalent command.

On the 16th January, 1778, Jones received his orders from the Commissioners. They were such as ever proved the most agreeable to him—unlimited—implying full confidence in his zeal and ability. The only caution he received, was, not to return *immediately* to the ports of France after making an attempt on the coasts of Britain, as the French court wished to shuffle a little longer.

The Ranger being now refitted, Jones sailed to Quiberon, and at that place displayed considerable professional address and characteristic firmness, in compelling the French Admiral to give the American flag—which Jones had been the first to hoist—the first salute it ever received. It was thus he wrote on this occasion:—

"February 14th, 1778.

"Dear Sir,

"I am extremely sorry to give you fresh trouble, but I think the Admiral's answer of yesterday requires an explanation. The haughty English return gun for gun to foreign officers of equal rank, and two less only to captains by flag-officers. It is true, my command at present is not important, yet, as the senior American officer at present in Europe, it is my duty to claim an equal return of respect to the flag of the United States that would be shown to any other flag whatever.

"I therefore take the liberty of enclosing an appointment, perhaps as respectable as any which the French Admiral can produce—besides which I have others in my possession.

"If, however, he persists in refusing to return an equal salute, I will accept of two guns less, as I have not the rank of Admiral.

"It is my opinion, that he would return four less to a privateer or a merchant ship; therefore, as I have been honoured oftener than once with a chief command of ships of war, I cannot in honour accept of the same terms of respect.

"You will singularly oblige me by waiting upon the Admiral; and I ardently hope you will succeed in the application, else I shall be under a necessity of departing without coming into the bay. I have the honour to be, &c. &c.

"To William Carmichael, Esq."

"N.B.—Though thirteen guns is your greatest salute in America, yet if the French Admiral should prefer a greater number, he has his choice, *on conditions*."

Of the triumphant recognition of the American flag obtained in the first instance by him, Jones was naturally very proud. "I am happy," he says, addressing the Marine Committee at home, "in having it in my power to congratulate you on my having seen the American flag recognised in the fullest and completest manner by the flag of France." And he relates how he accomplished this object.

On the 10th of April Jones sailed from Brest on that cruise which the assault on Whitehaven, the landing at the Earl of Selkirk's, and the capture of the Drake, afterwards rendered so celebrated. The account of that expedition will be best given in his own words. It is, however, worthy of notice, that the original log-book of the Ranger, and of his more famous ship, the Bon Homme Richard, which are now accidentally in the hands of gentlemen in Scotland wholly unconnected with Captain Jones, generally corroborate all his statements to the most minute particulars. It is thus his account commences:—

"I have now to fulfil the promise made in my last, by giving you an account of my late expedition.

"I sailed from Brest the 10th of April; my plan was extensive, I therefore did not at the beginning wish to encumber myself with prisoners. On the 14th I took a brigantine between Scilly and Cape Clear, bound for Ostend, with a cargo of flax-seed for Ireland—sunk her, and proceeded into St George's Channel.

"On the 17th I took the ship Lord Chatham, bound from London to Dublin, with a cargo consisting of porter, and a variety of merchandise, and almost within sight of her port; this ship I manned and ordered for Brest.

"Towards the evening of the day following the weather had a promising appearance, and, the wind being favourable, I stood over from the Isle of Man with an intention to make a descent at Whitehaven; at ten I was off the harbour with a party of volunteers, and had every thing in readiness to land; but before eleven the wind greatly increased and shifted, so as to blow directly upon the shore; the sea increased of course, and it became impossible to effect a landing. This obliged me to carry all possible sail so as to clear the land, and to await a more favourable opportunity.

"On the 18th, in Glentinebay, on the south coast of Scotland, I met with a revenue wherry; it being the common practice of these vessels to board merchant ships, the Ranger then having no external appearance of war, it was expected that this rover would have come alongside; I was, however, mistaken, for though the men were at their quarters, yet this vessel out-sailed the Ranger, and got clear in spite of a severe cannonade.

"The next morning, off the Mull of Galloway, I found myself so near a Scotch coasting schooner, loaded with barley, that I could not avoid sinking her. Understanding that there were ten or twelve sail of merchant ships, besides a Tender brigantine, with a number of impressed men on board, at anchor in Lochryan, in Scotland, I thought this an enterprise worthy my attention; but the wind, which at the first would have served equally well to have sailed in or out of the Loch, shifted in a hard squall, so as to blow almost directly in, with an appearance of bad weather. I was therefore obliged to abandon my project.

" Seeing a cutter off the lee-bow steering for the Clyde, I gave chase, in hopes of cutting her off; but finding my endeavours ineffectual, I pursued no farther than the Rock of Ailsa. In the evening I fell in with a sloop from Dublin, which I sunk, to prevent intelligence.

" The next day, the 21st, being near Carrickfergus, a fishing-boat came off, which I detained. I saw a ship at anchor in the road, which I was informed by the fishermen was the British ship-of-war Drake, of twenty guns. I determined to attack her in the night; my plan was to overlay her cable, and to fall upon her bow, so as to have all her decks open and exposed to our musquetry, &c.; at the same time, it was my intention to have secured the enemy by grapplings, so that, had they cut their cables, they would not thereby have attained an advantage. The wind was high, and unfortunately the anchor was not let go so soon as the order was given, so that the Ranger was brought to upon the enemy's quarter at the distance of half a cable's length. We had made no warlike appearance, of course had given no alarm; this determined me to cut immediately, which might appear as if the cable had parted, and at the same time enable me, after making a tack out of the Loch, to return with the same prospect of advantage which I had at the first. I was, however, prevented from returning, as I with difficulty weathered the lighthouse on the lee-side of the Loch, and as the gale increased. The weather now became so very stormy and severe, and the sea ran so high, that I was obliged to take shelter under the south shore of Scotland.

"The 22d introduced fair weather, though the three kingdoms were, as far as the eye could reach, covered with snow. I now resolved once more to attempt Whitehaven; but the wind became very light, so that the ship would not in proper time approach so near as I had intended. At midnight I left the ship with two boats and thirty-one volunteers; when we reached the outer pier the day began to dawn; I would not, however, abandon my enterprise, but despatched one boat under the direction of Mr Hill and Lieutenant Wallingsford, with the necessary combustibles to set fire to the shipping on the north side of the harbour, while I went with the other party to attempt the south side. I was successful in scaling the walls and spiking up all the cannon on the first fort; finding the sentinels shut up in the guard-house, they were secured without being hurt. Having fixed sentinels, I now took with me one man only, (Mr Green,) and spiked up all the cannon on the southern fort, distant from the other a quarter of a mile.

"On my return from this business, I naturally expected to see the fire of the ships on the north side, as well as to find my own party with everything in readiness to set fire to the shipping on the south; instead of this, I found the boat under the direction of Mr Hill and Mr Wallingsford returned, and the party in some confusion, their light having burnt out at the instant when it became necessary.*

---

* Jones did not soon surmount the disappointment occasioned by this misunderstanding on the part of his

" By the strangest fatality, my own party were in the same situation, the candles being all

---

officers. In a memorial to Congress, he says, " My first object was to secure an exchange of prisoners in Europe, and my second to put an end, by one good fire in England *of shipping*, to all the burnings in America. I succeeded in the first, even by means far more glorious than my most flattering ideas had expected when I left France. In the second I endeavoured to deserve success; but a wise officer of mine observed, that 'it was a rash thing, and that nothing could *be got* by burning poor people's property.' I must, however, do him the justice to mention his acknowledgment, that he had no turn for enterprise; and I must also do equal justice to my former officers in the Providence and the Alfred, by declaring, that had they been with me in the Ranger, two hundred and fifty, or three hundred sail of large ships at Whitehaven would have been laid in ashes." In answer to certain queries on this subject, proposed by the Board of Admiralty in 1781, he says, " I made a descent at Whitehaven with thirty men only, surprised and took two strong forts with thirty pieces of cannon, and set fire to the shipping where they lay, 300 or upwards, in the dry pier. That both the shipping and the town, containing from 40 to 50,000 inhabitants, was not burned, was owing to the backwardness of some persons under my command."

burnt out. The day too came on apace, yet I would by no means retreat while any hopes of success remained. Having again placed sentinels, a light was obtained at a house disjoined from the town, and fire was kindled in the steerage of a large ship, which was surrounded by at least an hundred and fifty others, chiefly from two to four hundred tons burthen, and lying side by side, aground, unsurrounded by the water.

"There were, besides, from seventy to an hundred large ships in the north arm of the harbour, aground, clear of the water, and divided from the rest only by a stone pier of a ship's height. I should have kindled fires in other places if the time had permitted; as it did not, our care was to prevent the one kindled from being easily extinguished. After some search, a barrel of tar was found, and poured into the flames, which now ascended from all the hatchways. The inhabitants began to appear in thousands, and individuals ran hastily towards us. I stood between them and the ship on fire, with a pistol in my hand, and ordered them to retire, which they did with precipitation. The flames had already caught the rigging, and began to ascend the main-mast; the sun was a full hour's march above the horizon, and as sleep no longer ruled the world, it was time to retire. We re-embarked without opposition, having released a number of prisoners, as our boats could not carry them. After all my people had embarked, I stood upon the pier for a considerable space, yet no person advanced: I saw all the eminences round the town covered with the amazed inhabitants.

"When we had rowed to a considerable distance from the shore, the English began to run in vast numbers to their forts; their disappointment may easily be imagined when they found, I suppose, at least thirty heavy cannon (the instruments of their vengeance) rendered useless. At length, however, they began to fire, having, as I apprehend, either brought down ships' guns, or used one or two cannon which lay on the beach at the foot of the walls, dismounted, and which had not been spiked. They fired with no direction, and the shot falling short of the boats, instead of doing us any damage, afforded some diversion, which my people could not help showing, by discharging their pistols, &c. in return of the salute.

"Had it been possible to have landed a few hours sooner, success would have been complete; not a single ship out of more than two hundred could possibly have escaped, and all the world would not have been able to save the town; what was done, however, is sufficient to show that not all their boasted navy can protect their own coasts, and that the scenes of distress which they have occasioned in America may soon be brought home to their own doors. One of my people was missing, and must, I fear, have fallen into the enemy's hands after our departure.* I was pleased that in this business we neither killed nor

---

* In the Ranger's log-book this man is named David Smith. He is probably the same person who, under the name of Freeman, gave information at several houses in a street adjoining the piers, that fire had been set to a ship, and afterwards other information that appears substantially correct. He must have remained on shore voluntarily.

wounded. I brought off three prisoners as a sample."

Jones has been severely censured, even by those who are willing to allow him merited praise in other respects, for his descent on Whitehaven, and St Mary's Isle,—as the seat of Lord Selkirk is named. The wanton burnings and destruction of private property on the coasts of America must have been sufficiently irritating, and must have naturally provoked a spirit of retaliation ; still the bulk of mankind must join in opinion with his cautious lieutenant, that "nothing was to *be got* by burning poor people's property,"—and with the biographer of Jones in the Edinburgh Encyclopædia, who truly states, that "there is something revolting in the idea of a man's deliberately stifling all his early associations, and availing himself of his familiar acquaintance with the place of his youthful enjoyments, to effect its destruction." Our feelings refuse to move in sympathy with this new-born vehement zeal felt by a man against that native land in which his mother, sisters, and relatives, were then living in peace and security. That young Paul had in boyhood imbibed an enthusiastic attachment to America, from the conversation of discontented seamen trading to the colonies, which has been urged in extenuation of the part he chose, is a mere gratuitous assumption. At the period of his boyhood there was no existing discontent which reached his class of society; and up to the time of his entering the American navy, he might in all probability, with equal good-will, have accepted a commission under his native sovereign. He was influenced by fortuitous circumstances; but, once fairly engaged in the service of the United States, he devoted himself to his new country with unshaken zeal and incorruptible integrity.

Besides the questionable nature of the assault on Whitehaven, in a private or abstract view, from a man circumstanced as was Jones, there is a startling discrepancy, a degree of exaggeration, and an air of rhodomontade, about all his accounts of that affair.

In all the contemporary accounts of the attempt on Whitehaven, and capture of the Drake, the Ranger is termed a privateer. This is a mistake; she was a ship of war belonging to the United States, and Jones was appointed her commander by a resolution of Congress on the 14th of June, 1777. The character of this vessel was, however, certainly anomalous in any regular navy. Her commander acted alone and single-handed; and such was his temper and the nature of the service for which he seemed most fitted, that he uniformly succeeded best when acting thus on his own judgment and responsibility, and never wholly failed, save in those combined operations where his opinions were opposed or fettered. With the unlimited command of the Ranger, and small as his force was, he determined to prove to France and America what, with adequate means placed at his disposal, he might achieve. But it is time to return to the narrative of this cruise, which resembled more the bold exploits of Morgan or Lolonnois than the operations of modern nautical warfare.

"We now stood over for the Scotch shore, and landed at noon on St Mary's Isle, with one boat only, and a very small party, (twelve men.) The motives which induced me to land there are explained in the within copy of a letter* which I have written to the Countess of Selkirk.

"On the morning of the 24th I was again off Carrickfergus, and would have gone in had I not seen the Drake preparing to come out; it was very moderate, and the Drake's boat was sent out to reconnoitre the Ranger. As the boat advanced I kept the ship's stern directly towards her, and, though they had a spy-glass in the boat, they came on within hail, and alongside. When the officer came on the quarter-deck, he was greatly surprised to find himself a prisoner!—although *an express had arrived from Whitehaven the night before.* I now understood what I had before imagined, that the Drake came out in consequence of this information with volunteers against the Ranger. The officer told me also, that they had taken up the Ranger's anchor.

"The Drake was attended by five small vessels full of people, who were led by motives of curiosity to see an engagement; but when they discovered the Drake's boat at the Ranger's stern

---

* See page 87.

they wisely put back. Alarm-smokes now appeared in great abundance, extending along both sides of the channel. The tide was unfavourable, so that the Drake worked out but slowly. This obliged me to run down several times, and to lay with courses up, and main-topsail to the mast. At length the Drake weathered the point, and having led her out to about mid-channel, I suffered her to come within hail. The Drake hoisted English colours, and at the same instant the American stars were displayed on board the Ranger. I expected that preface had been now at an end; but the enemy soon after hailed, demanding what ship it was. I directed the master to answer, the American continental ship Ranger; that we waited for them, and desired they would come on. The sun was now little more than an hour from setting, it was therefore time to begin. The Drake being rather astern of the Ranger, I ordered the helm up, and gave her the first broadside. The action was warm, close, and obstinate; it lasted an hour and five minutes, when the enemy called for quarters, her fore and main-top-sail yards being both cut away, and down on the cap; the fore-top-gallant-yard and mizen-gaff both hanging up and down along the mast; the second ensign which they had hoisted shot away, and hanging over the quarter-gallery, in the water; the jib shot away, and hanging into the water; her sails and rigging entirely cut to pieces, her masts and yards all wounded, and her hull also very much galled.

"I lost only Lieutenant Wallingsford, and one seaman (John Dongal) killed, and six wounded, among whom are the gunner, (Mr Falls,) and Mr Powers, a midshipman, who lost his arm. One of the wounded (Nathaniel Wills) is since dead; the rest will recover.

"The loss of the enemy in killed and wounded was far greater. All the prisoners allow that they came out with a number not less than an hundred and sixty men, and many of them affirm that they amounted to an hundred and ninety; the medium may perhaps be the most exact account, and by that it will appear that they lost in killed and wounded forty-two men.*

---

* This loss is stated by the other party at twenty-two.

" The captain and lieutenant were among the wounded; the former, having received a musket-ball in the head the minute before they called for quarters, lived and was sensible for some time after my people boarded the prize; the lieutenant survived two days. They were buried with the honours due to their rank, and with the respect due to their memory.

" The night, and almost the whole day after the action, being moderate, greatly facilitated the refitting of the ships. A large brigantine ran so near the Drake in the afternoon, that I was obliged to bring her to: she belonged to Whitehaven, and was bound to Norway.

" I had thoughts of returning by the south channel, but the wind shifting, I determined to pass by the north, and round the west coast of Ireland: this brought me once more off Belfast Loch on the evening of the day after the engagement.

" It was now time to release the honest Irishmen whom I took here on the 21st; and as the poor fellows had lost their boat, she having sunk in the late stormy weather, I was happy in having it in my power to give them the necessary sum to purchase every thing new which they had lost; I gave them also a good boat to transport themselves ashore, and sent with them two infirm men, on whom I had bestowed the last guinea in my possession, to defray their travelling expenses to their proper home at Dublin. They took with them one of the Drake's sails, which would sufficiently explain what had happened to the volunteers. The grateful Irishmen were enraptured, and expressed their joy in three huzzas as they passed the Ranger's quarter."

On the 26th April, Captain Jones placed Lieutenant Simpson under suspension and arrest; and on the 8th May he re-entered Brest roads, having been absent only twenty-eight days.*

---

* The worthy and cautious citizens of Aberdeen were the only persons greatly alarmed on this occasion. In the Scots Magazine for May, 1778, we find the following paragraph:—

"On receiving at Aberdeen intelligence of the plunder of Lord Selkirk's house and the landing at Whitehaven, a hand-bill was circulated by order of the Ma-

If the American plenipotentiaries were gratified by the success of this expedition, the Court of Versailles was still more delighted. France was now on the very eve of war. The plenipotentiaries of the United States had been publicly received at Versailles a month before—the treaty had been signed—and D'Estaing's squadron was ready for sea. The French ambassador had been ordered to leave London, and by the famous engagement between the Arethusa and La Belle Poule the first blow had been struck. In England the nation, much divided on the policy of the unsuccessful war with the colonies, were for the first time united in feelings of hostility to the "ancient foe," and of indignation at the insidious

---

gistrates, to set on foot an association of the inhabitants for defence, and in a few days 120 were enrolled."

The affair never went farther. Another American vessel, which landed a party, and plundered the house of Mr Gordon, near Banff, must have quickened their apprehensions; but no alarm was seriously felt till the squadron of Paul Jones appeared in the frith of Forth. Even then the panic was short-lived.

policy of the court of Versailles. The most active preparations were going on throughout the whole of the three kingdoms. All the winter and spring, in anticipation of a war with France, volunteer corps, defensive bands, and fencible regiments, had been raising; the navy was hastily augmented; addresses were sent from all quarters of the country; and the bulk of the nation was animated by the most ardent spirit of loyalty.

The first leisure of Captain Jones on arriving at Brest was employed in writing his celebrated letter to the Countess of Selkirk. His conduct throughout the whole of this delicate affair, though certainly on his part the spontaneous impulse of elevated feeling, was also good policy, as the descent on St Mary's Isle, which ultimately redounded to his honour, was liable to much misrepresentation. The explanatory chivalrous epistle to the Countess of Selkirk has been often talked of. It represents the character of the writer in a new and certainly not unpleasing light. How seldom does the romance of real life exist till the age of thirty!

But however romantic one class of the feelings of Jones might be, awakened and softened by his visit to the scenes of his boyhood, under circumstances so extraordinary, he was still much more at home in drawing up a clear memorial of his proceedings for Congress, or in bringing *to* a tardy and shuffling minister, than in addressing high-born dames. Though he had been a few weeks in Paris, the airs of a carpet-knight still sat awkwardly upon him, and his letter evinces more right feeling than good taste or knowledge of lady-life. But Franklin, the republican sage, to whom the epistle was enclosed, says, "It is a gallant letter, which must give her Ladyship a high and just opinion of your generosity and nobleness of mind;"—and he was right. The matter was admirable, whatever might be the faults of style. Had the same generous spirit of hostility been displayed throughout, how much of human misery, wantonly inflicted, might have been spared,—how much of that bitterness of feeling engendered between countries having in common so many powerful bonds of alliance might have been prevented!

"Ranger, Brest, 8th May, 1778.

"MADAM,

"It cannot be too much lamented, that, in the profession of arms, the officer of fine feelings and real sensibility should be under the necessity of winking at any action of persons under his command which his heart cannot approve; but the reflection is doubly severe, when he finds himself obliged, in appearance, to countenance such acts by his authority.

"This hard case was mine, when, on the 23d of April last, I landed on St Mary's Isle. Knowing Lord Selkirk's interest with the King, and esteeming, as I do, his private character, I wished to make him the happy instrument of alleviating the horrors of hopeless captivity, when the brave are overpowered and made prisoners of war.

"It was, perhaps, fortunate for you, Madam, that he was from home; for it was my intention to have taken him on board the Ranger, and to have detained him, until, through his means, a general and fair exchange of prisoners, as well in Europe as in America, had been effected. When

I was informed by some men whom I met at landing, that his Lordship was absent, I walked back to my boat, determined to leave the island. By the way, however, some officers, who were with me, could not forbear expressing their discontent, observing that, in America, no delicacy was shown by the English, who took away all sorts of moveable property, setting fire, not only to towns and to the houses of the rich, without distinction, but not even sparing the wretched hamlets and milch-cows of the poor and helpless, at the approach of an inclement winter. That party had been with me the same morning at Whitehaven; some complaisance, therefore, was their due. I had but a moment to think how I might gratify them, and at the same time do your Ladyship the least injury. I charged the officers to permit none of the seamen to enter the house, or to hurt anything about it; to treat you, Madam, with the utmost respect; to accept of the plate which was offered, and to come away without making a search, or demanding anything else.

"I am induced to believe that I was punctually obeyed, since I am informed that the plate which they brought away is far short of the quantity expressed in the inventory which accompanied it. I have gratified my men; and, when the plate is sold, I shall become the purchaser, and will gratify my own feelings by restoring it to you by such conveyance as you shall please to direct.

"Had the Earl been on board the Ranger the following evening, he would have seen the awful pomp and dreadful carnage of a sea-engagement; both affording ample subject for the pencil as well as melancholy reflection for the contemplative mind. Humanity starts back from such scenes of horror, and cannot sufficiently execrate the vile promoters of this detestable war—

'For *they*, 'twas *they*, unsheathed the ruthless blade,
'And Heaven shall ask the havoc it has made.'

"The British ship of war Drake, mounting twenty guns, with more than her full complement of officers and men, was our opponent. The ships met, and the advantage was disputed with great fortitude on each side for an hour and four minutes, when the gallant commander of the

Drake fell, and victory declared in favour of the Ranger. The amiable lieutenant lay mortally wounded, besides near forty of the inferior officers and crew killed and wounded,—a melancholy demonstration of the uncertainty of human prospects, and of the sad reverse of fortune which an hour can produce. I buried them in a spacious grave, with the honours due to the memory of the brave.

"Though I have drawn my sword in the present generous struggle for the rights of men, yet I am not in arms as an American, nor am I in pursuit of riches. My fortune is liberal enough, having no wife nor family, and having lived long enough to know that riches cannot ensure happiness. I profess myself a citizen of the world, totally unfettered by the little, mean distinctions of climate or of country, which diminish the benevolence of the heart, and set bounds to philanthropy. Before this war began I had at the early time of life withdrawn from the sea-service in favour of 'calm contemplation and poetic ease.' I have sacrificed not only my favourite scheme of life, but the softer affections of the heart and my prospects of domestic happiness, and I am ready to sacrifice my life also with cheerfulness, if that forfeiture could restore peace and good-will among mankind.

" As the feelings of your gentle bosom cannot but be congenial with mine, let me entreat you, Madam, to use your persuasive art with your husband's to endeavour to stop this cruel and destructive war, in which Britain can never succeed. Heaven can never countenance the barbarous and unmanly practice of the Britons in America, which savages would blush at, and which, if not discontinued, will soon be retaliated on Britain by a justly-enraged people. Should you fail in this, (for I am persuaded that you will attempt it, and who can resist the power of such an advocate?) your endeavours to effect a general exchange of prisoners will be an act of humanity which will afford you golden feelings on a deathbed.

" I hope this cruel contest will soon be closed; but should it continue, I wage no war with the fair. I acknowledge their force, and bend before it with submission. Let not, therefore, the amiable Countess of Selkirk regard me as an enemy; I am ambitious of her esteem and friendship, and would do any thing, consistent with my duty, to merit it.

"The honour of a line from your hand in answer to this will lay me under a singular obligation; and if I can render you any acceptable service in France or elsewhere, I hope you see into my character so far as to command me without the least grain of reserve.

"I wish to know exactly the behaviour of my people, as I am determined to punish them if they have exceeded their liberty. I have the honour to be, with much esteem and with profound respect, Madam, &c. &c.

"JOHN PAUL JONES.

"To the COUNTESS of SELKIRK."

It afterwards cost Jones much more trouble than he could have calculated upon to redeem the promise here given to the Countess of Selkirk. Once in the harpy claws of commissaries and prize-agents, it required all his energy, activity, and disinterestedness, to wrest the plate from them, even by paying, he says, "more than the value." It was valued and re-valued, and occasioned more trouble and expense than it was intrinsically worth, had not Jones conceived his honour pledged for its safe restoration.

Jones found a useful auxiliary in this affair in Father John, an Irish priest, the chaplain of Count D'Orvilliers, who then commanded a fleet lying off Brest, and whom he had already made his friend. So justly provoked was he about this affair, and the sordid spirit of the agents, that, in the very temper of Hotspur, we find him exclaiming, "I will not abate the thousandth part of a *sol* of three-twentieths of prizes, which no man in America ever presumed to dispute as being my just and proper right, and which no rascal in Europe shall presume to dispute with impunity! To whom, since I was myself Commander-in-Chief, would that old fool decree the three-twentieths? Perhaps to his dear self, who is puffed up with the idea of his right to secure 'the property of captures?'"

Though the plate came into the possession of Jones in 1780, it was nearly five years before he was able to return it to the owner. It was lodged with a friend during his absence in America; and in writing to Lord Selkirk in 1784, after the peace, he takes occasion to make a new avowal of the views and sentiments on which he had acted during the war:—

"Paris, February 12th, 1784.

"My Lord,

"I have just received a letter from Mr Nesbitt, dated at L'Orient the 4th instant, mentioning a letter to him from your son, Lord Daer, on the subject of the plate that was taken from your house by some of my people when I commanded the Ranger, and has been for a long time past in Mr Nesbitt's care. A short time before I left France to return to America, Mr W. Alexander wrote me from Paris to L'Orient, that he had, at my request, seen and conversed with your Lordship in England respecting the plate. He said you had agreed that I should restore it, and that it might be forwarded to the care of your sister-in-law, the Countess of Morton, in London. In consequence I now send orders to Mr Nesbitt to forward the plate immediately to her care.

When I received Mr Alexander's letter, there was no cartel or other vessel at L'Orient, that I could trust with a charge of so delicate a nature as your plate, and I had great reason to expect I should return to France within six months after I embarked for America; but circumstances in America prevented my returning to Europe during the war, though I had constant expectation of it. The long delay that has happened to the restoration of your plate has given me much concern, and I now feel a proportionate pleasure in fulfilling what was my first intention. My motive for landing at your estate in Scotland was to take *you* as an hostage for the lives and liberty of a number of the citizens of America, who had been taken in war on the ocean, and committed to British prisons, under an act of parliament, as *traitors*, *pirates*, and *felons*. You observed to Mr Alexander, that 'my idea was a mistaken one, because you were not (as I had supposed) in favour with the British ministry, who knew that *you favoured the cause of liberty*.' On that account I am glad that you were absent from your estate when I landed there, as I bore no personal enmity, but the contrary, towards you. I afterwards had the happiness to redeem my fellow-citizens from Britain, by means far more glorious than through the medium of any single hostage.

"As I have endeavoured to serve the cause of liberty, through every stage of the American revolution, and sacrificed to it my private ease, a part of my fortune, and some of my blood, I could have no selfish motive in permitting my people to demand and carry off your plate. My sole inducement was to turn their attention and stop their rage from breaking out, and retaliating on your house and effects the *too wanton* burnings and desolation that had been committed against their relations and fellow-citizens in America by the British; of which, I assure you, you would have felt the severe consequences had I not fallen on an expedient to prevent it, and hurried my people away before they had time for farther reflection. As you were so obliging as to say to Mr Alexander, that '*my people behaved with great decency at your house*,' I ask the favour of you to announce that circumstance to the public.

"I am, my Lord, wishing you always perfect freedom and happiness," &c. &c.

"PAUL JONES."

The answer that Jones received next year from the Earl was some indemnification for his trouble and anxiety:—

"London, 4th August, 1785.

"SIR,

"I received the letter you wrote me at the time you sent off my plate, in order for restoring it. Had I known where to direct a letter to you at the time it arrived in Scotland, I would have then wrote to you; but not knowing it, nor finding that any of my acquaintance at Edinburgh knew it, I was obliged to delay writing till I came here, when, by means of a gentleman connected with America, I was told Mr Le Grand was your banker at Paris, and would take proper care of a letter for you; therefore I enclose this to him.

"Notwithstanding all the precautions you took for the easy and uninterrupted conveyance of the plate, yet it met with considerable delays, first at Calais, next at Dover, then at London. However, it at last arrived at Dumfries, and, I dare say, quite safe, though as yet I have not seen it, being then at Edinburgh. I intended to have put an article in the newspapers about your having returned it; but before I was informed of its being arrived, some of your friends, I suppose, had put it in the Dumfries newspaper, whence it was immediately copied into the Edinburgh papers, and thence into the London ones.

" Since that time I have mentioned it to many people of fashion; and on all occasions, Sir, both now and formerly, I have done you the justice to tell, that you made an offer of returning the plate very soon after your return to Brest, and although you yourself were not at my house, but remained at the shore with your boat, that yet you had your officers and men in such extraordinary good discipline, that you having given them the strictest orders to behave well, to do no injury of any kind, to make no search, but only to bring off what plate was given them; that in reality they did exactly as ordered, and that not one man offered to stir from his post, on the outside of the house, nor entered the doors, nor said an uncivil word; that the two officers stood not a quarter of an hour in the parlour and butler's pantry while the butler got the plate together; behaved politely, and asked for nothing but the plate, and instantly marched their men off in regular order; and that both officers and men behaved in all respects so well, that it would have done credit to the best-disciplined troops whatever. Some of the English newspapers at that time having put in confused accounts of your expedition to *Whitehaven* and Scotland, I ordered a proper one of what happened in Scotland to be put in the London newspapers, by a gentleman who was then at my house, by which the good conduct and civil behaviour of your officers and men were done justice to, and attributed to your orders, and the good discipline you maintained over your people.

"I am, Sir, your most humble servant,

"SELKIRK."

The plate was returned exactly as it had been taken away; even the tea leaves, it is said, remained in the tea-pot.

CHAPTER IV.

The success of Jones, and the temporary vogue into which it raised him at the court of France on his return to Brest, did not free him from many embarrassments. To provide for his crew, to secure the two hundred prisoners he had brought in, and to obtain a new command for himself, all occupied and distracted his attention at the same time. The dilatoriness or cupidity of the prize-agents, and the straitened funds at the disposal of the Commissioners, excited open discontents among the seamen,—who, after their exertions, saw themselves neglected and forgotten, and even in want of the common necessaries of food and clothing. Captain Jones had now obtained the right of speaking out, and also of being heard; and he used his newly-acquired influence with equal anxiety for the comfort of his own men, and of the sick, the wounded, and prisoners whom the fortune of war had placed at his mercy.

Before quitting America, Jones had, under the sanction of the Marine Committee, made himself accountable to his crew for the regular payment of their wages. With this circumstance Mr Lee, one of the Commissioners, who afterwards gave both of his own colleagues much trouble, was acquainted; yet he concurred with those who were in ignorance of this arrangement in dishonouring the draft which Jones made on the Commissioners on his return to Brest, under circumstances which should have compelled them to attend to his wants, in humanity and good policy as well as justice. "I was left," he says, "with two hundred prisoners of war, a number of sick and wounded, an almost naked crew, and a ship, after a severe engagement, in want of stores and provisions, from the 9th May till the 13th of June, destitute of any public support." "To make me completely wretched," he says, on another occasion, "M. de Bersolle has told me that he now stops his hand, not only of the necessary articles to refit the ship, but also of the *daily provisions.* I know not where to find to-morrow's dinner for the great number of mouths that depend on me for food. Are the continental ships of war to depend on the sale of their prizes for a daily dinner to their men? Publish it not in Gath!"

But from all these pressing difficulties Jones contrived to extricate himself with little aid, in the first instance, from the harassed Commissioners, who, at this time, had their hands full of business, and their purses empty of money.

Shortly afterwards we find Captain Jones interfering to protect his prisoners from the rapacity of the persons who were intrusted with supplying their wants. By his exertions and credit with the French government and its functionaries, he had already ensured their safe custody in order to an exchange,—an object for which Franklin was now negotiating, and which at all times was one of prime importance to Jones, as appears on the face of his whole correspondence. The letter enclosing the memorial of his prisoners is very creditable to his feelings.

"The fellow," he says, "who holds the rod over their wretched heads, has menaced them 'if they dare to complain,' and would have intercepted their memorial, had I not prevented it. This Riou is the scoundrel who, by his falsehood, promoted discord in the Ranger, and got the deluded people to appoint him their particular agent. Before that time he never could call twenty louis his own,—and he is now too rich for his former profession of King's interpreter. He does not deny that he is a scoundrel, for so I have called him more than once before witnesses, and so every person of sense thinks him at Brest. If the exchange of prisoners does not take place immediately, I conceive it would be the most eligible method to have the people on board the Patience landed. They are convinced that if you should think fit to return them an answer, it will never come to their hands through the means of any person who calls himself an agent at Brest, and they having full confidence in the honour and humanity of Father John, professor of English, and chaplain to Comte D'Orvilliers at Brest, have desired me to inform you, that through that gentleman they beg you to favour them with an answer. In granting their request you will confer a very singular obligation on me."

Though Jones had just cause of anger in the hardship and indignity to which he was exposed by the Commissioners dishonouring his drafts, and in the conduct of the prize-agents, and the discontents which in consequence arose among his crew, who naturally all looked to him for justice, if not reward, he was cheered by many marks of private friendship and esteem. The Comte D'Orvilliers, Commander-in-Chief at Brest, showed him the utmost kindness, untinctured by any of that professional jealousy with which he was afterwards regarded by the horde of inferior officers of the French navy. The Duc de Chartres seemed friendly; and, above all, the wise and venerable Franklin, who, from first to last, appears to have appreciated his character, proved a friend as steady as he was judicious.

Jones had not been three weeks in Brest when Franklin wrote him, congratulating him on his late success, and proposing another expedition. "The Jersey privateers," he says, "do us a great deal of mischief by intercepting our supplies. It has been mentioned to me, that your small vessel, commanded by so brave an officer, might render great service, by following them where greater ships dare not venture their bottoms; or, being accompanied and supported by some frigates from Brest, at a proper distance, might draw them out and then take them. I wish you to consider of this, as it comes from *high authority*."

To be made the decoy-duck of French frigates could not be peculiarly agreeable to a man whose first and vehement object at all times was "a separate command," "unlimited orders," and to be his "own counsellor." Yet in reply he says, "Nothing could give me more pleasure than to render essential service to America in any way which you may find expedient." He then hints his desire of still obtaining the command of the ship building at Amsterdam. "I demand nothing," he adds, "and though I know that it was the intention of Congress to give me that ship, I am now ready to go wherever the service calls me." "If two or three fast-sailing ships could be collected together, there is a great choice of *private enterprises* that I can name, some of which might effectually succeed, and would be far more for the interest and honour of America than cruising with twice the force. It appears to me to be the province of our infant navy to surprise and spread alarms with fast-sailing ships. When we grow stronger we can meet their [the British] fleets, and dispute with them the sovereignty of the ocean."

These plans and speculations were forgotten in the more dazzling prospects which the following letter from Franklin opened to Jones; though what at first promised so fair, afterwards became to him the source of much trouble and vexation:—

(Private.)

"Dear Sir,

"I have the pleasure of informing you, that it is proposed to give you the command of the great ship we have built at Amsterdam. By what you wrote to us formerly, I have ventured to say in your behalf, that this proposition would be agreeable to you. You will immediately let me know your resolution; which, that you may be more clear in taking, I must inform you of some circumstances. She is at present the property of the King; but as there is no war yet declared, you will have the commission and flag of the States, and act under their orders and laws. The Prince de Nassau will make the cruise with you. She is to be brought here under cover as a French merchantman, to be equipped and manned in France. We hope to exchange your prisoners for as many American sailors; but if that fails, you have your present crew to be made up here with other nations and French. The other Commissioners are not acquainted with this proposition as yet; and you see by the nature of it, that it is necessary to be kept a secret till we have got the vessel here, for fear of difficulties in Holland, and interception; you will therefore direct your answer to me alone. It being desired that the affair should rest between you and me, perhaps it may be best for you to take a trip up here to concert matters, if in general you approve the idea.

"I was much pleased with reading your journal, which we received yesterday."

A few days after this, Franklin had this affair so well matured as to write again in the following terms:—

"Passy, June 10th, 1778.

"DEAR SIR,

"I received yours of 1st instant, with the papers enclosed, which I have shown to the other Commissioners, but have not yet had their opinion of them; only I know that they had before (in consideration of the disposition and uneasiness of your people) expressed an inclination to order your ship directly back to America. You will judge from what follows, whether it will not be advisable *for you to propose* their sending her back with her people, and under some other command. In consequence of the high opinion the Minister of the Marine has of your conduct and bravery, it is now settled (observe, that is to be a secret between us, I being expressly enjoined not to communicate it to any other person,) that you are to have the frigate from Holland, which actually belongs to government, and will be furnished with as many good French seamen as you shall require. But you are to act under Congress commission. As you may like to have a number of Americans, and your own are home-sick, it is proposed to give you as many as you can engage out of two hundred prisoners, which the ministry of Britain have at length agreed to give us in exchange for those you have in your hands. They propose to make the exchange at Calais, where they are to bring the Americans. Nothing is wanting to this but a list of yours, containing their names and rank; immediately on the receipt of which an equal number are to be prepared, and sent in a ship to that port, where yours are to meet them.

"If by this means you can get a good new crew, I think it would be best that you are quite free of the old; for a mixture might introduce the infection of that sickness you complain of. But this may be left to your own discretion. Perhaps we shall join you with the Providence, Captain Whipple, a new continental ship of 30 guns, which, in coming out of the river of Providence, gave the two frigates that were posted to intercept her each of them so heavy a dose of her 18 and 12 pounders, that they had not the courage, or were not able, to pursue her. It seems to be desired that you will step up to Versailles, (where one will meet you,) in order to such a settlement of matters and plans with those who have the direction as cannot well be done by letter. I wish it may be convenient to you to do it immediately.

"The project of giving you the command of this ship pleases me the more, as it is a probable opening to the higher preferment you so justly merit."

Jones must have been exceedingly gratified by this information. It was placing him at once at the summit of his wishes. The French Minister of Marine notified the wishes of his Most Christian Majesty to employ the American captain; and the Commissioners as formally signified their acquiescence. They say, "We readily consent that he should be at your Excellency's disposition, and shall be happy if his services may be in any respect useful to the designs your Excellency has in contemplation."

Though Jones had already some experience of Marine Committees, and of the delays and insolence of office, it was quite impossible that he could have anticipated all the torture and vexation laid up in store for him by a proposal which at first sight appeared so fair and flattering. He made his acknowledgments to the minister in his best style; but probably thought less of the "dignity of human nature," the slang of that day, long before all official connexion was finished between them. "I have no doubt," he says, "that many projects might be formed from the hints which I had the honour of sending lately for your inspection: had I been intrusted with the chief command, I would have held myself responsible for consequences."

"I am bound in honour to communicate faithfully to Congress the generous offer which the King now makes, of lending the Epervier in the meantime to be employed under my command, under the flag of America. I have now under my command a ship bound to America. On my arrival there, from the former confidence of Congress, I have reason to expect an immediate removal into one of their best ships. I have reason to expect the chief command of the first squadron destined for an expedition, having in my possession several similar appointments; and when Congress see fit to appoint admirals, I have assurance that my name will not be forgot. These are flattering prospects to a man who has drawn his sword only upon principles of philanthropy, and in support of the dignity of human nature. But as I prefer a solid to a shining reputation, a useful to a splendid command, I hold myself ready, with the approbation of the Commissioners, to be governed by you in any measures that may tend to distress and humble the common enemy."

This letter, in several of its hints, shows some address on the part of Jones, who, it must be acknowledged, seldom, unless stirred by indignation or a sense of injury, slipped the opportunity of forwarding his own interests by an opportune hint or leading suggestion: of hints and projects of a public nature his brain was at all times singularly fertile. At this moment of excitement it teemed with bold ideas or fancies. To effect the destruction of Whitehaven was, as we have seen, one project. To take the Bank of Ayr, destroy that town, and probably Greenock and Port-Glasgow, with the shipping in the Clyde, was a yet bolder design. "Much," he says, "might be done in Ireland, where ships worth 150,000 *livres, or even* 200,000, might be seized,—London might be distressed, by cutting off the supply of coals carried from Newcastle,—the fishing at Campbelton might be destroyed, and many towns on the north-east coasts of England and Scotland might be burnt or laid under contribution." A more feasible project was the capture or destruction of the Baltic fleet. "The success of any of these, or of like enterprises," says Jones, in a letter to the French Minister of Marine, "will depend in surprising well, and on despatch both in the attack and in the retreat; therefore it is necessary the ships should *sail fast*, and that their forces should be sufficient to repel any of the enemy's cruising frigates, two of which may perhaps be met at a time. It is scarcely conceivable how great a panic the success of any one of these projects would occasion in England. It would convince the world that their coasts are vulnerable, and would, consequently, hurt their public credit.

"If alarming the coast of Britain should be thought inexpedient, to intercept the enemy's West India or Baltic fleets, or their Hudson's Bay ships, or to destroy their Greenland fishery, are capital objects."

There is much in these plans that must either have been conceived in ignorance, or suggested by Jones for the purpose of merely amusing, or of quickening the motions of the French marine department. Even when, long afterwards, a force was obtained, not one of them was attempted save the abortive attack on Leith.

It has been noticed, that, after the engagement with the Drake, Captain Jones ordered Lieutenant Simpson under arrest for what appeared very satisfactory reasons. He had afterwards been annoyed by the Commissioners' dishonouring his draft, and he was now enraged by their conduct regarding Simpson, the offending officer. Indeed no excuse can be offered for their proceedings, save that these distracted Commissioners had not power at all times to administer rigid justice, whatever might have been their wishes. The account of this proceeding is given in the words of the memorial, long afterwards prepared by Captain Jones for the information of the King of France. It was an insult the memory of which did not soon leave him.

"The lieutenant under arrest on board the Drake had constant intercourse with the crew; who thereby became so insolent as to refuse duty, and go all hands below repeatedly before the Captain's face. It was impossible to trifle at that time, as Count D'Orvilliers had assured Captain Jones, unless he could get the Drake ready to transport the prisoners to America before orders arrived from Court, they would in all probability be given up without an exchange, to avoid immediate war with England. It therefore became impossible to suffer the lieutenant to remain any longer among them. Captain Jones had him removed to the ship called the Admiral, where the French confine even the first officers in the service. He had there a good chamber to himself, and liberty to walk the deck. The lieutenant endeavoured to desert out of the Admiral, and behaved in a manner so extravagant, that Count D'Orvilliers (without the knowledge of Captain Jones) ordered him to the prison of the port, where he also had a good chamber, and Captain Jones paid his expenses out of his own pocket.

"About this time Captain Jones, finding the lieutenant appeared more reasonable than formerly, took his parole in writing, not to serve again in the navy before he was acquitted by a court-martial, and set him at liberty. A day or two afterwards the Commissioners thought fit to interfere respecting the lieutenant of the Ranger, which, it is presumed, they had no authority to do, as it laid the axe to the root of subordination."

On returning from Versailles, whither he had gone, as has been noticed, on the invitation of Franklin, Captain Jones feeling himself dreadfully aggrieved, wrote as follows:—

"Brest, August 13th, 1778.

"GENTLEMEN,

"I have been five days in this place since my return from Passy, during which time I have neither seen nor heard from Lieutenant Simpson; but Mr Hill, who was last winter at Passy, and who sailed with me from Nantes, informs me truly, that it is generally reported in the Ranger, and of course throughout the French fleet, and on shore, that I am turned out of the service; that you, gentlemen, have given Mr Simpson my place, with a captain's commission, and that my letter to you of the 16th July was involuntary on my part, and in obedience only to your orders.

"That these reports prevail is not an idle conjecture, but a melancholy fact. Therefore I beseech you,—I demand of you to afford me redress,—redress by a court-martial; to form which we have now, with the assistance of Captain Hinman, Captain Read, as also them at Nantes, a sufficient number of officers in France, exclusive of myself. The Providence and Britain are expected here very soon from Nantes, and I am certain that they neither can nor will again depart, before my friend Captain Hinman can come down here; and it is his unquestioned right to succeed me in the Ranger.

"I have faithfully and personally supported and fought the dignified cause of human nature ever since the American banners first waved on the Delaware and on the ocean. This I did when that man did not call himself a republican, but left the continent, and served its enemies; and this I did when this man appeared backward, and did not support me as he ought.

"I conclude by requesting you to call before you, and examine for your own satisfaction, Mr Edward Meyers, who is now at the house of the Swedish Ambassador, and who, having been with me as a volunteer, can and will, I am persuaded, represent to you the conduct of the officers and men towards me, both before I left Brest, and afterwards in the Irish Channel, as well as my conduct towards them.—I have the honour to be, &c. &c.

"Their Excellencies the
American Plenipotentiaries."

He received no immediate satisfaction, and resolved to digest his chagrin as he best could, and at least avoid the odium of a squabble among the Americans in France.

In the spring of the following year, he, however, received a slight atonement to his wounded feelings, in an official letter signed by Franklin and Adams, stating, that as his removal from the Ranger, and the appointment of Lieutenant Simpson to the command of that ship, might be liable to misrepresentations and misinterpretations, they certified it to be done by them, that, on the request of M. de Sartine, he might be employed on some public service; and that Simpson had been appointed by his (Jones's) consent after he had released that officer from an arrest under which he had placed him.

The prospect of immediate active service, of getting afloat with unlimited orders, and a larger force than he had ever yet commanded, so flattering and near in July, became more doubtful in the end of August; and by September, as war was now declared with England, the French officers were in the first place to be provided for;

and the promised, or rather offered, frigates dwindled down to a much smaller force. Even that was delayed. After repeatedly applying to the American Commissioners, and using all the personal influence which his enlarged acquaintance in the court circles enabled him to obtain, Jones found it needful to remonstrate with M. de Sartine. He had, however, lost another powerful hold of the Minister. The Prince of Nassau, who in the outset had eagerly desired to accompany him in his expedition, either from caprice or change of views, abandoned the scheme, without scruple or apology, and to the letters of Jones did not even deign the civility of a reply.

That his time might not be wholly consumed in idleness, and in the sickness of hope deferred, Jones again addressed the Minister in what he calls "an explicit letter," which explains his situation better than could be done in many words.

"Brest, September 13th, 1778.

"HONOURED SIR,

"When his Excellency Doctor Franklin informed me that you had condescended to think me worthy of your notice, I took such pleasure in reflecting on the happy alliance between France and America, that I was really flattered, and entertained the most grateful sense of the honour which you proposed for me, as well as the favour which the king proposed for America, by putting so fine a ship of war as the Indian under my command, and under its flag, with unlimited orders.

"In obedience to your desire, I came to Versailles, and was taught to believe that my intended ship was in deep water, and ready for the sea; but when the Prince (de Nassau) returned I received from him a different account; I was told that the Indian could not be got afloat within a shorter period than three months at the approaching equinox.

"To employ this interval usefully, I first offered to go from Brest with Count D'Orvilliers, as a volunteer, which you thought fit to reject. I had then the satisfaction to find that you approved in general of a variety of hints for private enterprises which I had drawn up for your consideration, and I was flattered with assurances from Messieurs de Chaumont and Bandonin, that three of the finest frigates in France, with two tenders, and a number of troops, would be immediately put under my command; and that I should have unlimited orders, and be at free liberty to pursue such of my own projects as I thought proper. But this plan fell to nothing in the moment when I was taught to think that nothing was wanting but the King's signature.

"Another much inferior armament from L'Orient was proposed to be put under my command, which was by no means equal to the services that were expected from it; for speed and force, though both requisite, were both wanting. Happily for me this also failed, and I was thereby saved from a dreadful prospect of ruin and dishonour.

"I had so entire a reliance that you would desire nothing of me inconsistent with my honour and rank, that the moment you required me to come down here, in order to proceed round to St Malo, though I had received no written orders, and neither knew your intention respecting my destination or command, I obeyed with such haste, that although my curiosity led me to look at the armament at L'Orient, yet I was but three days from Passy till I reached Brest. Here too I drew a blank; but when I saw the Lively, it was no disappointment, as that ship, both in sailing and equipment, is far inferior to the Ranger.

"My only disappointment here was my being precluded from embarking in pursuit of marine knowledge with Count D'Orvilliers, who did not sail till seven days after my return. He is my friend, and expressed his wishes for my company; I accompanied him out of the road when the fleet sailed; and he always lamented that neither himself nor any person in authority in Brest had received from you any order that mentioned my name. I am astonished therefore to be informed that you attribute my not being in the fleet to my stay at L'Orient.

"I am not a mere adventurer of fortune. Stimulated by principles of reason and philanthropy, I laid aside my enjoyments in private life, and embarked under the flag of America when it was first displayed. In that line my desire of fame is infinite, and I must not now so far forget my own honour, and what I owe to my friends and America, as to remain inactive.

"My rank knows no superior in the American marine: I have long since been appointed to command an expedition with five of its ships, and I can receive orders from no junior or inferior officer whatever.

"I have been here in the most tormenting suspense for more than a month since my return; and agreeable to your desire, as mentioned to me by Monsieur Chaumont, a lieutenant has been appointed, and is with me, who speaks the French as well as the English. Circular letters have been written, and sent the 8th of last month from the English Admiralty, because they expected me to pay another visit with four ships. Therefore I trust that, if the Indian is not to be got out, you will not, at the approaching season, substitute a force that is not at least equal both in strength and sailing to any of the enemy's cruising ships.

"I do not wish to interfere with the harmony of the French marine; but if I am still thought worthy of your attention, I shall hope for a separate command, with liberal orders. If, on the contrary, you should now have no further occasion for my services, the only favour I can ask is, that you will bestow on me the Alert, with a few seamen, and permit me to return, and carry with me your good opinion in that small vessel, before the winter, to America."

This letter was submitted to the Duc de Rochefoucault, and enclosed to Franklin, who, while he omitted no opportunity of serving Jones, still counselled patience. To Franklin he says, " It is in vain for the minister to pretend that he has not ships to bestow. I know the contrary. He has bestowed the *Renommée* and others here since my return; and there are yet several new ships unbestowed at St Malo and elsewhere. I know too, that unless the States of Holland oppose it, the Indian can be got afloat with a tenth part of the difficulty that has been represented. If I was worth his notice at the beginning I am not less so now. After all, you have desired me to have patience, and I promise you that I will wait your kind advice, and take no step without your approbation. If it were consistent and convenient for you to see M. de Sartine, I should hope that such an explanation would be the consequence as might remove every cause of uneasiness."

Day after day he continued to write Franklin, mentioning vessels that he might command if the minister were sincere in his professions. Meanwhile Franklin procured the minister's order that he should be received on board the French fleet; but, either intentionally or by accident, it came too late to admit of his embarking to gain that knowledge of naval tactics, and of governing a fleet, which was his object. It was indeed surmised that the jealousy of the French service was the true obstacle, both to his promised command and desire of increasing his knowledge of his profession on the great scale. "I think of going to L'Orient," he says, "being heartily sick of Brest, and an eyesore to the marine." In another letter he says, "I have excited the jealousy of many officers in our young navy, because I have pursued honour while they sought after profit."

Gradually as his hopes decreased, Jones lowered his demands. He proposed many different vessels, the chief object being fast-sailing ships. "I wish to have no connexion with any ship that does not sail fast," he says, "for I intend to *go in harm's way*. You know, I believe, that this is not every one's intention; therefore buy a frigate that sails fast, and that is sufficiently large to carry twenty-six or twenty-eight guns on one deck." "I have, to show my gratitude to France," he adds, "lost so much time, and with it such opportunities as I cannot regain,—I have almost half killed myself with grief. Give me but an assurance that the command of the Indian will be reserved for me, and bestowed on no other person on any pretence whatsoever, and I will say I am satisfied. This I pledge myself will be no loss to France—America is not ungrateful. The noble-minded Congress know not the little mean distinctions of climate or place of nativity, nor have they adopted any *rule* which can preclude them from encouraging or rewarding the merit of a stranger, by raising him even to the first posts of honour. In the army there are many instances of this. In the navy, young as it is, it gives me particular pleasure to inform you that Congress have given the command of *the best ship* in their service to a French officer, and called the ship the *Alliance*."

Many vessels were proposed in succession, and all were abandoned. The anger and impatience of Jones got beyond control, and he never appears to have been of the temper which makes a proud man disdain to reveal his chagrin and disappointment. M. de Sartine accordingly, on his part, felt equally annoyed by the incessant importunity of the man who held him to his word.

To the Duc de Rochefoucault, whom he always found friendly, Jones writes,—" The minister's behaviour towards me has been and is really astonishing. At his request (for I sought not the connexion) I gave up absolute certainties, and far more flattering prospects than any of those which he proposed. What inducement could I have for this but gratitude to France for having first recognized our independence? And having given my word to stay for some time in Europe, I have been and am unwilling to take it back, especially after having communicated the circumstances to Congress. The minister, to my infinite mortification, after possessing himself of my *schemes* and *ideas*, has treated me like a child five times successively, by leading me on from great to little, and from little to less. Does such conduct do honour either to his head or to his heart? He has not to this moment offered me the least apology for any of these five deceptions; nor has he, I believe, assigned any good reason to that venerable and great character, his Excellency Doctor Franklin, whom he has made the instrument to entrap me in this cruel state of inaction and suspense.

"The minister has lately written a letter to Count D'Orvilliers, proposing to send me home in 'une bonne voiture.' This is absolutely adding insult to injury, and it is the proposition of a man whose *veracity* I have not experienced in former cases.

"I could in the summer, with the Ranger, joined with the two other American frigates, have given the enemy sufficient foundation for their fears in Britain as well as Ireland, and could since have been assisting Count D'Estaing, or acting separately with an American squadron. Instead of this I am chained down to shameful

F 2

inactivity here, after having written to Congress to reserve no command for me in America.

"Convinced as I am, that your noble and generous breast will feel for my unmerited treatment, I must beseech you to interest yourself with the Duke de Chartres, that the King may be made acquainted with my situation. I have been taught to believe that I have been detained in France with his Majesty's knowledge and approbation, and I am sure he is too good a prince to detain me for my hurt or dishonour.

"M. de Sartine may think as he pleases, but Congress will not thank him for having thus treated an officer who has always been honoured with their favour and friendship. I entertained some hopes of his honourable intentions till he gave the command of the Fox to a lieutenant, after my friends had asked for me only that ship with the Alert cutter. He was the asker *at the beginning*, and ought to be so now; he has, to my certain knowledge, ships unbestowed, and he is bound in honour to give me the Indian, as he proposed at the first, or an equivalent command, immediately."

To M. Ray de Chaumont, Jones says about the same period,—

"Although the minister has treated me like a child five successive times, by leading me on from great to little, and from little to less, yet I had some dependence on his honourable intentions until he refused the small command which you asked for me the 23d ultimo, and afterwards bestowed the Fox *on a lieutenant* who, to my certain knowledge, does not thank him for the favour, and thinks that ship far short of his right. I say I verily believed the minister at the beginning, and afterwards; but now having deceived me so often, I wish him to know that I doubt him, though he swears even '*by the stix*.'* I have written to him several respectful letters of some consequence, none of which he has condescended to answer. This is a piece of incivility and disrespect to me as a stranger which he has not shown even to subalterns in the French marine, in whose hands I have seen his answers to

* At an interview M. Chaumont had with the minister, he swore by Styx! that Paul Jones should have a frigate, were he even to buy it.

letters of little importance. The secrecy which I was required to observe respecting what seemed his first intention in my favour has been inviolable; and I have been so delicate with respect to my situation, that I have been, and am considered everywhere as an officer disgraced and cast off for private reasons. I have of course been in actual disgrace here ever since my return, which is more than two months. I have already lost near five months of my time, the best season of the year, and such opportunities of serving my country, and *acquiring honour, as I cannot again expect this war*, while I have been thus shamefully entrapped in inaction. My duty and sensibility cannot brook this unworthy situation. If the minister's intentions have been honourable from the beginning, he will make a direct written apology to me, suitable to the injury which I have sustained, otherwise, in vindication of my sacred honour, painful as it will be, I must publish in the Gazettes of Europe the conduct he has held towards me."

The compatriots of Jones in France sympathized in his disappointment and indignation; particularly Dr Bancroft and Mr William Temple Franklin, the grandson and secretary of Benjamin Franklin. "I have felt for you most sincerely," says young Franklin; "Monsieur S.'s conduct towards you has been as remarkable as it has been unjust, and has altered in a great degree the good opinion many have had of him. I have been asked in several companies, *où est le brave Capitaine Jones? que fait-il?* and have felt myself (as your compatriot) in a manner ill-treated, when I can only answer that you are still at Brest. On the receipt of your letter, I asked Mr Chaumont 'whether he thought any thing would be done for you?' He answered, 'that to his certain knowledge M. S. was ashamed of the conduct he had held towards you, and that he was now occupied to make up for it. Bancroft,' says he, 'is assured that the minister had all along felt good dispositions, but had been prevented from carrying them into execution by the intrigues of 487,557,* (the marine,) among whom multitudes were mak-

* These numbers refer to a cipher that Bancroft and young Franklin had got from Paul Jones for their private correspondence with him.

ing interest, and caballing to obtain 303, (ships,) and opposing the disposal of any except among their own body; but 710 (M. de Sartine) had assured him that you should soon have one, if he were even to purchase it.' Mr Bandonin desired me also to make you his best compliments, to assure you that he would not suffer your business to rest much longer, and in the mean time to beg your patience a little longer. In this situation I know not what we can do, but wait a week or two, when, if nothing comes, I think 299 (Doctor Franklin) will declare his utmost resentment, and nothing that any of us can say will be too bad."

Worn out with waiting, "half killed," as he strongly expresses himself, with suspense and inaction, Jones now formed the design of directly addressing the king, and of soliciting the kindness of the family of *Chartres*, (Orleans,) in presenting his letter. He, as usual, took the precaution of enclosing all these epistolary compositions to Franklin,—a course which preserved him from ever going too far wrong, even while under the greatest irritation.

In his letter to Franklin, he says, "The Duchesse de Chartres will, I am persuaded, undertake to deliver my letter into the King's hands; and as you may not yet think fit to appear in the business, either the Duc de Rochefoucault, or your grandson, will oblige me by waiting on her at the Palais Royal. The Duc de Rochefoucault, as he understands English well, and is acquainted with the circumstances, would oblige me much if he would be present when the letter is presented to the King. I do not wish to trouble the Duc de Chartres about this affair, as that brave prince has undeservedly met with vexations of his own."

The following is the letter which Captain Jones wrote to the King of France, and which was to be presented to his Majesty by the Duchess of Chartres, afterwards the Duchess of Orleans:—

"Brest, October 19th, 1778.

"SIRE,

"After my return to Brest in the American ship of war the Ranger, from the Irish Channel, his excellency Dr Franklin informed me by letter, dated June the 1st, that M. de Sartine, having a high opinion of my conduct and bravery, had determined, with your Majesty's consent and approbation, to give me the command of the ship of war the Indian, which was built at Amsterdam for America, but afterwards, for political reasons, made the property of France.

" I was to act with unlimited orders under the commission and flag of America; and the Prince de Nassau proposed to accompany me on the ocean.

" I was deeply penetrated with the sense of the honour done me by this generous proposition, as well as of the favour your Majesty intended thereby to confer on America. And I accepted the offer with the greater pleasure, as the Congress had sent me to Europe in the Ranger, to command the Indian before the ownership of that vessel was changed.

" The minister desired to see me at Versailles to settle future plans of operation, and I attended him for that purpose. I was told that the Indian was at the Texel completely armed and fitted for sea; but the Prince de Nassau was sent express to Holland, and returned with a very different account. The ship was at Amsterdam, and could not be got afloat or armed before the September equinox. The American plenipotentiaries proposed that I should return to America; and as I have repeatedly been appointed to the chief command of an American squadron to execute secret enterprises, it was not doubted but that Congress would again show me a preference. M. de Sartine, however, thought proper to prevent my departure, by writing to the plenipotentiaries, (without my knowledge,) requesting that I might be permitted to remain in Europe, and that the Ranger might be sent back to America under another commander, he having special services which he wished me to execute. This request they readily granted, and I was flattered by the prospect of being enabled to testify, by my services, my gratitude to your Majesty, as the first prince who has so generously acknowledged our independence.

"There was an interval of more than three months before the Indian could be gotten afloat. To employ that period usefully, when your Majesty's fleet was ordered to sail from Brest, I proposed to the minister to embark in it as a volunteer, in pursuit of marine knowledge. He objected to this, at the same time approved of a variety of hints for private enterprises, which I had drawn up for his consideration. Two gentlemen were appointed to settle with me the plans that were to be adopted, who gave me the assurance that three of the best frigates in France, with two tenders, and a number of troops, should be immediately put under my command, to pursue such of my own projects as I thought proper; but this fell to nothing, when I believed that your Majesty's signature only was wanting.

"Another armament, composed of cutters and small vessels, at L'Orient, was proposed to be put under my command, to alarm the coasts of England and check the Jersey privateers; but, happily for me, this also failed, and I was saved from ruin and dishonour, as I now find that all the vessels sailed slow, and their united force is very insignificant. The minister then thought fit that I should return to Brest to command the Lively, and join some frigates on an expedition from St

Malo to the North Sea. I returned in haste for that purpose, and found that the Lively had been bestowed at Brest before the minister had mentioned that ship to me at Versailles. This was, however, another fortunate disappointment, as the Lively proves, both in sailing and equipment, much inferior to the Ranger; but, more especially, if it be true, as I have since understood, that the minister intended to give the chief command of the expedition to a lieutenant, which would have occasioned a very disagreeable misunderstanding: for, as an officer of the first rank in the American marine, who has ever been honoured with the favour and friendship of Congress, I can receive orders from no inferior officer whatever. My plan was the destruction of the English Baltic fleet, of great consequence to the enemy's marine, and then only protected by a single frigate! I would have held myself responsible for its success had I commanded the expedition.

"M. de Sartine afterwards sent orders to Count D'Orvilliers to receive me on board the fleet, agreeably to my former proposal; but the order did not arrive until after the departure of the fleet the last time from Brest, nor was I made acquainted with the circumstance before the fleet returned here.

" Thus have I been chained down to shameful inactivity for nearly five months. I have lost the best season of the year, and such opportunities of serving my country and acquiring honour as I cannot again expect this war; and, to my infinite mortification, having no command, I am considered everywhere an officer cast off and in disgrace for secret reasons.

" I have written respectful letters to the minister, none of which he has condescended to answer; I have written to the Prince de Nassau with as little effect; and I do not understand that any apology has been made to the great and venerable Dr Franklin, whom the minister has made the instrument of bringing me into such unmerited trouble.

" Having written to Congress to reserve no command for me in America, my sensibility is the more affected by this unworthy situation in the sight of your Majesty's fleet. I, however, make no remark on the treatment I have received.

"Although I wish not to become my own panegyrist, I must beg your Majesty's permission to observe, that I am not an adventurer in search of fortune, of which, thank God, I have a sufficiency.

"When the American banner was first displayed, I drew my sword in support of the violated dignity and rights of human nature; and both honour and duty prompt me steadfastly to continue the righteous pursuit, and to sacrifice to it, not only my private enjoyments, but even life, if necessary. I must acknowledge that the generous praise which I have received from Congress and others exceeds the merit of my past services; therefore I the more ardently wish for future opportunities of testifying my gratitude by my activity.

"As your Majesty, by espousing the cause of America, hath become the protector of the rights of human nature, I am persuaded that you will not disregard my situation, nor suffer me to remain any longer in this insupportable disgrace.

I am, with perfect gratitude
and profound respect,
SIRE,
Your Majesty's very obliged,
very obedient, and
very humble servant,
J. PAUL JONES."

There is no satisfactory evidence that the above letter was ever presented, or indeed that it ever came into the hands of the Duchess of Chartres; yet the fact appears to be assumed by the American biographer of Jones; and the letter itself, as expressive of his sentiments at this crisis, is too important to be suppressed. The correspondence and journals of Jones contain no allusion to any effect produced by that letter,—not even the extract of his journal made long afterwards, expressly for the perusal of the King; and the postscript of a letter written by Mr Temple Franklin is at least complete proof that, if the letter to the King was ever delivered, it was decidedly against the judgment of Franklin. The letter of the younger Franklin is dated the 22d October, the postscript the 24th. It says, " Since writing the above, I have received yours of the 19th instant (the letter to the King.) I would willingly do every thing you there desire of me, but it is my grandfather's opinion that there will be no occasion to send those letters; and I imagine they were wrote before you heard of the minister's final determination. If, however, you still think they ought to be sent, you have only to order it."

From this it would appear that the minister's " final determination" to buy Jones " a suitable ship" had preceded the letter to the King, and was not a consequence of it. In a letter to M. de Chaumont, of the 30th November, Jones thus expresses himself with regard to M. de Sartine:—" My best respects and most grateful thanks await the minister for the very honourable things he said of me to the Duc de la Rochefoucault. It shall be my ambition, when he gives me opportunities, to merit his favour and affection."

CHAPTER V.

The gratitude of Jones to the minister of marine was premature. But it would be tiresome to follow the train of petty disappointments which this brave man had yet to encounter before he got once again fairly afloat. From the month of June, 1778, till the month of February of the following year, he was condemned to feel to its utmost extent the misery there is—

"In suing long to bide."

In this interval some proposals were made to Captain Jones while at Brest to take the command of privateers. This he decidedly declined; and he even resented the supposition that, bearing, as he did, the commission of Congress, he should act at any time as the commander of privateers. So nice was he on this point, that in one instance we find Franklin himself condescending to sooth his hasty feelings. "Depend upon it," says the sage, "I never wrote Mr Gillon that the Bon Homme Richard was a privateer. I could not write so, because I never had such a thought. I will next post send you a copy of my letter to him, by which you will see that he has only forced that construction from a vague expression I used, merely to conceal from him (in answering his idle demand that I would order your squadron, then on the point of sailing, to go with him to Carolina,) that the expedition was at the expense and under the direction of the King, which it was not proper or necessary for him to know." And to the proposal that he would take the command of an armament of privateers, Jones says, "*Were I in pursuit of profit* I would accept it without hesitation; but I am under such obligations to Congress, that I cannot think myself my own master,—and as a servant of the Imperial Republic of America, honoured with the public approbation of my past services, I cannot, from my own authority or inclination, serve either myself or even my best friends, in any private line whatsoever." With these feelings, his indignation at being long afterwards offered a letter-of-marque by the French government, in requital of his services, may be easily imagined. But this belongs to a more advanced stage of his history.

Every thing appeared in a fair way in November; yet Jones found it necessary to repair once more to Versailles, and to Passy, the seat of the American legation. "As nothing was done," he says in his memorial to the King, "Captain Jones determined to go himself to court." When he got there, the minister offered him the Marshal de Broglio, a large ship; but as his Americans had all left the service during the long period of idleness, he was unable to man this vessel, and the Duc de Duras was bought for him, which, among many other vessels, he had acquainted his friends, was on sale at L'Orient.

On the 6th of February Jones had at last the satisfaction of making, from Passy, his acknowledgments to the minister Sartine. His gratitude was quite as lively as the treatment he had received required. He obtained leave to change the name of the ship to *Bon Homme Richard*, "in compliment," he says, "to a saying of Poor Richard," (of which, by the way, he had just experienced the truth,) " If you would have your business done, come yourself—if not, send."

Jones now went to Nantes to engage seamen, and to obtain cannon to arm his ship. On his late journey he had been introduced to M. Garnier, in order to concert a plan of operations for a combined naval and military force. Four or five sail were to be added to the Bon Homme Richard, of which two vessels were to be fire-ships. Five hundred picked men, taken from the Irish regiment, were to embark under the command of Mr Fitzmaurice. All were to be under the entire command of Jones. " A plan,"* he says, " was laid, which promised perfect success, and had it succeeded, would have astonished the world."

In an evil hour he solicited that the Alliance, a new American frigate, of which the command had been given by Congress to one Landais, a Frenchman, should be added to his force. As Dr Franklin had just been formally appointed

* This plan was directed against Liverpool.

ambassador to the Court of France, Jones imagined that not only the disposal of the frigate, but the power of displacing its commander at pleasure, was vested in him, as the guardian of American interests in Europe.

About this time the Marquis de la Fayette returned from America, and he wished to go on the projected expedition. Jones was summoned to court; and it was arranged that the Marquis de la Fayette was to command a body of about 700 troops, assigned him by the King. The Alliance was made part of the squadron by the American minister plenipotentiary, at the particular desire of the French government.

The squadron was now to consist of the Bon Homme Richard, the Alliance, the Pallas, the Vengeance brig, and the Cerf, a fine cutter, well fitted and manned. "A person," (M. Chaumont,) says Jones, "was appointed commissary, and unwisely intrusted with the secret of the expedition. The commissary took upon himself the whole direction at L'Orient; but the secret was too big for him to keep. All Paris rang with the expedition from L'Orient; and government was obliged to drop the plan when the squadron lay ready for sea, and the troops ready to embark."

In the expectation that Jones was to be joined by the Marquis de la Fayette, his judicious friend Franklin wrote him thus, actuated, no doubt, both by anxiety for the public cause and regard to the individual he addressed:

"I have, at the request of M. de Sartine, postponed the sending of the Alliance to America, and have ordered her to proceed immediately from Nantes to L'Orient, where she is to be furnished with her complement of men, join your little squadron, and act under your command.

"The Marquis de la Fayette will be with you soon. It has been observed that joint-expeditions of land and sea forces often miscarry through jealousies and misunderstandings between the officers of the different corps. This must happen where there are little minds, actuated more by personal views of profit or honour to themselves, than by the warm and sincere desire of good to their country. Knowing you both, as I do, and your just manner of thinking on these occasions,

I am confident nothing of the kind can happen between you, and that it is unnecessary for me to recommend to either of you that condescension, mutual good-will, and harmony, which contribute so much to success in such undertakings. I look upon this expedition as an introduction only to greater trusts and more extensive commands, and as a kind of trial of both your abilities and of your fitness in temper and disposition for acting in concert with others. I flatter myself, therefore, that nothing will happen that may give impressions to the disadvantage of either of you, when greater affairs shall come under consideration.

" As this is understood to be an American expedition, under the Congress commission and colours, the Marquis, who is a Major-General in that service, has of course the step in point of rank, and he must have the command of the land-forces, which are committed by the King to his care; but the command of the ships will be entirely in you, in which I am persuaded that whatever authority his rank might in strictness give him, he will not have the least desire to interfere with you. There is honour enough to be got for both of you if the expedition is conducted with a prudent unanimity. The circumstance is indeed a little unusual; for there is not only a junction of land and sea forces, but there is also a junction of Frenchmen and Americans, which increases the difficulty of maintaining a good understanding; a cool, prudent conduct in the chiefs is therefore the more necessary, and I trust neither of you will in that respect be deficient. With my best wishes for your success, health, and honour, I remain, dear Sir, your affectionate and most obedient servant."

This excellent counsel was not thrown away on Jones. His letter to La Fayette, written a few days afterwards, re-echoes the sentiments of the republican sage. "Where men of fine feelings are concerned," he says, "there is very seldom any misunderstanding,—and I am sure I should do the greatest violence to my sensibility if I were capable of giving you a moment's pain by any part of my conduct; therefore, without any apology, I shall expect you to point out my errors, when we are alone together, with perfect freedom,—and I think I dare promise you that your reproof shall not be lost. I have received from the good Dr Franklin instructions at large, which do honour to his liberal mind, and which it will give me the greatest satisfaction to execute. I cannot ensure success,—but we will endeavour to deserve it."

Some of the instructions of Dr Franklin to which Jones refers, and of which he says, "your noble-minded instructions would make a coward brave," deserve to be made known as widely as possible.*

"You are to bring to France all the English seamen you may happen to take prisoners, in order to complete the good work you have already made such progress in, of delivering, by an exchange, the rest of our countrymen now languishing in the gaols of Great Britain.

* It is a pleasing trait in the history of that period, that all the naval commanders of the countries at war with England had particular orders "not to molest the ships of the brave navigator Captain Cook," if they chanced to fall in with them.

"As many of your officers and people have lately escaped from English prisons, either in Europe or America, you are to be particularly attentive to their conduct towards the prisoners which the fortune of war may throw in your hands, lest resentment of the more than barbarous usage by the English in many places towards the Americans, should occasion a retaliation, and an imitation of what ought rather to be detested and avoided, for the sake of humanity and for the honour of our country.

"In the same view, although the English have wantonly burnt many defenceless towns in America, you are not to follow this example, unless where a reasonable ransom is refused; in which case your own generous feelings, as well as this instruction, will induce you to give timely notice of your intention, that sick and ancient persons, women and children, may be first removed."

Jones attributes the failure of the expedition so much talked of to the tattling of the commissary; but he probably over-rates that circumstance. The truth is, that the French government never continued for one week of the same mind; and they had, about this time, been seized with that *grand idea* by which the court and people of France seem to be periodically infatuated—the design of invading England. The expedition which was "to astonish the world" was abandoned, according to La Fayette, "for political and military reasons." Instead of Commodore Jones burning towns and shipping, taking hostages and levying contributions, an invasion was to be attempted on that grand scale so congenial to the Gallic character.

Another service was in consequence allotted to Jones. He was to act as convoy to troops, stores, and private merchandize, for Bordeaux and other ports in the Bay of Biscay. This trifling service he performed, and cruised about with little aim or effect for some days.

On the night of the 20th June the Alliance ran foul of the Bon Homme Richard, and injured the vessel. The character of Landais, the commander of the Alliance, and his after conduct, which was marked by the grossest degree of insubordination, insolence, and even treachery, gave rise to a suspicion that this accident was of a doubtful character. The head and bowsprit of the Bon Homme Richard were carried away, and the Alliance lost her mizen-mast. The lieutenant of the Bon Homme Richard, who had the watch that night, was afterwards broke by a court-martial.

Even at this busy period Jones had not forgotten his relations in Scotland, though his correspondence with them necessarily required some management. It does not appear by what channel the following letter, received at Dumfries, was transmitted to Cork. The person on whom the bill (for £30) was drawn could not be heard of in Carlisle. Other remittances made by Jones to his friends were in like manner never received. In reply to a letter from his sister, Mrs Taylor, informing him of the death of his mother and eldest sister, he says with true feeling, "The loss of those dear friends is the more affecting to me, as they never received the remittances I intended for them, and as they had not perhaps a true idea of my affection." The following letter is addressed to Jones's eldest sister, Elizabeth Paul:—

"Cork, June 1st, 1779.

"If ever my dear girl had any doubts of the sincerity of my friendship, I hope the enclosed bill will remove them. You find it drawn in favour of my dearest departed brother, Captain Plaince. However, as it is made payable to his order, my sister-in-law's signature will make it quite the same. Had the bill been drawn on any place of commerce, I would have negotiated it myself, and then got a bill on Dumfries for you; however, as Carlisle is near you, you will sooner get the money, as I must have sent it there for acceptance. The half is for Mrs Paul, and the other half for your use. You will immediately get some gentleman to present it for acceptance: you will find it payable ten days after. Adieu, my dear girl; number me with the sincerest of your friends, write me of your health, and be assured of the good wishes of

"Your humble servant,

"Judith Plaince."

On the 30th of June, Jones came into the road of Groix. The Alliance and Bon Homme Richard both required to be refitted; the other vessels meanwhile looked after prizes. On that day the log-book of the Bon Homme Richard has the following entry:—

"At half-past 7, P. M., saw two sail bearing down upon us, one with a flag at each mast-head. Hove about and stood from them to get in readiness for action; then hove mizen-topsail to the mast, down all stay-sails and up mizen-sail. Then they hove about and stood from us. Immediately we tacked ship and stood after them.

"After which they wore ship and stood for us. Captain Jones, *gentleman-like*, called all his officers, and consulted them whether they were willing to see them. They all said yes. Made sail after them; but they, being better sailers than we, got from us. At 1, A. M., tacked ship."

At the isle of Groix Jones lay for six weeks,—a period not without its vexations. In anticipating his earlier arrival, and unconscious of the damage received by the shock of the Alliance, Dr Franklin, in the following letter of the 30th June, directed him to set out on a long cruise.

"Passy, June 30, 1779.

"Dear Sir,

"Being arrived at Groix, you are to make the best of your way, with the vessels under your command, to the west of Ireland, and establish your cruise on the Orcades, the cape of Derneus, and the Dogger-Bank, in order to take the enemy's property in those seas.

"The prizes you may make send to Dunkirk, Ostend, or Bergen in Norway, according to your proximity to either of those ports. Address them to the persons M. De Chaumont shall indicate to you.

"About the 15th August, when you will have sufficiently cruised in these seas, you are to make route for the Texel, where you will meet my further orders.

"If, by any personal accident, you should be rendered unable to execute these instructions, the officer of your squadron next in rank is to endeavour to put them in execution.

"With best wishes for your prosperity, I am ever, dear Sir, your affectionate friend and humble servant, B. Franklin.

"The Honourable Captain Jones."

The preceding letter was crossed by that in which Jones gave an account of his cruise, and of the Alliance running foul of the Bon Homme Richard. In this letter he again hinted his desire to obtain the Indian, to cruise towards the Texel, and bring her out with the crew he now had. But Franklin had no mind to change his original orders. " I have no other orders to give," he says ; " for as the court are at the chief expense, I think they have the best right to direct." —" I observe what you say about a change of destination ; but when a thing has been once considered and determined on in council, they don't care to resume the consideration of it, having much business on hand." This epistle has the following pithy postscript :—" N. B. If it should fall in your way, remember that the Hudson's Bay ships are very valuable. B. F."

Again Jones complained bitterly of the tattling commissary, (Chaumont,) who had formerly frustrated the expedition with La Fayette, and was now busied at similar work. Perhaps Commodore Jones might be over sensitive or suspicious on this point. " I have another proof," he says, "this day, of the communicative disposition of M. De Chaumont. He has written to an officer under my command a whole sheet on the subject of your letter, and has even introduced more than perhaps was necessary to a person commanding in chief. I have also strong reasons to think that this officer is not the only improper person here to whom he has written to the same effect. This is surely a strange infatuation, and it is much to be lamented that one of the best hearts in the world should be connected with a mistaken head, whose errors can afford him neither pleasure nor profit, but may effect the ruin and dishonour of a man whom he esteems and loves. Believe me, my worthy sir, I dread the thoughts of seeing this subject too soon in print, as I have done several others of greater importance, with which he was acquainted, and which I am certain he communicated too early to improper persons, whereby very important services have been impeded and set aside."

In a marginal note, in the handwriting of Jones, he says,—"I found it in print before I reached Holland!" And in another marginal note on a letter of Dr Franklin's of the 19th July, he writes, "It is clear I saw my danger, and sailed with my eyes open, rather than return to America dishonoured."

Jones was farther annoyed by reports which had reached head-quarters, and which were indeed too well-founded, that a mutinous disposition had shown itself among the crew of the Bon Homme Richard. He had at this time gone back to L'Orient. It was not deemed expedient to permit the ship to sail without inquiry and a change of men; and, what was worse, the Court saw no reason to detain the Alliance because the Bon Homme Richard was unfit for sea; and Franklin did not think proper to prevent what appeared so reasonable. This, however, did not take place; and holding out the prospect of capturing the Jamaica fleet,* then expected, escorted by a fifty-gun ship and two strong frigates, Jones solicited and obtained leave for the Monsieur privateer to join him, and his leave was extended

* In his memorial to the King of France, Jones says, "that it was his intention to cruise off the south-west of Ireland for 12 or 15 days, to intercept the enemy."

till the end of September. The captains of the Monsieur and Grandville privateers had at this time requested to be permitted to follow him and share his fortunes, offering to bind themselves to remain attached to his squadron; but this the disinterested Commissary would not permit. The consequences were soon obvious; the privateers remained attached to the squadron exactly as long as suited themselves.

Having given the necessary orders and signals, and appointed various places of rendezvous for every captain in case of separation, Commodore Jones sailed from the road of Groix on the 14th of August, exactly one day short of the time he had been desired to come into the Texel, after ending his cruise; so uncertain and precarious are all nautical movements. The squadron consisted of seven sail: the Bon Homme Richard, of 40 guns; the Alliance, of 36; the Pallas, of 32; the Cerf, of 18; and the Vengeance, of 12 guns; besides the privateers, Monsieur, of 40 guns, and the Grandville, of 14 guns;—" a force which might have effected great services," says Jones himself, in his memorial to the King of France, " and done infinite injury to the enemy, had there been *secrecy and due subordination.* Unfortunately there was neither. Captain Jones saw his danger; but his reputation being at stake, he put all to the hazard."

The effects of this want of subordination were soon felt. The captain of the privateer Monsieur, as might have been expected, acted as he thought proper, and in a few days left the squadron. And Captain Landais, a man of the most unhappy temper, not only behaved with disrespect to the Commander, but soon assumed to act as he pleased, and as an independent commander, refusing to obey the signals of the Commodore, giving chase where or how he thought fit, and availing himself of any pretext to leave the squadron, which he finally abandoned. Several prizes were made on the first days of the cruise, and more might have been captured, had a good understanding subsisted among the commanders.

From the 3d of September till the 13th the weather was stormy, and Jones continued to beat about the coasts of Scotland. The Alliance had again separated from the Bon Homme Richard;

and there remained of the squadron only the Commodore's ship, with the Pallas and Vengeance. "Yet," says Jones, "I did not abandon the hope of performing some essential service."

It was at this time he offered that attempt on Leith, by which, in one quarter of Scotland, the formidable name of "Paul Jones" is still best remembered. The following particulars are taken from his letter to Dr Franklin, giving an account of his cruise to be transmitted to Congress. The letter is dated October 3, 1779, on board the ship of war Serapis, at anchor without the Texel :—

"The winds continued to be contrary, so that we did not see the land till the evening of the 13th, when the hills of Cheviot, in the south-east of Scotland, appeared. The next day we chased sundry vessels, and took a ship and a brigantine, both from the frith of Edinburgh, laden with coal. Knowing that there lay at anchor in Leith Road an armed ship of 20 guns, with two or three fine cutters, I formed an expedition against Leith, which I purposed to lay under contribution, or otherwise to reduce it to ashes. Had I been alone, the wind being favourable, I would have proceeded directly up the frith, and must have succeeded, as they lay then in a state of perfect indolence and security, which would have proved their ruin. Unfortunately for me, the Pallas and Vengeance were both at a considerable distance in the offing, they having chased to the southward. This obliged me to steer out of the frith again to meet them. The captains of the Pallas and Vengeance being come on board the Bon Homme Richard, I communicated to them my project, to which many difficulties and objections were made by them. At last, however, they appeared to think better of the design, after I had assured (them) that I hoped to raise a contribution of £200,000 sterling on Leith, and that there was no battery of cannon there to oppose our landing. So much time, however, was unavoidably spent in pointed remarks and sage deliberations that night, that the wind became contrary in the morning."

That nothing might be wanting, Commodore Jones meanwhile prepared his summons to the Magistrates of Leith. In that locality it must still be an interesting document; and as such we give it at full length, not doubting that the worshipful persons for whom it was intended, if any of them should haply still survive, will see it for the first time with more satisfaction in these harmless pages than had it reached its destination fifty years back. Jones felt greatly chagrined and disappointed at the failure of this enterprise.

"The Honourable J. Paul Jones, Commander-in-Chief of the American Squadron now in Europe, &c., to the Worshipful the Provost of Leith, or, in his absence, to the Chief Magistrate who is now actually present and in authority there.

"Sir,

"The British marine force that has been stationed here for the protection of your city and commerce being now taken by the American arms under my command, I have the honour to send you this summons by my officer, Lieutenant-Colonel De Chamillard, who commands the vanguard of my troops. I do not wish to distress the poor inhabitants; my intention is only to demand your contribution towards the reimbursement which Britain owes to the much-injured citizens of the United States,—for savages would blush at the unmanly violation and rapacity that has marked the tracks of British tyranny in America, from which neither virgin-innocence nor helpless age has been a plea of protection or pity.

"Leith and its port now lies at our mercy; and did not our humanity stay the hand of just retaliation, I should, *without advertisement*, lay it in ashes. Before I proceed to that stern duty as an officer, my duty *as a man* induces me to propose to you, by the means of a reasonable ransom, to prevent such a scene of horror and distress. For this reason, I have authorized Lieutenant-Colonel De Chamillard to conclude and agree with you on the terms of ransom, allowing you exactly half an hour's reflection before you finally accept or reject the terms which he shall propose (£200,000.) If you accept the terms offered within the time limited, you may rest assured that no further debarkation of troops will be made, but that the re-embarkation of the vanguard will immediately follow, and that the property of the citizens shall remain unmolested.

"I have the honour to be, with sentiments of due respect, Sir, your very obedient and very humble servant,

"PAUL JONES.

"On board the American ship-of-war the Bon Homme Richard, at anchor in the Road of Leith, September the 17th, 1779."

The copy of the letter now lying before us contains the N.B. subjoined to it, in his own handwriting:—

"N.B.—The sudden and violent storm which arose in the moment when the squadron was abreast of Keith Island,* which forms the entrance of the Road of Leith, rendered impracticable the execution of the foregoing project."

The three ships had lain so long off and on the coast, that alarm was general; and on the 15th an express reached Edinburgh, sent to the Commander-in-Chief and to the Board of Cus-

* Inchkeith Island.

toms, with accounts that three strange ships were seen off Eyemouth on the afternoon of the 14th, which had made two prizes; and that a ship, supposed to mount 40 or 50 guns, was seen off Dunbar. At 5, P. M., on the 16th, they were distinctly seen from Edinburgh sailing up the Frith of Forth; but whether they were French vessels or the squadron of Paul Jones was not yet ascertained. The alarm along the coast was become general; batteries were hastily erected at Leith, and the incorporated trades bravely petitioned for arms, which were supplied from the castle of Edinburgh. Yet the audacity of the American commander so far blinded some of the spectators on the northern shores, that on the 17th a boat with five men came off from the coast of Fife to the Bon Homme Richard, soliciting powder and shot in name of a certain landed proprietor, who wished "to have the means of defending himself from the expected visit of the pirate Paul Jones." So far as powder went, this request was politely complied with; but the Commodore declined sending any shot.

On the 15th a small collier had been captured,

the master of which, from his knowledge of the coast, and subserviency to his captor, was of the greatest use to Jones in his intended project.—When he afterwards abandoned the enterprise, he gave this man up his vessel, "on account of his attachment to America, and the faithful information and important services he rendered me," says Jones, "by his general knowledge of the east coast of Britain. I had given orders to sink the old vessel, when the tears of this honest* man prevailed over my intention."

* This "honest man," but very bad patriot, was Andrew Robertson, master of the Friendship of Kirkcaldy. After being for two days kept on board the Bon Homme Richard, and having his ship given up to him for "faithful information" and "important services," he pretended that Commodore Jones had put it to ransom. This indeed was the face necessary to put on the affair; but the Commodore had previously declared that he had no authority to ransom prizes. The ransom-passport is amusing, from its date, and the circumstances under which it was granted. It is written by a French marine officer, who probably acted as the secretary of Commodore Jones, but is signed by himself:—

The narrative of this bold though abortive attempt will be best given in Jones's own words:—

"We continued working to windward of the frith, without being able to reach the road of Leith till, on the morning of the 17th, when, being almost within cannon-shot of the town, having every thing in readiness for a descent, a

---

"L'Honorable Capitaine John Paul Jones, Ecuyer, commandant en chef l'escadre Americaine actuellement en Europe,

"A tous ceux qui ces presentes verront, spécialement les sujets de la France:—

"Je certifie par le présent passeport, que le vaisseau Friendship, commandé par André Robertson, du port de Kirkcaldy, et venant du dit lieu pour aller à Riga, a été pris par l'escadre Americaine que je commande, et qu'il est ransonné: C'est pourquoi je prie et requiers tous les sujets de la France et de l'Amérique, de laisser librement passer le dit vaisseau Friendship, et continuer son voyage, sans le troubler en façon quelconque.

"Donné à la mer à bord du Bon Homme Richard, le dix-sept Septembre, mil sept cent soixante dix-neuf.

"J. PAUL JONES."

very severe gale of wind came on, and, being directly contrary, obliged us to bear away, after having in vain endeavoured for some time to withstand its violence. The gale was so severe, that one of the prizes that were taken on the 14th sunk to the bottom, the crew being with difficulty saved. As the clamour had by this time reached Leith by means of a cutter that had watched our motions that morning, and as the wind continued contrary, (though more moderate in the evening,) I thought it impossible to pursue the enterprise with a good prospect of success, especially as Edinburgh, where there is always a number of troops, is only a mile distant from Leith: therefore I gave up the project."*

* The prodigious sensation caused by the appearance of the squadron of Paul Jones in the Frith of Forth is hardly yet forgotten on the coast of Fife. There are various accounts of the manner in which this daring attempt was defeated. The 17th September, when Jones advanced to Leith, happened to be a Sunday. His ship, the Bon Homme Richard, stood at times so near the northern shores as to be distinctly seen by the crowds assembled on the beach, and on the commanding heights in the

It was the misfortune of Paul Jones, in almost every important crisis of his life, to be either

---

neighbourhood. At one time the Bon Homme Richard was not more than a mile from Kirkcaldy, a thriving and wealthy seaport. The alarm was naturally very great in that town; and the Rev. Mr Shirra, a worthy and very eccentric dissenting clergyman, remarkable for his quaint humour, instead of holding forth in the church as at ordinary times, where on this day he would have had but a thin audience, repaired to the fine level sandy beach of Kirkcaldy, and soon attracted a very numerous congregation. Here he prayed most fervently and earnestly, with that homely and familiar eloquence by which his sermons and prayers were distinguished, that the enterprise of "the piratical invader Paul Jones might be defeated." For once, it may be believed, the hearts of a congregation went with their minister. That violent gale, so much lamented by Paul Jones, suddenly arose,—the alleged consequence of Mr Shirra's powerful intercession. Such was long the popular belief. When, in after periods, this good old man was questioned on the subject, and complimented on the prevailing spirit of his prayer, which had so opportunely raised the wind that blew off Paul Jones, his usual reply, disclaiming the full extent of the compliment, was,—"I prayed,—but the LORD sent the wind."

clogged by the timid counsels of those about him, whose genius and courage could not keep pace with his, or to be thwarted by the baser feelings of ignoble rivalship. In no other service than that of America, still struggling for a doubtful existence as an independent state, and without either power or means to enforce due obedience throughout the gradations of the public service, could such insubordination as was displayed by

---

A gentleman, writing shortly afterwards from Amsterdam to his friend in Leith, says,—" You may count it a very fortunate circumstance that this gentleman (Commodore Jones) was prevented from hurting you when he was in your frith by a *strong westerly wind,* and the springing of a mast, as, in a conversation I had with him in this city, he assured me that his intention was to seize the shipping in the harbour, and to set fire to such as he could not carry off. He seemed to be well acquainted with the coast, and knew" (thanks to ' honest' Andrew Robertson !) " that there was no force to oppose him." Jones is described at this time, by those who saw him, as being " dressed in the American uniform, with a Scotch bonnet, edged with gold,—as of a middling stature, stern countenance, and swarthy complexion."

his force have been tolerated. The French officers under Jones at this time, besides the feelings of national and professional rivalship, had also too little experience of the capacity of their commander to give him that entire confidence so indispensable to success. His ill-fortune, with these uncongenial associates, was the more distressing, as their opposition or fears, while they baffled his enterprises, averted no real danger to which the loitering squadron might be exposed. The conduct of the agents of the court of France had also promoted and even authorised this unhappy insubordination of which the Commodore, after his return to the Texel, bitterly complained. "I must," he says, "speak plainly; as I have been always honoured with the full confidence of Congress, and as I also flattered myself with enjoying, in some measure, the confidence of the court of France, I could not but be astonished at the conduct of M. de Chaumont, when, in the moment of my departure from Groix, he produced a paper or *concordat* for me to sign in common with the officers whom I had commissioned but a few days before. Had this paper, or even a less dishonourable one, been proposed to me at the beginning, I would have rejected it with just contempt."

The other enterprise, which, after having failed at Leith, Jones so reluctantly abandoned, is not exactly known. It might have been against Hull or Newcastle. It had been a favourite project with him in the former year to distress London by destroying the coal-shipping.

Jones had now the mortifying prospect of going into the Texel with merely a few prizes, the sole fruit of a long cruise with a formidable maritime armament, when fortune threw in his way the most brilliant achievement of his public life.

CHAPTER VI.

THE engagement between the Serapis and the Bon Homme Richard was, previous to the last war, one of the most desperate in naval chronicles. As a close and deadly fight, hand to hand, and accompanied by all the dreadful circumstances that can attend a sea-engagement, it has even yet few parallels. Its incidents have been selected as the foundation of fictitious narratives of maritime combats, from exceeding in intense interest the boldest imaginings of the poet and the novelist.*

* Mr Cooper, the celebrated American novelist, and Allan Cunningham, have both chosen PAUL JONES as the hero of romances, very different in character, but equally admirable each in its peculiar style. Mr Cunningham has certainly in many instances made wild work with the sober facts of history; and, considering the very recent period in which his hero flourished, takes larger poetical license than is quite admissible. The charms and accom-

This battle was fought on the 23d September, under a full harvest-moon,—thousands of spectators, we are told, watching the engagement from the English shore, with anxiety corresponding to the deep interest of the game. No account of this memorable engagement can equal the simple and animated narrative of the main actor, which we purpose to adopt. It is to be noticed, that while Jones engaged the Serapis, the Pallas fought the Countess of Scarborough. The commencement of the engagements was simultaneous,

---

plishments allotted to some of Paul's female relatives would probably have been disclaimed by these ladies if purchased at the expense of the fair and spotless fame of their maternal ancestor. However, if Mr Cunningham imagined this cast of character best suited to his purposes, there is no great harm done. Few live to feel offence,—none to believe in those romantic *passages*, which owe their existence solely to the imagination of the poet. In painting Scottish scenery, and embodying romantic tradition, Mr Cunningham is in his work as much at home as is the author of "THE PILOT" in those fields of ocean which, as a novelist, he at present "possesses as his own domain."

but the Countess of Scarborough had struck while the Serapis still held desperately out.

"On the 21st," says Jones, "we saw and chased two sail off Flamborough Head; the Pallas chased in the N. E. quarter, while the Bon Homme Richard, followed by the Vengeance, chased in the S. W.; the one I chased, a brigantine collier in ballast, belonging to Scarborough, was soon taken, and sunk immediately afterwards, as a fleet then appeared to the southward. This was so late in the day, that I could not come up with the fleet before night; at length, however, I got so near one of them as to force her to run ashore between Flamborough Head and the Spurn. Soon after I took another, a brigantine from Holland, belonging to Sunderland, and at daylight the next morning, seeing a fleet steering towards me from the Spurn, I imagined them to be a convoy bound from London for Leith, which had been for some time expected. One of them had a pendant hoisted, and appeared to be a ship of force. They had not, however, courage to come on, but kept back all except the one which seemed to be armed, and that one also kept to windward, very near the land, and on the edge of dangerous shoals, where I could not with safety approach. This induced me to make a signal for a pilot, and soon afterwards two pilots' boats came off. They informed me that a ship that wore a pendant was an armed merchantman, and that a king's frigate lay there in sight, at anchor, within the Humber, waiting to take under convoy a number of merchant ships bound to the northward. The pilots imagined the Bon Homme Richard to be an English ship of war, and consequently communicated to me the private signal which they had been required to make. I endeavoured by this means to decoy the ships out of the port; but the wind then changing, and, with the tide, becoming unfavourable for them, the deception had not the desired effect, and they wisely put back. The entrance of the Humber is exceedingly difficult and dangerous, and as the Pallas was not in sight, I thought it imprudent to remain off the entrance, therefore steered out again to join the Pallas off Flamborough Head. In the night we saw and chased two ships until three o'clock in the morning, when, being at a very small distance from them, I made the private signal of reconnoissance, which I had given to each captain before I sailed from Groix: one half of the answer only was returned. In this position both sides lay to till daylight, when the ships proved to be the Alliance and the Pallas.

"On the morning of that day, the 23d, the brig from Holland not being in sight, we chased a brigantine that appeared laying to, to windward. About noon we saw and chased a large ship that appeared coming round Flamborough Head from the northward, and at the same time I manned and armed one of the pilot-boats to send in pursuit of the brigantine, which now appeared to be the vessel that I had forced ashore. Soon after this a fleet of forty-one sail appeared off Flamborough Head, bearing N. N. E. This induced me to abandon the single ship which had then anchored in Burlington Bay; I also called back the pilot-boat, and hoisted a signal for a general chase. When the fleet discovered us bearing down, all the merchant ships crowded sail towards the shore. The two ships of war that protected the fleet at the same time steered from the land,

and made the disposition for battle. In approaching the enemy, I crowded every possible sail, and made the signal for the line of battle, to which the Alliance showed no attention. Earnest as I was for the action, I could not reach the Commodore's ship until seven in the evening, being then within pistol-shot, when he hailed the Bon Homme Richard. We answered him by firing a whole broadside.

"The battle being thus begun, was continued with unremitting fury. Every method was practised on both sides to gain an advantage, and rake each other; and I must confess that the enemy's ship, being much more manageable than the Bon Homme Richard, gained thereby several times an advantageous situation, in spite of my best endeavours to prevent it. As I had to deal with an enemy of greatly superior force, I was under the necessity of closing with him, to prevent the advantage which he had over me in point of manœuvre. It was my intention to lay the Bon Homme Richard athwart the enemy's bow; but as that operation required great dexterity in the management of both sails and helm, and some of our braces being shot away, it did not exactly succeed to my wish. The enemy's bowsprit, however, came over the Bon Homme Richard's poop by the mizen-mast, and I made both ships fast together in that situation, which, by the action of the wind on the enemy's sails, forced her stern close to the Bon Homme Richard's bow, so that the ships lay square alongside of each other, the yards being all entangled, and the cannon of each ship touching the opponent's. When this position took place, it was eight o'clock, previous to which the Bon Homme Richard had received sundry eighteen-pound shots below the water, and leaked very much. My battery of twelve-pounders, on which I had placed my chief dependence, being commanded by Lieutenant Dale and Colonel Weibert, and manned principally with American seamen and French volunteers, was entirely silenced and abandoned. As to the six old eighteen-pounders that formed the battery of the lower gun-deck, they did no service whatever, except firing eight shot in all. Two out of three of them burst at the first fire, and killed almost all the men who were stationed to manage them. Before this time, too, Colonel de Chamillard, who commanded a party of twenty soldiers on the poop, had abandoned that station after having lost some of his men. I had now only two pieces of cannon, (nine-pounders,) on the quarter-deck, that were not silenced, and not one of the heavier cannon was fired during the rest of the action. The purser, M. Mease, who commanded the guns on the quarter-deck, being dangerously wounded in the head, I was obliged to fill his place, and with great difficulty rallied a few men, and shifted over one of the lee quarter-deck guns, so that we afterwards played three pieces of nine-pounders upon the enemy. The tops alone seconded the fire of this little battery, and held out bravely during the whole of the action, especially the main-top, where Lieutenant Stack commanded. I directed the fire of one of the three cannon against the main-mast, with double-headed shot, while the other two were exceedingly well served with grape and canister shot, to silence the enemy's musketry and clear her decks, which was at last effected. The enemy were, as I have since understood, on the instant of calling for quarters, when the cowardice or treachery of three of my under-officers induced them to call to the enemy. The English Commodore asked me if I demanded quarters, and I having answered him in the most determined negative, they renewed the battle with double fury. They were unable to stand the deck; but the fire of their cannon, especially the lower battery, which was entirely formed of ten-pounders, was incessant; both ships were set on fire in various places, and the scene was dreadful beyond the reach of language. To account for the timidity of my three under-officers, I mean the gunner, the carpenter, and the master-at-arms, I must observe, that the two first were slightly wounded, and, as the ship had received various shot under water, and one of the pumps being shot away, the carpenter expressed his fears that she would sink, and the other two concluded that she was sinking, which occasioned the gunner to run aft on the poop, without my knowledge, to strike the colours. Fortunately for me, a cannon-ball had done that before, by carrying away the ensign-staff; he was therefore reduced to the necessity of sinking, as he supposed, or of calling for quarter, and he preferred the latter.

"All this time the Bon Homme Richard had sustained the action alone, and the enemy, though much superior in force, would have been very glad to have got clear, as appears by their own acknowledgments, and by their having let go an anchor the instant that I laid them on board, by which means they would have escaped, had I not made them well fast to the Bon Homme Richard.

"At last, at half-past nine o'clock, the Alliance appeared, and I now thought the battle at an end; but, to my utter astonishment, he discharged a broadside full into the stern of the Bon Homme Richard. We called to him for God's sake to forbear firing into the Bon Homme Richard; yet they passed along the off-side of the ship, and continued firing. There was no possibility of his mistaking the enemy's ships for the Bon Homme Richard, there being the most essential difference in their appearance and construction. Besides, it was then full moonlight, and the sides of the

Bon Homme Richard were all black, while the sides of the prize were all yellow. Yet, for the greater security, I showed the signal of our reconnoissance, by putting out three lanterns, one at the head, another at the stern, and the third in the middle, in a horizontal line. Every tongue cried that he was firing into the wrong ship, but nothing availed; he passed round, firing into the Bon Homme Richard's head, stern, and broadside, and by one of his volleys killed several of my best men, and mortally wounded a good officer on the forecastle only. My situation was really deplorable; the Bon Homme Richard received various shot under water from the Alliance; the leak gained on the pumps, and the fire increased much on board both ships. Some officers persuaded me to strike, of whose courage and good sense I entertain a high opinion. My treacherous master-at-arms let loose all my prisoners without my knowledge, and my prospects became gloomy indeed. I would not, however, give up the point. The enemy's mainmast began to shake, their firing decreased fast, ours rather increased, and the British colours were struck at half an hour past ten o'clock.

"This prize proved to be the British ship of war the Serapis, a new ship of forty-four guns, built on the most approved construction, with two complete batteries, one of them of eighteen-pounders, and commanded by the brave Commodore Richard Pearson. I had yet two enemies to encounter, far more formidable than the Britons,—I mean fire and water. The Serapis was attacked only by the first, but the Bon Homme Richard was assailed by both; there was five feet water in the hold, and though it was moderate from the explosion of so much gunpowder, yet the three pumps that remained could with difficulty only keep the water from gaining. The fire broke out in various parts of the ship in spite of all the water that could be thrown in to quench it, and at length broke out as low as the powder-magazine, and within a few inches of the powder. In that dilemma I took out the powder upon deck, ready to be thrown over-board at the last extremity, and it was ten o'clock the next day (the

24th) before the fire was entirely extinguished. With respect to the situation of the Bon Homme Richard, the rudder was cut entirely off, the stern-frame and transoms were almost entirely cut away, and the timbers by the lower deck, especially from the main-mast towards the stern, being greatly decayed with age, were mangled beyond my power of description, and a person must have been an eye-witness to form a just idea of the tremendous scene of carnage, wreck, and ruin, which everywhere appeared. Humanity cannot but recoil from the prospect of such finished horror, and lament that war should be capable of producing such fatal consequences.

"After the carpenters, as well as Captain Cottineau and other men of sense, had well examined and surveyed the ship, (which was not finished before five in the evening,) I found every person to be convinced that it was impossible to keep the Bon Homme Richard afloat, so as to reach a port, if the wind should increase, it being then only a very moderate breeze. I had but little time to remove my wounded, which now became unavoidable, and which was effected in the course of the night and next morning. I was determined to keep the Bon Homme Richard afloat, and, if possible, to bring her into port. For that purpose, the first lieutenant of the Pallas continued on board with a party of men, to attend the pumps, with boats in waiting, ready to take them on board in case the water should gain on them too fast. The wind augmented in the night, and the next day, the 25th, so that it was impossible to prevent the good old ship from sinking. They did not abandon her till after nine o'clock; the water was then up to the lower deck, and a little after ten I saw, with inexpressible grief, the last glimpse of *the Bon Homme Richard.* No lives were lost with the ship, but it was impossible to save the stores of any sort whatever. I lost even the best part of my clothes, books, and papers; and several of my officers lost all their clothes and effects.

"Having thus endeavoured to give a clear and simple relation of the circumstances and events that have attended the little armament under my command, I shall freely submit my conduct therein to the censure of my superiors and the impartial public. I beg leave, however, to observe, that the force that was put under my command was far from being well composed, and as the great majority of the actors in it have appeared bent on the pursuit of *interest* only, I am exceedingly sorry that they and I have been at all concerned."

Such is the despatch which Commodore Jones transmitted from the Texel to Dr Franklin, and afterwards to Congress. It is painful to observe how often he is forced to complain of the sordidness or cowardice of his associates. To a generous and elevated mind nothing could have been more humiliating than this necessity. The pursuit of "interest alone," with which he so frequently charges his associates, is, however, a positive virtue compared with the gratuitous villany imputed to Landais, the commander of the Alliance. The alleged conduct of this person, particularly during the engagement between the Bon Homme Richard and the Serapis, was so daring in atrocity and treachery as to exceed all reasonable belief, were it not solemnly asserted, as beyond all doubt it was firmly believed, by Jones.

The general conduct of Landais was that of a malignant madman, as much incited by the prevailing influence of frenzy as actuated by deliberate villany. His behaviour during the whole cruise was made the subject of a set of charges* drawn up by Jones in coming into the Texel, which were attested, in whole or in part, by most of the officers of the Bon Homme Richard and the Alliance. The fact of Landais firing into the Bon Homme Richard is also confirmed by the log-book,† which was preserved when the ship sunk, and by a very interesting and seaman-like narrative of the engagement, drawn up by Mr Dale,‡

* See Appendix A.

† This battered volume, after many adventures by land and water, in Europe and America, is now in the possession of Mr George Napier, advocate.

‡ This gentleman, long since a Commodore in the service of the United States, is, or very lately was, still alive. He has for many years lived in retirement at Philadelphia, in the bosom of his family. It is but fair to state, in exculpation of Landais, that Captain Pearson, commander of the Serapis, in his despatch to the Admiralty, (see Appendix B,) repeatedly asserts, and assigns as the main cause of

then first lieutenant of the ship. The brilliant success of Jones at this time, though far short of his own hopes and projects, gave him a right to

---

his defeat, that while one frigate—the Bon Homme Richard—engaged him "muzzle to muzzle," the other—the Alliance—kept sailing round him during the whole action, and raking him fore and aft, by which means she killed or wounded almost every man on the quarter-deck and main-deck. It is not easy to judge of these contradictory statements.

From the variety of unusual circumstances which occurred during the heat and confusion of this memorable affair, there can be little doubt that both commanders may have given what he honestly believed a fair relation of facts. The gunner calling for quarter, as noticed by Jones, might have induced Captain Pearson to believe that the Bon Homme Richard had struck, especially as her flag so fortuitously disappeared at the same instant. The voice of Jones, who, according to Lieutenant Dale's narrative, decidedly denied that he struck, calling out that "he had not yet begun to fight," may have been lost in the bustle and noise of the moment, or construed into words of surrender; and where could any British officer have learned to imagine the atrocity of a commander pointing his guns in the heat of a close action, not speak out on affairs which left a deeper sting in his mind than even the perfidy of Landais. He thus concludes his despatch:—

---

against the enemy, but against his own consort, as is alleged of Landais?

If any reader take the trouble to turn up the Edinburgh Review for June, 1818, referring to the loss of the Alceste and the Medusa, he will obtain a view of the character of French seamen, which will go far to verify the assertions of Paul Jones and his officers regarding Landais. Franklin either really remained, or from policy was willing to appear, sceptical as to these revolting facts, though he entertained a very bad opinion of this man. He says, " It was not at all likely either that he should have given orders to fire into the Bon Homme Richard, or that his officers would have obeyed such orders had they been given them."

If Landais was really guilty—which there is every reason to believe—his is no solitary instance of such disgraceful perfidy on the part of French seamen. After the battle of Trafalgar, it is notorious that the flying French ships, as they escaped, poured broadsides into the Spanish vessels. " The ships," says Mr Southey, " which were thus flying, were four of the enemy's van, *all French*, under Rear Admiral Dumanoir. They had borne

"I am in the highest degree sensible of the singular attentions which I have experienced from the Court of France, which I shall remember with perfect gratitude until the end of my life, and will always endeavour to merit, while I can consistent with my honour continue in the public service. I must speak plainly; as I have been always honoured with the full confidence of Congress, and as I also flattered myself with enjoying in some measure the confidence of the court of France, I could not but be astonished at the conduct of Monsieur de Chaumont, when, in the moment of my departure from Groix, he produced a paper, *a concordat*, for me to sign, in common with the officers whom I had commis-

---

no part in the action; and now, when they were seeking safety in flight, they fired not only into the Victory and Royal Sovereign, (English ships,) but poured their broadsides into the captured Spanish vessels; and they were seen to back their sails, for the purpose of firing with more precision. The indignation of the Spaniards at this detestable cruelty from their allies, for whom they had fought so bravely and so profusely bled, may well be conceived."

sioned but a few days before. Had that paper, or even a less dishonourable one, been proposed to me at the beginning, I would have rejected it with just contempt, and the word *deplacement*, among others, should have been necessary. I cannot, however, even now suppose that he was authorized by the Court to make such a bargain with me. Nor can I suppose that the Minister of the Marine meant that M. de Chaumont should consider me merely as a colleague with the commanders of the other ships, and communicate to them not only all he knew but all he thought respecting our destination and operations. M. de Chaumont has made me various reproaches on account of the expense of the Bon Homme Richard, wherewith I cannot think I have been justly chargeable. M. de Chamillard can attest that the Bon Homme Richard was at last far from being well fitted or armed for war. If any person or persons who have been charged with the expense of that armament have acted wrong, the fault must not be laid to my charge. I had no authority to superintend that armament, and the persons who had authority were so far from giving me what I thought necessary, that M. de Chaumont even refused, among other things, to allow me irons to secure the prisoners of war.

"In short, while my life remains, if I have any capacity to render good and acceptable services to the common cause, no man will step forth with greater cheerfulness and alacrity than myself; but I am not made to be dishonoured, nor can I accept of the *half-confidence* of any man living. Of course I cannot, consistent with my honour, and a prospect of success, undertake future expeditions, unless when the object and destination is communicated to me alone, and to no other person in the marine line. In cases where troops are embarked, a like confidence is due alone to their commander-in-chief. On no other condition will I ever undertake the chief command of a private expedition; and when I do not command in chief, I have no desire to be in the secret."

In the memorial drawn up for the private perusal of the King of France, Jones says that it was his intention at this time to cruise off the south-west of Ireland for twelve or fifteen days, in order to intercept the English homeward-bound East India ships, which he had been informed would return without convoy, and sail for this point of land. This purpose, which he confined to his own breast, and which would have been rendered abortive by the misconduct of Landais, was quite compatible with the other objects of the cruise, whether these were the West India, or Hudson's Bay ships, or the Baltic fleet.

The earliness and accuracy of the information which Jones procured while he lay in the various harbours of France is not a little remarkable. Instead of receiving intelligence from the American ministers, he was enabled, through his own private channels in England and other quarters, to transmit to them information of the sailing of fleets and of the strength of convoys. His former connexions and mode of life may have given him some facilities; and money, the universal agent, never appears to have been with him an object of any consideration beyond its value as a means of obtaining professional advancement. He was able to supply the French Admiral, Count d'Orvilliers, with important information from London, of the sailing of a large West India fleet, and even to acquaint him with private transactions on board the squadrons of Keppel and Byron.

Meanwhile the squadron of Jones, which the narrative has left behind, continued to be tossed about till the 3d of October, when it came to anchor in the Texel, contrary to the judgment of the Commodore, who wished to gain the French harbour of Dunkirk, but was, he says, overruled by his officers. The rendezvous he found, was the cause of much personal vexation to himself, though it proved of ultimate advantage to America, by hurrying on the period when the Dutch were forced from their politic neutrality. The political importance of this measure might have been foreseen by Franklin, when in the previous summer he directed Jones, on finishing his northern cruise, to take shelter in the Texel. By doing so, the American minister greatly increased the perplexity of their High Mightinesses, on whom the cabinet of London already—and with good reason—looked with suspicious eyes. By this step the Dutch were in effect precipitated into the war rather sooner than suited their crafty and selfish policy, which, in shuffling with all parties, sought to profit by all. By compelling England to declare war, and the Dutch to declare openly for the United States, an end was virtually put to a contest, in which Britain was left to contend single-handed with her refractory colonies, then backed by France, Spain, and Holland.

Though the squadron of Jones had failed in its main purpose, and had neither captured fleets, nor put wealthy cities to ransom, the blow struck at the maritime pride of England could not fail to be highly gratifying to the Americans. Dr Franklin immediately wrote, warmly congratulating the victor.—" For some days," says Franklin, " after the arrival of your express, scarce any thing was talked of at Paris and Versailles, but your cool conduct and persevering bravery during that terrible conflict. You may believe that the impression on my mind was not less strong than that on others,—but I do not choose to say in a letter to yourself all I think on such an occasion.

" The ministry are much dissatisfied with

Captain Landais, and Monsieur de Sartine has signified to me in writing, that it is expected that I should send for him to Paris, and call him to account for his conduct, particularly for deferring so long his coming to your assistance; by which means, it is supposed, the States lost some of their valuable citizens, and the king lost many of his subjects, volunteers in your ship, together with the ship itself.

"I have, accordingly, written to him this day, acquainting him, that he is charged with disobedience of orders in the cruise, and neglect of his duty in the engagement; that a court-martial being at this time inconvenient, if not impracticable, I would give him an earlier opportunity of offering what he has to say in his justification, and for that purpose direct him to render himself immediately here, bringing with him such papers or testimonies as he may think useful in his defence. I know not whether he will obey my orders, nor what the ministry would do with him if he comes; but I suspect that they may, by some of their concise operations, save the trouble of a court-martial. It will, however, be well for you to furnish me with what you may judge proper to support the charges against him, that I may be able to give a just and clear account to Congress. In the mean time it will be necessary, if he should refuse to come, that you should put him under an arrest, and in that case, as well as if he comes, that you should either appoint some person to the command, or take it upon yourself; for I know of no person to recommend to you as fit for that station.

"I am uneasy about your prisoners, (504 in number,)—I wish they were safe in France. You will then have completed the glorious work of giving liberty to all the Americans that have so long languished for it in the British prisons."

Jones also received the thanks of the Duc de la Vauguyon, the French ambassador at the Hague, and the congratulations of numerous friends and admirers.

And now commenced those scenes of diplomatic altercation between the States of Holland and the British ambassador, Sir Joseph Yorke, which in the following year ended in the declaration of war. The Dutch had already committed many virtual infractions of the treaty of alliance with Britain. It was from Holland that France openly obtained her maritime stores. But a greater eyesore was the American squadron and its daring commander, with the captured frigates, riding in triumph in the Texel. Jones also appeared openly at Amsterdam. He was allowed to establish an hospital in the forts of the Texel for his wounded men and his wounded prisoners; though in this object of common humanity Sir Joseph Yorke readily concurred.

The squadron came into the Texel on the 3d October, and on the 13th Sir Joseph Yorke presented a brief and energetic memorial, peremptorily demanding that the captured frigates should be stopped in the Texel—the frigates "taken by one Paul Jones, a subject of the King of Great Britain, who, according to treaties and the laws of war, falls under the class of rebels and pirates."

Jones, though he must have been prepared for the demand, was, it may be presumed, not a little indignant at the unceremonious style in which he was designated by the English ambassador,—

"that little thing Sir Joseph," as he pettishly terms him. In this emergency he endeavoured to secure the friendship of certain powerful individuals. With a young, brave, and, above all, a successful commander, there is ever a ready sympathy; and even at this time, though the show of peace was still sedulously kept up, the cause of America had many warm friends among the Dutch, especially in the maritime towns.

It would have required greater magnanimity than most men are endowed with, had Jones forgiven the appellations bestowed on him, especially if any lurking consciousness rankled in his mind that his character and position were equivocal, and apt, at least in England, to be misconstrued. The distrust evinced by Le Ray Chaumont, and the consequent restraints imposed on his freedom as a commander, had already been sufficiently galling; and this was a fresh corrosion of the same sore. In a statement made long afterwards, Jones mentions that Sir Joseph Yorke having failed to obtain his person from the Dutch government, endeavoured to have him privately kidnapped,—a thing in itself extremely improbable, and for which there was, in all likelihood, no other foundation than the gossip of Amsterdam. Sir Joseph never even directly asked that Jones should be given up, while he loudly reiterated his demand for the restitution of the captured frigates.

The firmness and address displayed by Sir Joseph Yorke on this occasion did credit to his diplomatic abilities. He had resided long at the Hague, and had obtained great influence with the Prince of Orange and what may be called the court-party. His services on this occasion were afterwards rewarded by a peerage. Captain Pearson was also subsequently distinguished by many marks of the confidence and approbation of his sovereign. The defeated party were indeed more highly rewarded than the victor; for the subsequent honours heaped on Jones were more the consequence of dexterous management at Versailles, six months after the affair took place, than the natural and spontaneous fruits of his brilliant achievement. Immediately on his exchange, Captain Pearson received the honour of knighthood, which, following this period of eclipse, must have been peculiarly gratifying to his feelings; and the Royal-Exchange Assurance Company presented him and Captain Piercy of the Countess of Scarborough with services of plate "for their gallant defence of the Baltic fleet."

The peremptory demand of Sir Joseph Yorke threw their High Mightinesses into no little perplexity. They were not yet prepared for war with England, nor did they wish to risk offending France, and alienating the affections of the young Transatlantic republic, which might long remember unkindness, but would feel doubly grateful for succour shown in the season of adversity, and the struggle for existence. The States of Holland in those awkward circumstances temporized with much dexterity, sheltering themselves under those cautious maxims of policy which had hitherto governed the United Provinces in questions of the like nature. These maxims dictated that they should decline deciding on the validity of captures in the open seas of vessels not belonging to their own subjects. They afforded at all times shelter in their harbours to all ships whatsoever, if driven in by stress of weather; but compelled armed ships with their prizes to put to sea again as soon as possible, without permitting them to dispose of their cargoes; and this conduct they were to follow in the case of Jones.

This did not, however, extricate the Dutch government from the dilemma. As an American officer they durst not protect Jones, which would have been in effect a recognition of the rebellious colonies; and the French commission under which it was alleged he acted could never be forthcoming. They therefore were compelled to order him to put to sea with his squadron forthwith, though they "declined to pass judgment on the person and prizes of Paul Jones." They also publicly forbade the ships to be furnished with naval or warlike stores, save such as were absolutely necessary to carry them to the first foreign port, "that all suspicion of their being furnished *here* may drop."*

It was even agreed, though the measure met with strong opposition, that the American squadron should be expelled by force from the Texel.

---

* See manifesto, Appendix.

This much was obtained by the firmness of Sir Joseph Yorke.

The situation of Jones, all along unpleasant, was now become highly critical. The Dutch government, whom Sir Joseph neither suffered to slumber nor sleep, incessantly annoyed the French ambassador, who in his turn assailed Jones. He was thus placed between two fires, threatened by the Dutch to be driven from the Texel, while English ships were placed at its entrance to interrupt his exit, and while, to "make assurance double sure," light squadrons were cruising about in all directions to prevent his gaining any French or Spanish port, should he be fortunate enough to escape the vessels on the more immediate watch. So deep and galling was the wound this individual had inflicted on the national pride, that the capture of "one Paul Jones" would at this time have been more welcome to England than if she had conquered a rich argosy.

One main object of Jones being ordered to the Texel on the termination of his northern cruise, was, as has been noticed, to convoy a French fleet with naval stores to Brest, and to get out the Indian. The same officious commissary, whose talkative propensities and suspicious disposition had so frequently baffled the projects of Jones, had again been at work ; and although the Dutch government might have winked at the sailing of the fleet under his convoy, the measure would have been rendered abortive by premature disclosure. Jones complained to Franklin, and to Sartine, the minister of the French marine, to whom during the time he lay in the Texel he had, as usual, been transmitting some of the many projects for maritime expeditions of which his scheming brain was ever so fertile. He also in this interval drew up a refreshing memorial for Congress, containing a narrative of his professional life and services.

Before receiving any answer to his communication to Sartine, Jones was ordered to attend the French ambassador at the Hague, the Duc de la Vauguyon. He went privately to the Hague to avoid unnecessary offence, and at a long conference it was agreed that he should forthwith sail for Dunkirk with his numerous prisoners. As they were now situated they could scarcely be considered in security, and both Franklin and Jones, as a personal kindness, had solicited and obtained the consent of the French government that these prisoners should be exchanged for the Americans, then prisoners in England.

The Serapis had been dismasted in the late engagement, and as it was probable that, even on the short voyage to Dunkirk, Jones might encounter his watchful foe in some force, it was necessary to refit his ship. For this purpose he went to Amsterdam. Thus time wore on. The English ambassador from remonstrances came to threats. The Dutch, driven to their wit's end, remonstrated and menaced by turns; and Jones, unable to be longer silent, wrote as follows to the French ambassador:—

"On board the Bon Homme Richard's Prize the Ship of War Serapis, at the Texel, November 4th, 1779.

"My Lord,

"This morning the commandant of the Road sent me word to come and speak to him on board his ship. He had before him on the table a letter which he said was from the Prince of Orange.

He questioned me very closely whether I had a French commission, and, if I had, he almost insisted upon seeing it. In conformity to your advice "Cet avis donné au commencement n'etoit plus de saison depuis l'admission de l'escadre sous Pavillon Americain," I told him that my French commission not having been found among my papers since the loss of the Bon Homme Richard, I feared it had gone to the bottom in that ship; but that, if it was really lost, it would be an easy matter to procure a duplicate of it from France. The commandant appeared to be very uneasy and anxious for my departure. I have told him that as there are eight of the enemy's ships laying wait for me at the south entrance, and four more at the north entrance of the port, I was unable to fight more than three times my force, but that he might rest assured of my intention to depart with the utmost expedition, whenever I found a possibility to go clear.

"I should be very happy, my Lord, if I could tell you of my being ready. I should have departed long ago, if I had met with common assistance; but for a fortnight past I have every day expected the necessary supply of water from Amsterdam in cisterns, and I am last night informed that it cannot be had without I send up water-casks. The provision, too, that was ordered the day I returned to Amsterdam from the Hague, is not yet sent down; and the spars that have been sent from Amsterdam are spoiled in the making. None of the iron-work that was ordered for the Serapis is yet completed, so that I am, even to this hour, in want of hinges to hang the lower gun-ports. My officers and men lost their clothes and beds in the Bon Homme Richard, and they have yet got no supply. The bread that has been twice a week sent down from Amsterdam to feed my people, has been, literally speaking, *rotten*, and the consequence is that they are falling sick.

" It is natural also that they should be discontented, while I am not able to tell them that they will be paid the value of their property in the Serapis and Countess of Scarborough, if either or both of them should be lost or taken after sailing from hence.

" Thus you see, my Lord, that my prospects are

far from pleasing. I have but few men, and they are discontented. If you can authorize me to promise them, at all hazards, that their property in the prizes shall be made good, and that they shall receive the necessary clothing and bedding, &c. or money to buy them, I believe I shall soon be able to bring them again into a good humour. In the meantime I will send a vessel or two out to reconnoitre the offing and to bring me word. Whatever may be the consequence of my having put into this harbour, I must observe that it was done contrary to my opinion, and I consented to it only because the majority of my colleagues were earnest for it," &c. &c.

The French government, to rid themselves of farther importunity, now fell on a new expedient. The cruise was suddenly declared at an end, and the ships were dismissed; Franklin agreed to place the captured frigates under the flag of France, and that Jones should be removed to the only ship now ostensibly American, the Alliance, which, on Landais having been ordered to Paris to answer to the plenipotentiaries for his misconduct on the cruise, had been left without a commander.

Jones received this intimation with disgust and

chagrin; but such were the orders of Sartine and Franklin, such the course sound policy dictated; and after an altercation lasting, he states, for thirteen hours, with the French ambassador at the Hague, he most reluctantly left the Serapis, whose deck seemed the theatre of his glory, and went on board the Alliance. The squadron soon afterwards sailed under a Dutch convoy, and Jones was left alone in his new ship. His French commission had never yet been produced; the English ambassador had repeatedly alleged that he held no legal commission from any sovereign;* and to relieve the Dutch government from their

* About this time, a seaman's wife of Burlington addressed a letter to Sir Joseph Yorke at the Hague, imploring tidings of her husband, of whom, since the engagment of Jones with the Serapis, she had never heard, and who, she feared, had fallen in that fight. Sir Joseph gallantly and humanely complied with the poor Englishwoman's request, and as he was aware that his epistle to Mrs Burnot would appear in all the English and French newspapers, he, with considerable covert-humour, contrived to have a hit at the shuffling policy of the Dutch, and the chamelion character of the squadron they sheltered, while he replied to the seaman's wife:—" Mrs Burnot, As soon

dilemma, and, probably to ensure the personal safety of Jones in case of the worst, a regular commission was now tendered him by the ministers of his Most Christian Majesty, but of a kind so degrading that there is no doubt he would,

---

as I received your letter of the 7th instant, I lost no time in making inquiries after your gallant husband, Mr Richard Burnot; and have now great pleasure in congratulating you upon his being alive and well, on board the Countess of Scarborough, at the Texel. I find he had been burnt with an explosion of gunpowder, but is now quite recovered. He sends me word, that he, as you know, could not write, and therefore hoped I would let you know he was well, which I do with infinite satisfaction. It will still be greater, if I can get him exchanged, which I am doing my best endeavours for; but as the people who took him are sometimes French and sometimes rebels, as it suits their convenience, that renders this affair more difficult than it would be if they allowed themselves to be French, because I could then settle the exchange at once. I am happy to be able to give such agreeable news to the wife of my brave countryman, and I am very sincerely your most faithful humble servant,

"JOSEPH YORKE.

"*Hague, Nov.* 26, 1779."

far rather than have accepted it, have chosen the alternative of falling into the power of the English. Whatever were his personal difficulties, he was at this time in "the blaze of his fame," "talked of," says Franklin, "at Paris and Versailles," celebrated throughout Europe and America. His temper and blood were at no time very cool on sudden excitement, and the excess of his indignation may be imagined when he received the insulting offer of a Letter of Marque. We know not what to make of the frequent boasts of Jones in after-periods of life, of never accepting any commission save from Congress. The concordat of Le Ray Chaumont, and the Letter of Marque of Sartine and the Duc de la Vauguyon, it must be confessed, offered but slight temptation. Jones, though far from being naturally inclined either to conceal or depreciate his professional talents and personal services, never over-estimated himself half so much as he was at this time undervalued by the vacillating and capricious government with which he had to do. If the true ability of a statesman is best seen in his capacity for selecting and managing the instruments of his power, Sartine in this instance, as in many others, sadly betrayed his own incapacity. Under the first galling feelings of this insult, Jones wrote the following spirited letter to the French ambassador. It is one of the best productions of his pen, precisely because it is the spontaneous dictate of the most honourable impulses of his spirit :—

" *To His Excellency the Duc de la Vauguyon, Ambassador from France at the Hague.*

" Alliance, Texel, December 13th, 1779.

" My Lord,

" Perhaps there are many men in the world who would esteem as an honour the commission that I have this day refused. My rank from the beginning knew no superior in the marine of America, how then must I be humbled were I to accept a letter-of-marque!—I should, my Lord, esteem myself inexcusable, were I to accept even a commission of equal or superior denomination to that I bear, unless I were previously authorized by Congress, or some other competent authority in Europe. And I must tell you, that, on my arrival at Brest from the Irish Channel, Count D'Orvilliers offered to procure for me from Court a commission of "Captain de Vaisseaux," which I did not then accept for the same reason, although the war between France and England was not then begun, and of course the commission of France would have protected me from an enemy of superior force.

"It is a matter of the highest astonishment to me, that, after so many compliments and fair professions, the Court should offer the present insult to my understanding, and suppose me capable of disgracing my present commission. I confess that I never merited all the praise bestowed on my past conduct, but I also feel that I have far less merited such a reward. Where profession and practice are so opposite, I am no longer weak enough to form a wrong conclusion. They may think as they please of me; for where I cannot continue my esteem, praise or censure from any man is to me a matter of indifference.

"I am much obliged to them, however, for having at last fairly opened my eyes, and enabled me to discover truth from falsehood.

"The prisoners shall be delivered agreeable to the orders which you have done me the honour to send me from his Excellency the American ambassador in France.

"I will also with great pleasure, not only permit a part of my seamen to go on board the ships under your Excellency's orders, but I will also do my utmost to prevail with them to embark freely; and if I can now or hereafter, by any other honourable means, facilitate the success or the honour of his Majesty's arms, I pledge myself to you as his ambassador, that none of his own subjects would bleed in his cause with greater freedom than myself, an American.

"It gives me the more pain, my Lord, to write this letter, because the Court has enjoined you to prepare what would destroy my peace of mind, and my future veracity in the opinion of the world.

"When, *with the consent of Court* and by order of the American ambassador, I gave American commissions to French officers, I did not fill up those commissions to command privateers, nor even for a rank *equal* to that of their commissions in the marine of France. They were promoted to rank *far superior*,—and why?—not from personal friendship, nor from my knowledge of their services and abilities, (the men and their characters being entire strangers to me,) but from the respect which I believed America would wish to show for the service of France.

"While I remained eight months seemingly forgot by the Court at Brest, many commissions such as that in question were offered to me; and I believe, (when I am in pursuit of *plunder*,) I can still obtain such an one without application to Court.

"I hope, my Lord, that my behaviour through life will ever entitle me to the continuance of your good wishes and opinion, and that you will take occasion to make mention of the warm and personal affection with which my heart is impressed towards his Majesty.

"I am," &c. &c.

This letter Jones enclosed to Franklin, to whom he gave his passionate feelings fuller breath in an epistle very characteristic both of the man and the seaman. "I hope," he says, "that the within copy of my letter to the Duc de la Vauguyon will meet your approbation; for I am persuaded that it never could be your intention or wish that I should be made the tool of any great r—— whatever; or that the commission of America should be overlaid by the dirty piece of parchment which I have this day rejected! They have played upon my good humour too long already, but the spell is at last dissolved. They would play me off with assurance of the personal and particular esteem of the King, to induce me to do what would render me contemptible even in the eyes of my own servants! Accustomed to speak untruths themselves, they would also have me to give under my hand that I am a liar and a scoundrel. They are mistaken, and I would tell them what you did to your naughty servant. 'We have too contemptible an opinion of one another's understanding to live together.' I could tell them too, that if M—— de C——* had not taken such

* De la Ray Chaumont.

safe precautions to keep me honest by means of his famous *concordat*, and to support me by so many able colleagues, these great men would not have been reduced to such mean shifts; for the prisoners could have been landed at Dunkirk the day that I entered the Texel, and I could have brought in double the numbers."

The whole of these effusions were submitted to M. Dumas, a new friend Jones had acquired, who had lately been appointed agent for American affairs at Amsterdam.*

* This gentleman is a most amusing specimen of the diplomatist in the small way, busy and bustling about nothing, shrouding every trifle in mystery;—one who writes about "the great man," and hints obscurely at "the certain friend in high station," and intimates dark meanings through which every body could see, in any way save simply and directly. America was at this early stage of her history singularly prolific of these mysterious personages. Bancroft, Mr W. Temple Franklin, who was, however, still a lad, and even Commodore Jones, disported themselves in this sort of innocent diplomacy, employing a cipher, or numbers, in their correspondence about their own personal affairs, as if the eyes of all the world had

The letter of Jones to the ambassador of France produced the desired effect. A soothing epistle was despatched to the sturdy and indignant Anglo-American. " I perceive with pain, my dear Commodore," says the Duke, " that you do not view your situation in the right light; and I can assure you that the ministers of the King have no intention to cause you the least disagreeable feeling, as the honourable testimonials of the esteem of his Majesty which I send you ought to convince you. I hope you will not doubt the sincere desire with which you have inspired me to procure you every satisfaction you may merit. It cannot fail to incite you to give new proofs of your zeal for the common cause of France and America. I flatter myself to renew, before long, the occasion, and to procure you the means to increase still more the glory you have already acquired. I am already occupied with all the interest I promised you; and if my views are

---

been watchful of their motions. Franklin alone kept clear of this folly. His letters contain no blanks, no ominous stars, no mystification of important nothings.

realized, as I have every reason to believe, you will be at all events perfectly content; but I must pray you not to hinder my project by delivering yourself to the expression of those strong sensations to which you appear to give way, and for which there is really no foundation. You appear to possess full confidence in the justice and kindness of the King; rely also upon the same sentiments on the part of his ministers."

The "dear Commodore" of the Duke was somewhat mollified by this apology, but far from being satisfied; nor did he slip so inviting an opportunity of proclaiming his grievances. "Were I to form," he says, "my opinion of the ministry from the treatment that I experienced while at Brest, or from their want of confidence in me afterwards, exclusive of what has taken place since I had the misfortune to enter this port, I will appeal to your Excellency, as a man of candour and ingenuity, whether I ought to desire to prolong a connexion that has made me so unhappy, and wherein I have given so very little satisfaction. M. le Chevalier de Lironcourt has lately made me reproaches on account of the expense that, he says, France has been at to give me reputation, in preference to twenty captains of the royal navy, better qualified than myself, and who, each of them, solicited for the command that was lately given to me!

"This, I confess, is quite new, and indeed surprising to me; and, had I known it before I left France, I certainly should have resigned in favour of the twenty men of superior merit. I do not, however, think that his first assertion is true; for the ministers must be unworthy of their places were they capable of squandering the public money only to give an individual reputation; and as to the second, I fancy the Court will not thank him for having given me that information, whether true or false. I may add here, that with a force so ill composed, and with powers so limited, I ran ten chances of ruin and dishonour for one of gaining reputation; and had not the plea of humanity in favour of the unfortunate Americans in English dungeons superseded all consideration of self, I faithfully assure you, my Lord, that I would not have proceeded under such circumstances from Groix. I do not imbibe hasty prejudices against any individuals ; but when many and repeated circumstances, conspiring in one point, have inspired me with disesteem towards any person, I must see convincing proof of reformation in such person before my heart can beat again with affection in his favour; for the mind is free, and can be bound only by kind treatment."

The insult, as he justly conceived it, which Jones had received from France, did not increase his inclination to hoist the flag of that nation on board of the Alliance; nor had he longer any secret motive to refuse, or at least to delay obedience to the reiterated and peremptory mandate of the Dutch government, ordering him to leave the Texel. America was now his sole hope—to reach its coasts his only aim. "I am not sorry," he writes his friend Morris, "that my connexion with them (the French government) is at an end. In the course of that connexion I ran ten chances of ruin and dishonour for one of reputation; and all the honour or profit that France could bestow should not tempt me again to undertake the same service, with an armament equally ill composed and with powers equally limited. It affords me the most exalted pleasure to reflect, that when I return to America I can say I have served in Europe at my own expense, and without the fee or reward of a court. When the prisoners we have taken are safely lodged in France, I shall have no further business in Europe, as the liberty of all our fellow-citizens who now suffer in English prisons will then be secured."

He was now detained only by contrary winds, and eagerly waited for a fair opportunity of eluding the vigilance of those on the watch to intercept him. After three months spent in continual altercation, imbittered by the animosity of Landais, the babbling and suspicions of Le Ray Chaumont, the conduct of the French ministers, and the discontents of his officers and men respecting the prize-money, Jones sailed from the Texel on the 27th December, 1779.

The only consolation Jones received at this period was effecting the exchange of the American prisoners in England. This was, he said, "all the reward he wished." He had also wrung some promises from the ambassador in behalf of his discontented officers and crew, who, as the prizes had not been valued in Holland, and were liable to be retaken in getting into a French port, had no assurance that they would ever obtain any reward for their courage and their toil. The prizes sent into Bergen in Norway by Landais had been claimed by the English consul, and given up by the Danish government, who were very unlikely to grant the Americans any indemnity. Even more severely than these incidental hardships, Jones felt the grumbling of the French agents at the expense he necessarily incurred in refitting his ships. "It had cost France too much to give him fame," was the taunting observation bitterly felt and not easily forgotten.

It must, under all the circumstances, have been with considerable anxiety that Jones sailed from the Texel, with the alternative of rashly braving or fortunately eluding the English: he was not in condition to meet them even in equal force. The Alliance, by the gross misconduct of Landais, who was as bad a seaman as he was an officer, was in the worst condition. The officers were, as Jones states, "idle and drunken; the men filthy and in bad subordination, and many of them sick of an epidemic illness;" the vessel was, besides, badly armed, and the powder of bad quality. The last evil Jones remedied; and, putting a bold face on the matter, whatever might be his secret feelings, he thus exultingly wrote Dumas on leaving the Texel:—" Alliance at sea, 27th December:—I am here, my dear Sir, with a good wind at east, under my best American colours. So far you have your wish. What may be the event of this critical moment I know not; I am, not however, without good hopes."

The memorial, drawn up by Jones himself for the King of France, contains the best account that is extant of his escape and of the progress of this ticklish voyage. " He passed," he states, " along the Flemish banks, and, getting the windward of the enemy's fleet of observation in the North Sea, he the next day passed through the Straits of Dover, in full view of the enemy's fleet in the Downs. The day following Captain Jones ran the Alliance past the Isle of Wight, in view of the enemy's fleet at Spithead, and in two days more got safe through the Channel, having passed by windward in sight of several of the enemy's large two-decked cruising ships. Captain Jones wished to carry with him some prizes and prisoners to France; but the Alliance, by the arrangement Captain Landais had made of the ballast at L'Orient, was out of trim, and could not sail fast, her sails being too thin and old for cold latitudes. He steered to the southward, and cruised for some days without success off Cape Finisterre. On the 16th of January, 1780, Captain Jones, to shun a gale of wind, and procure a sound anchor, (for he had left the Texel with only one,) ran into Corogne. He was very kindly received in Spain, but sailed again, and arrived at Groix on the 10th February, having taken no prizes."

On gaining L'Orient, Jones lost no time in beginning to refit his ship and obtain military stores. A board of Admiralty had by this time been established by Congress, and one of its first acts was to order home the Alliance. In making the ships under his command fit for sea, whether "in battle or in breeze," Jones never grudged or even thought of expense, and on the present occasion his professional liberality of spirit far outran the frugal genius of Franklin. The anxious and almost pathetic remonstrances addressed to him by the republican sage are as amusing as they are characteristic. The court of France had demurred to incurring farther expense for this refractory hero and his American ship. "The whole expense will fall upon me," cries Franklin, "and I am ill provided to bear it, having so many unexpected calls upon me from all quarters. I therefore beg you would have mercy on me, put me to as little charge as possible, and take nothing you can possibly do without. As to sheathing with copper it is totally out of the question."

By the middle of April, the Alliance (notwithstanding the prayers of Franklin) was, by the care of her commander, pronounced by himself one of the most complete frigates in France.

Nearly a month before the Alliance having been, as was said, ordered home to America with certain supplies of arms and warlike stores furnished by France, Franklin urged the immediate sailing of the ship as strongly as he could with propriety, and wished its commander a prosperous voyage. He even stretched a point to furnish those of the former crew of the Bon Homme Richard, now on board the Alliance, with a small sum of money, as they had not yet realized a *sou* of their prize-money. This was done to allay discontent and send the men home in good humour. But neither the Commodore nor his crew were yet in trim for sea.

Jones had made repeated attempts to obtain an adjustment of the prize-money, and now meditated a journey to Court ostensibly to solicit a final settlement. A person in office had about this time excited his indignation by meanly claiming the merit of some or all of his manifold projects; and it is probable that various other motives and personal interests disposed him to undertake this memorable journey. Having on a former occasion verified the truth of the maxim, which led him to give the celebrated name of Bon Homme Richard to his ship, he determined once more to speed his errand by doing it himself. He was aware that, though disliked or envied by the marine service of France, he was popular with the Court and the nation, who were about this time in the very height and fervour of the American mania. On this knowledge he proceeded to Versailles.

CHAPTER VII.

Jones at no time neglected to keep himself alive in the memory of his Court friends and official patrons,—a species of attention necessary to a professional man everywhere, at least in the commencement of his career, and particularly so at that period in France. While superintending the refitting of the Alliance, he had been corresponding with La Fayette, the Duke de la Rochefoucault, and others of his former great friends, and by them he might have been advised to repair to Versailles to claim justice for his people in the affair of the prize-money. If such was his only business, it does not appear to have been much advanced by his appearance at this crisis; but the reception he personally met from many individuals among the higher classes of society and the leaders of fashion, when Americans and republicanism were the infatuating novelties of the day, must have been highly gratifying to his feelings and to his insatiable love of distinction. The American Commodore, the conqueror of the haughty English, insulted by the degrading offer of a letter-of-marque at Amsterdam, became the hero, and, what was nearly the same thing, the *lion* of the day in Paris. He was everywhere feasted and caressed; and, as if to make ample amends for the gratuitous insult offered him by the ministers, he was presented by the King with a gold sword, bearing the following honourable inscription:—"VINDICATI MARIS LUDOVICUS XVI. REMUNERATOR STRENUO VINDICI." Leave was requested from Congress to invest him with the military Order of Merit,—an honour which had never been conferred on any one before who had not actually borne arms under the commission of France. An official letter was also addressed to him by his ancient tormentor, M. Sartine, expressive of the highest approbation of his conduct, and esteem for his personal character. This much was to be gained by a man of talent and address appearing in his own cause at the Court of France; nor is there any lack of charity in supposing that, had Jones remained quiet at L'Orient, the victor of the Serapis, and the generous and patriotic liberator of the American prisoners, would not have sunk beneath the load of Court honours. The secret history of the manner in which services of plate, knighthoods, and letters of thanks, are sometimes obtained, would form a curious and not unedifying chapter in the story of many a professional man's life. In the present instance they were amply merited. They were as proudly received; and did equal honour to the royal donor and the individual distinguished by his favour. Jones was exactly of the sanguine, ambitious, and loyal cast of character, which leads men to prize at their full value those coveted marks of princely approbation. The gold sword and the accompanying Order were the pride and the boast of his future life.

Testimonies of kindness and esteem, of a kind even more gratifying to his private feelings, were not wanting. Of this brilliant period he long afterwards says, in speaking of himself, " he received at Paris, and other parts of the kingdom, the most flattering applause and public approbation wherever he appeared. Both the great and the learned sought his acquaintance in private life, and honoured him with particular marks of friendship. At Court he was always received with a kindness which could only have arisen from a fixed esteem."

While the French Court were thus in the vein of caressing and bestowing, Jones solicited and obtained the Ariel frigate to accompany the Alliance to America, with stores for Washington's army. Nor in all probability was he averse to an increase of force, should fortune throw any English ships in his way on the homeward voyage. The Ariel he intended to man from the supernumeraries of the Alliance and the lately exchanged American prisoners. The affair of the prize-money was put in train, as far as fair promises and preliminary orders may go, and in high spirits Jones took leave of the French Court and capital, and returned to L'Orient, ready, as he conceived, to quit France, and furnished, by dint of his indefatigable genius, with an official letter from the Minister of Marine to Congress, enumerating his services in Europe, and recommending him to favour, and consequently to advancement.

While Jones was absent in Paris, his ship had been the scene of a mutinous intrigue, of which the wretched Landais, though apparently the promoter, was in reality at first only the tool.

This intrigue originated with Mr Arthur Lee, who had held a subordinate diplomatic appointment in France, and was now about to return to America. The real cause of this person's conduct at this time appears to have been dislike of Franklin, and a mean jealousy of the consideration in which this truly great man was held, both by friend and foe, in Europe as well as in America, while the vast merits of the patriotic Mr Lee were overlooked. When the affair of Landais had been originally discussed, Lee, in the spirit of factious opposition, had gone openly against the opinion of Franklin and the other plenipotentiaries, and taken part with the mutinous, and, as it afterwards turned out, mad Frenchman, on what he was pleased to call constitutional grounds.

Landais had originally received the command of the Alliance from Congress. When ordered to head-quarters to account for his conduct, he voluntarily left his ship, and soon afterwards Jones was officially ordered to quit the Serapis, and assume command of the Alliance, which, as has been seen, he did much against his inclination. Meanwhile Landais was ordered to return to America, that cognizance might be taken of his conduct before the proper tribunal. In this order he appeared to acquiesce; and he was furnished with money by Franklin to bear his charges. On his arrival at L'Orient, it seems to have been adroitly insinuated into his naturally ricketty brains, that Franklin and the other plenipotentiaries had exceeded their powers in superseding him and ordering him to America; and that Congress having bestowed his commission, to Congress alone was he bound to surrender it. The same doctrine was diligently promulgated among the seamen of the Alliance, and readily received by many of the officers. The delay of the prize-money, and the non-payment of the seamen's arrears, gave a strong handle to the discontented and designing. It was artfully represented to the disaffected crew, that while Jones, their new commander, basked in the sunshine of Court favour at Versailles, he either neglected or compromised their rights and interests, and hesitated to demand justice for his men from those who heaped favours on himself, and loaded him alone with benefits and honours, while those who had shared his toils and achieved the glory he claimed were neglected and forgotten. There was some colour for complaint. Jones felt his error, and, in writing to a friend about the discontent of his crew, says, "I have been to blame for having returned from Paris without having absolutely insisted on the previous payment of my men." These men he had found on his return sullen, alienated, and almost in open mutiny.

Landais had now determined, to assume by force the command of the Alliance, unjustly, as he said, wrested from him; and the officers and men prepared a memorial, addressed to the plenipotentiaries, setting forth their grievances and their wishes. Landais, to do the business with becoming modesty, and propriety, expressed a desire to be formally reinstated* in his command.

---

* Franklin's letter in reply to the modest demand of this Frenchman is as indicative of his strong good sense and clear-sighted integrity as any thing that ever issued from his pen. Of this sagacious person one might almost think it was because "honesty was the best policy" that he loved it. He admired truth for its utility more than its native beauty; and employed it accordingly with singular success in his dealings with men, where others more short-sighted, if not less sincere, would have used subterfuge and trick only to counteract their own purposes. It is thus he wrote Landais:—"No one ever learned the opinion I formed of you from inquiry made into your conduct. I kept it entirely to myself. I have not even hinted it in my letters to America, because I would not hazard giving to any one a bias to your prejudice. By communicating *a part of that opinion* privately to you I can do no harm, for you may burn it. I should not give you the pain of reading it, if your demand did not make it necessary. I think you then so imprudent, so litigious, and quarrelsome a man, even with your best friends, that peace and good order, and consequently the quiet and regular subordination so necessary to success, are, where you preside, impossible. These are within my observation and apprehension. Your military operations I leave to

Franklin, whose feelings, whether as a public or private man, must have been grossly outraged by this proceeding, stifled his indignation, and, by every argument likely to convince their reason, or influence their passions, endeavoured to recall these misled men to a sense of their duty.

No minister ever took half the pains to conciliate a set of wrongheaded malcontents, whom the power of France could have enabled him to crush at once. Some of the arguments he addressed to their professional feelings and pride are exceedingly subtle. The officers and crew of the Alliance were naturally indignant at the charge of having fired into the Bon Homme Richard during the engagement with the Serapis. In relation to this affair, Franklin states, "though I declined any judgment of his (Landais's) manœu-

---

more capable judges. If, therefore, I had twenty ships of war in my disposition, I should not give one of them to Captain Landais. The same temper which *excluded* him from the French marine would weigh equally with me; of course I shall not replace him in the Alliance."

vres in the fight, I have given it as my opinion, (to Congress,) after examining the affair, that it was not at all likely, either that he should have given orders to fire into the Bon Homme Richard, or that his officers would have obeyed such an order had it been given them. Thus I have taken what care I could of your honour in that particular. You will therefore excuse me if I am a little concerned for it in another. If it should come to be publicly known that you had the strongest aversion to Captain Landais, who had used you basely, and that it is only since the last year's cruise, and the appointment of Commodore Jones to the command, that you request to be again under your old captain, I fear suspicions and reflections may be thrown upon you by the world, as if this change of sentiment may have arisen from your observation during the cruise, that Captain Jones loved close fighting, that Captain Landais was skilful in keeping out of harm's way, and that you therefore thought yourself safer with the latter. For myself, I believe you to be brave men, and lovers of your country and its glorious cause; and I am persuaded you have only been ill-advised, and misled by the artful and malicious misrepresentations of some persons I guess at. Take in good part this friendly counsel from an old man who is your friend. Go home peaceably with your ship. Do your duty faithfully and cheerfully. Behave respectfully to your commander, and I am persuaded he will do the same to you. Thus you will not only be happier in your voyage, but recommend yourselves to the future favours of Congress and of your country."

Such was the conciliatory tone in which Franklin addressed these turbulent and discontented men. It were to be wished that his good temper and calmness of reason had produced the effect that might have been expected. The failure proves that something besides reason is at times necessary in governing seamen.

In a letter to Jones he explains the affair, and relates the measures he had taken in consequence. "Saturday morning," he says, "I received a letter signed by about 115 of the sailors of the Alliance, declaring that they would not raise the anchor, nor depart from L'Orient, till they had six months' wages paid them, and the utmost farthing of their prize-money, including the ships sent into Norway, and until *their legal captain, P. Landais,* was restored to them. This mutiny has undoubtedly been excited by that captain; probably by making them believe that satisfaction has been received for those Norway prizes delivered up to the English," &c. &c. "That he is concerned in this mutiny he has been foolish enough to furnish us with proofs, the sailors' letter being not only enclosed under a cover directed to me in his hand-writing, but he also, in the same writing, interlined the words, *their legal captain, P. Landais,* which happens to contain his signature. I immediately went to Versailles to demand the assistance of government, and on showing the letter, by which his guilt plainly appeared, an order was immediately granted, sent away the same evening, for apprehending and imprisoning him, and orders were (promised to be) given at the same time to the commissary of the port to afford you all kind of assistance to facilitate your departure." The promises thus given were very ill kept. The mutiny had now reached the crisis. On the morning of the 13th June, before going on shore to superintend the equipment of the Ariel, Jones caused his appointment to the Alliance to be read on the deck of that ship, and, addressing the assembled crew, demanded that whoever had any complaint to prefer against him should now speak out. "There was," he says, "every appearance of contentment and subordination;" and again, "I am certain the people love me and would readily obey me." The proofs of this affection were of a very unusual kind. No sooner had Jones quitted the ship, than Landais came on board and usurped the command.

As soon as intelligence of this wild measure reached Franklin, Landais was ordered to quit the ship, and the officers were commanded to obey Jones alone. To Jones, who was in the greatest perplexity, he wrote, "You are likely to have great trouble. I wish you well through it. You have shown your abilities in fighting,—you have now an opportunity of showing the other necessary part, in the character of a great chief,—your abilities in policy."

Landais, backed and instigated by Lee, and supported by the officers and seamen, refused to yield one jot; and, holding the mandate of Franklin and the arrest of the King alike in defiance, he resolved to sail for America, captain of the Alliance. In this singular juncture, Jones posted back to Versailles, to solicit the assistance of government. Orders, he was told, had been previously sent to L'Orient to compel Landais and his crew to obedience, or, if he attempted to quit the port, to fire on him, and, if necessary, sink the ship. Confiding in this statement, Jones immediately returned to L'Orient, and found that the orders which were said to have preceded him, if they had ever been despatched, had at least never arrived,—a circumstance somewhat singular, though, in French diplomacy, by no means unaccountable. The local authorities, however, with whom Jones, in the course of his long stay in that port, had acquired considerable influence, were strongly disposed to support his authority and to enforce the orders of Franklin. Acting under the sanction of the American ministers, and supported by the local authorities at L'Orient, as well as by the promises and countenance of the government, had Jones at this time listened to the dictates of passion or revenge, irreparable mischief might have been done, which his magnanimity and prudence averted.

Basely as he had been used, and irritated as he must have been, he would not be even the indirect cause of shedding American blood. It is thus he notices the part he had taken, and relates the consequences of the mutiny to Franklin:

"L'Orient, June 21, 1780.

"SIR,

"I was detained at Versailles forty hours from the time of my arrival, and was then informed by M. de Genet, that an express had been sent from Court with the necessary orders to the King's officers at L'Orient, respecting Captain Landais and the Alliance. I found myself here early yesterday morning, fifty-four hours after leaving Versailles. The Alliance had, the evening and night before, been warped and towed from the road of L'Orient to Port Louis; and no express from Court had arrived here. M. de Thevenard, the commandant, however, made every necessary preparation to stop the Alliance, as appears by the enclosed document on the subject. He had even sent orders in the evening, before I was aware, to fire on the Alliance, and sink her to the bottom, if they attempted to approach and pass the barrier that had been made across the entrance of the port. Had I even remained silent *an hour* longer, the dreadful work would have been done. Your humanity will, I know, justify the part I acted in preventing a scene that would have rendered me miserable for the rest of my life. The Alliance has this morning been towed and warped through the rocks, and is now at anchor without, between Port Louis and Groix. In this situation I at noon sent out Lieutenant Dale with a letter to Captain Landais, whereof the within is a copy.

"Yesterday morning the within letter was brought me from Mr Lee, though I had never even hinted that his opinion or advice would be acceptable. He has, however, pulled off the mask, and, I am convinced, is not a little disappointed that his operations have produced no bloodshed between the subjects of France and America. Poor man!

“ Yesterday every thing that persuasion or threatening could effect was attempted * * * * * * * * * * *

“ M. de Thevenard, on his part, sent the deputy of M. Sweighauser on board with your letters, *under his own cover*, to Captain Landais, and to the officers and men of the Alliance. The one was delivered to Captain Landais, the other to Lieutenant Digges. M. de Thevenard also sent on board an officer with the King's order to arrest Captain Landais, who refused to surrender himself. Mr Lee and his party pretend to justify their measures, because they say you did not put Captain Landais under arrest. According to them, you cannot displace him, however great his crimes! If the government does not interfere to crush this despicable party, France and America have much to fear from it. I verily believe them to be *English* at the bottom of their hearts.”*

* In a marginal note, affixed to this letter many years afterwards, Jones says, “ In this opinion I was not singular, though perhaps I was mistaken.”

To a lady in Paris, one of the friends he had lately made, he sent a much fuller account of this unpleasant affair, wishing, no doubt, to stand clear in the opinion of his powerful and fashionable patrons in the capital, and reasonably concluding that his exculpatory epistle might make the round of the circles. "I confess to you," he writes to Madame Tellison, "that I feel rather ashamed that such an event should have happened, although, God knows, it was not owing to any fault of mine. The true reason was, that M. Ray de Chaumont unjustly detained from the brave Americans, who had so bravely served in the squadron under my command, not only their wages, but also their prize-money; and he has not, even to this hour, given me the means of paying them their just claims. One or two envious persons here, taking advantage of these circumstances, persuaded these poor people that I had joined M. Ray de Chaumont to detain from them their just dues, and that it was, besides, my intention to carry them on new expeditions in Europe, and not to suffer them to return to their families in America during the war.

These insinuations were false and groundless; I had disapproved the conduct of M. Ray de Chaumont so much as neither to speak or write to him after my return to France. My sole business at Court was to obtain the free sale of the prizes, which I effected; and, far from being then bound on new expeditions in Europe, I was ordered by the board of admiralty in America to return forthwith to Congress, and had in consequence received the public despatches both from Dr Franklin and the Court. The Alliance, however, was hurried out of this port before the crew had time for reflection; yet, before they sailed from the road of Groix, many of them, seeing their error, refused to weigh anchor, and were carried to sea, confined hands and feet in irons. The government of France had taken measures to stop the ship; but I interposed, to prevent bloodshed between the subjects of the two allied nations. I am now again almost ready to sail in the Ariel, and I know, soon after my arrival in America, that Congress will do me impartial justice. I will then have the happiness to furnish you with the account I promised, and the circumstances will be supported by the fullest evidence. I dare promise that it will then appear that I have only been to blame for having returned here from Paris without having insisted absolutely on the previous payment of my men."

Franklin could at this time do no more to support the authority of the officer he had appointed. His anxious thoughts were in America, occupied with the distressed condition of Washington's troops. His first object, therefore, was to remedy as far as possible the mischief done to the public cause by Landais's mutiny, and the consequent delay in forwarding the military stores. Jones, however, appears to have felt his own crippled command at least as pressingly as the exigencies of the distant troops, and attempted to obtain a larger vessel than the Ariel.

The Serapis was now refitted. From the hour of her capture his pride and his affections had been fixed on this command, and he very plausibly enumerated to Franklin the advantages that might result to the public cause, were he enabled, with this vessel armed for war, the Ariel, and certain American frigates, to undertake some of those daring expeditions he had so often proposed to government. This project failed, and he begged for the Terpsichore, another French ship, and engaged his personal friends to lend their influence to obtain it for him. Their solicitations did not succeed. France was now in the heat of the war,—the ministry were occupied with other subjects, and also evidently a little tired of the importunity of the Chevalier Jones,—and Franklin was disappointed and vexed at the delays which had taken place in forwarding those stores it had cost him so much to obtain, and of which the army stood in such pressing want. No sooner, however, had the Alliance left port, than, without wasting another thought on the affair, which no thought could amend, Franklin writes with the most business-like promptitude, "That affair is over, and the business is now to get the goods out as well as we can. I am perfectly bewildered with the different schemes that have been proposed to me for this purpose by Mr Williams, Mr Ross, yourself, and M. de Chaumont. Mr Williams was for purchasing ships. I told him I had not the money, but he still urges it. You and Mr Ross proposed borrowing the Ariel. I joined in the application for that ship. We obtained her. She was to convey all that the Alliance could not take. Now you find her insufficient. An additional ship has already been asked, and could not be obtained. I think therefore it will be best that you take as much into the Ariel as you can, and depart with it. For the rest I must apply to the government to contrive some means of transporting it in their own ships. This is my present opinion; and when I have once got rid of this business, no consideration shall tempt me to meddle again with such matters, as I never understood them."

Before Jones could get off on this errand, so necessary to America, but not much calculated, as he felt, to increase his glory, and therefore, on his part, not very zealously managed, a change took place in the French ministry which revived his hopes. The Marquis de Castries succeeded Sartine at the head of the marine department, and the virtuous Maurepas became prime minister. To both of these distinguished persons Jones lost no time in recommending himself by congratulatory letters; along with which were transmitted fresh copies of the maritime projects formerly sent to their predecessors in office. He also wished, before leaving Europe, to obtain from them, as the persons in actual power, testimonies in his favour, addressed to Congress, equivalent to those he had obtained from Sartine. His philanthropy, patriotism, and disinterested services, were once more duly set forth to the new ministers. He endeavoured to bring Mr Silas Dean and Dr Bancroft into his views, and again employed the influence of his friend the Duke of Rochefoucault. The ship so earnestly solicited was not obtained, nor does it appear that the American ministers concurred in the request.

Though on an after investigation Jones came clear out of this affair, it is obvious that, had he been half as anxious to forward the military stores as to serve the republic in a way more consonant to his own taste, the Ariel might long before this period have reached the shores of America.

Towards the end of June the Alliance had put to sea, and Jones still remained in port, when in

November accounts were received of the arrival of that ship at Boston. From his friend Dr Cooper of that town Dr Franklin received an account of the issue of Lee's factious proceedings, and of Landais's mutiny, which he instantly transmitted to the person most likely to sympathize with his feelings regarding that mortifying affair. The extract of Dr Cooper's letter was enclosed to the Commodore in a letter from Mr Temple Franklin, the grandson and secretary of Franklin, the minister himself being at this time confined to bed:

"Boston, September 8, 1780.

"The Alliance arrived here some weeks ago, with Dr Lee, who is still in town. This vessel appears to me to have left France in an unjustifiable manner, though I cannot yet obtain the particular circumstances. Landais did not hold his command through the voyage, which was either relinquished by him or wrested from him. All the passengers, as well as officers and sailors, are highly incensed against him, and Dr Lee as much as any one. A court of inquiry is now sitting upon this matter, in which the Doctor has given a full evidence against the captain, which represents him as *insane*."

It was unfortunate that Dr Lee was so late in making this discovery.

The tardy and inauspicious voyage of the Ariel, so long delayed and so often obstructed, was at length commenced on the 8th of October. On the following night the ship encountered a tremendous gale, which was felt over almost all Europe. She rode out the storm for two days dismasted, and the waters around her covered with the wrecks of other vessels; and on the 13th put back, in a very disabled condition, to L'Orient. The arms, the most important part of the stores, were so much damaged, that it was necessary they should be unshipped and left; and before the vessel could be repaired and freshly provisioned, it was the middle of December. Franklin, though too reasonable to complain of a delay occasioned by the violence of the elements, grudged, nevertheless, the expense to which he had been repeatedly put for new outfits,—grudged, but passed the bills drawn on him; giving, however, his less considerate friend sundry precautionary hints.

"I suppose," he writes, "you thought it for the good of the service, as you say you did, to order that great quantity of medicine for the 74-gun ship, yet, after what I had written to you of my difficulties, it still seems to me that you ought not to have done it without informing me and obtaining my consent; and I have only to be thankful that you did not order all her stores, sails, and rigging, anchors, powder, &c. I think you must be sensible, on reflection, that with regard to me it was wrong, and that it ought not to be expected from me to be always ready and able to pay the demands that every officer in the service may saddle me with. This affair, however, is done with, and I shall say and think no more about it."

Jones gave such an explanation as was at least meant to satisfy the frugal statesman; to whom, on the 18th December, he once again addressed a farewell letter. He also took leave once more of his friends and patrons in the capital. One of his valedictory epistles, addressed to Madame D'Ormoy, may be received as the best exposition that can be given of his feelings at the close of his short but brilliant career in Europe :—" I cannot leave France without expressing how much I feel myself honoured and obliged by the generous attention that you have shown to my reputation in your journal. I will ever have the most ardent desire to merit the spontaneous praise of beauty and her pen ; and it is impossible to be more grateful than I am for the very polite attentions I lately received at Paris and Versailles. My particular thanks are due to you, madam, for the personal proofs I had received of your esteem and friendship, and for the happiness you procured me in the society of the charming countess, and other ladies and gentlemen of your circle. But I have a favour to ask of you, madam, which I hope you will grant me. You tell me in your letter, that the inkstand I had the honour to present you, as a small token of my esteem, shall be reserved for the purpose of writing what concerns me ; now I wish you to see my idea in a more expanded light, and would have you make use of that inkstand to instruct mankind, and support the dignity and rights of human nature."

"By the enclosed declaration of my officers," he writes to the same lady, "you will see, my dear madam, that I was in a ticklish situation in the moment while you were employed in writing to me on the 9th ultimo. It is impossible to be more sensible than I am of the obligation conferred on me by your attentions and kind remembrance, joined to that of the belle comtesse, your fair daughters, and the amiable ladies and gentlemen of your society. I have returned without laurels, and, what is worse, without having been able to render service to the glorious cause of liberty. I know not why Neptune was in such anger, unless he thought it an affront in me to appear on his ocean with so insignificant a force. It is certain, that till the night of the 8th I did not fully conceive the awful majesty of tempest and of shipwreck. I can give you no just idea of the tremendous scene that nature then presented, which surpassed the reach even of poetic fancy and the pencil. I believe no ship was ever before saved from an equal danger off the point of the Penmark rocks. I am extremely sorry that the young English lady you mention should have imbibed the national hatred against me. I have had proofs that many of the first and finest ladies of that nation are my friends. Indeed I cannot imagine why any fair lady should be my enemy, since, upon the large scale of universal philanthropy, I feel, acknowledge, and bend before the sovereign power of beauty. The English nation may hate me, but *I will force them to esteem me too.*"

Jones had other, or at least one other fair correspondent about this period, who, under the assumed name of Delia, makes some figure in his private history. The day of the Amintas and Delias was not then quite gone by; and, under this pastoral and poetic appellation, a lady chose to conceal herself, of whose real name and situation the multitudinous papers left by the commodore, though they include many of her letters, afford no satisfactory trace. In America, Delia has been discovered to be a young lady of the Court. In Scotland we are not so quick-sighted.

But as the claims of love and gallantry were ever postponed by the Commodore to those of professional duty and ambition, we shall in so far follow his example as to defer the introduction of Delia and her fair contemporaries, till a a more convenient season.

Besides the enthusiastic epistles of Delia, Jones carried out the following letter, already noticed as written by De Sartine on the order of the King of France, and approved by his Most Christian Majesty in council. This of itself would have ensured him that honourable reception in the country of his adoption, to which his zeal and services gave him yet stronger claims.

Translation of the Letter addressed to Mr Hantenydon, President of the Congress of the United States, by M. de Sartine, Minister of the French Marine.

"Versailles, 20th May, 1780.

"Commodore Paul Jones, after having given to all Europe, and, above all, to the enemies of France and of the United States, high proofs of his valour and of his talents, is about to return to

America, to give an account to Congress of the success of his military operations. I am aware, Sir, that the reputation he has so justly acquired will go before him, and that the history of his campaigns will be sufficient to prove to his countrymen, that his abilities are equal to his courage; but the King has thought it right to join to the public voice his approbation and his bounty. He has charged me expressly to make known to you how much he is satisfied with the services of the Commodore, persuaded that Congress will do him like justice. His Majesty gives him a pledge of his esteem in bestowing on him the gift of a sword, which could not be placed in better hands, and now offers to Congress to decorate this brave officer with the cross of the order of Military Merit. His Majesty thinks that these peculiar distinctions, associating together in the same honours the subject of two countries united by similar interests, may be regarded as another tie between them, and excite them to emulation in the common cause. If, after having approved the conduct of the Commodore, it is judged fit to intrust him with any new expedition to Europe, his Majesty will see him return with pleasure; and he presumes Congress will refuse nothing that may be deemed necessary to promote the success of his enterprises. My personal esteem for the Commodore induces me to recommend him in a particular manner to you, Sir; and I venture to hope that, in the reception which he may receive from Congress, he will perceive the fruits of the sentiments with which he has inspired me.

"I have the honour to be, &c.

"De Sartine."

CHAPTER VIII.

On the 18th February, 1781, Commodore Jones reached Philadelphia. The principal adventure of this voyage is thus related by himself in the memorial to the King of France, and in the third person:—" After a variety of rencounters, he, in the latitude 26° north, and longitude of Barbadoes, met with a remarkably fast-sailing frigate belonging to the enemy's navy. Captain Jones endeavoured to avoid speaking with that ship, and as the night approached, he hoped to succeed, notwithstanding her superior sailing. He was, however, mistaken, for next morning the ships were at less distance asunder than they had been the evening before, although during the night the officers of the watch had always informed Captain Jones the sail continued out of sight. An action now became unavoidable, and the Ariel was prepared for it. Every thing was thrown overboard that interfered with the defence and safety of the ship. Captain Jones took particular care, by the management of sails and helm, to prevent the enemy from discovering the force of the Ariel, and worked her so well as not to discover any warlike appearance or preparation. In the afternoon the Ariel fired now and then a light stern-chaser at the enemy from the quarter-deck, and continued to crowd sail as if very much alarmed. This had the desired effect, and the enemy pursued with the greater eagerness. Captain Jones did not suffer the enemy to come close up till the approach of night, when, having well examined his force, he shortened sail, to meet his approach. When the two ships came within hail of each other they both hoisted English colours. The person whose duty it was to hoist the pendant on board the Ariel had not taken care to make the other end of the halliards fast, to haul it down again to change the colours. This prevented Captain Jones from an advantageous manœuvre he had intended, and obliged him to let the enemy range up along the lee-side of the Ariel, where he saw a battery lighted for action. A conversation now took place between the two ships, which lasted near an hour; by which Captain Jones learned the situation of the enemy's affairs in America. The captain of the enemy's ship said his name was John Pindar. His ship had been constructed by the famous Mr Peck of Boston, built at New-bury-Port, owned by Mr Tracey of that place, commanded by Captain Hopkins, the son of the late Commodore Hopkins, and had been taken and fitted out at New York, and named the Triumph, by Admiral Rodney. Captain Jones told him he must put out his boat, and come on board and show his commission, to prove whether or not he really did belong to the British navy. To this he made some excuses, because Captain Jones had not told him who he was; and his boat, he said, was very leaky. Captain Jones told him to consider the danger of refusing. Captain Pindar said he would answer for twenty guns, and that himself and every one of his people had shown themselves Englishmen. Captain Jones said he would allow him five minutes only to make his reflection. That time being elapsed,

Captain Jones backed a little on the weather-quarter of the enemy, ran close under her stern, hoisted American colours, and being within short pistol-shot on the lee-beam of the enemy, began to engage. It was past seven o'clock, and as no equal force ever exceeded the vigorous and regular fire of the Ariel's battery and tops, the action while it lasted made a glorious appearance. The enemy made a feeble resistance for about ten minutes. He then struck his colours. The enemy then begged for quarter, and said half his men were killed. The Ariel's fire ceased; and the crew, as usual after a victory, gave cries of joy, to "show themselves Englishmen." The enemy filled their sails, and got on the Ariel's weather-bow before the cries of joy had ended on board the Ariel. Captain Jones, suspecting the base design of the enemy, immediately set every sail he could to prevent her escape; but the enemy had so much advantage in sailing, that the Ariel could not keep up, and they soon got out of gun-shot. The English Captain may properly be called a knave, because, after he surrendered his ship, begged for, and obtained quarter, he basely ran away, contrary to the laws of naval war and the practice of civilized nations. A conspiracy was discovered among the English part of the Ariel's crew immediately after sailing from France. During the voyage every officer, and even the passengers, had been constantly armed, and kept a regular watch, besides a constant guard with fixed bayonets. After the action with the Triumph the plot was so far discovered, that Captain Jones confined twenty of the ringleaders in irons till his arrival. Captain Jones arrived at Philadelphia on the 18th February, 1781, having been absent from America three years, three months, and eighteen days."

The clamour excited in America by the detention of the army stores, and the real evils which had by this means been occasioned to the public service, compelled Congress to institute an immediate inquiry into the cause of the delay. This in common fairness was the more necessary, as Landais, who was arrested in coming to America with the Alliance, had now been tried, and for ever dismissed the service.

A Board of Admiralty had been for some time

organized, and on this Board devolved the duty of inquiry, while Congress almost simultaneously took up the affair. A string of questions, forty-seven in number, were proposed by the Board to Jones, to which he was required to give answers in writing. He lost no time in complying with this order; nor, it is to be presumed, in securing such powerful and useful friends as his brilliant reputation and the testimonials he brought from Europe had already predisposed in his favour. Admired and caressed at the Court of Versailles, and more dreaded by the vulgar of the English nation than was very creditable either to their judgment or courage, Paul Jones could not, at this period of agitation and imbittered hostility, fail to find friends in America, had his public services been even less valuable and important than they really were.

His answers to the official interrogatories were on all points ample, and, it appears, satisfactory; and the subsequent report of the Board, so far from being condemnatory, was highly flattering. Another report of the same Board will show the exact footing on which he now stood.

"Admiralty Office, June 16th, 1781.

"The Board, to whom was referred the letters and other papers relative to the conduct of John Paul Jones, Esq., beg leave to report, that they have carefully perused said letters and papers, wherein they find favourable mention is made of his abilities as an officer by the Duke de Vauguyon, M. de Sartine, and Dr Franklin; and this is also corroborated by that valour and intrepidity with which he engaged his Britannic Majesty's ship, the Serapis, of forty-four cannon, twelve and eighteen pounders, who, after a severe contest for several hours, surrendered to his superior valour, thereby acquiring honour to himself and dignity to the American flag.

"The Board therefore humbly conceive that an honourable testimony should be given to Captain Paul Jones, commander of the Bon Homme Richard, his officers and crew, for their many singular services in annoying the enemy on the British coasts, and particularly for their spirited behaviour in an engagement with his Britannic Majesty's ship of war, the Serapis, on the 23d of

September, 1779, and obliging her to surrender to the American flag."

The following is a farther extract from another of these reports:—

"With regard to Captain Jones, the Board beg leave to report, that the views of the Marine Committee in sending Captain Jones, and his views in going in the Ranger to France, were, that he might take the command of the Indian, a ship that was building at Amsterdam on a new construction, under a contract made by the Commissioners of these States at Paris, and with her, in concert with the Ranger, annoy the coasts and trade of Great Britain. When he arrived at Nantes, the Commissioners sent for him to Paris. After remaining there some time, he was informed that they had assigned their property in the ship Indian to the King of France. Captain Jones returned to Nantes, plans and undertakes a secret expedition in the Ranger," &c. &c. The report goes on to enumerate the various services of Captain Jones, and then proceeds, "ever since Captain Jones first became an officer in the navy of those States, he hath shown an unremitted attention in planning and executing enterprises calculated to promote the essential interests of our glorious cause. That in Europe, although in his expedition through the Irish Channel in the Ranger he did not fully accomplish his purpose, yet he made the enemy feel that it is in the power of a small squadron, under a brave and enterprising commander, to retaliate the conflagrations of our defenceless towns. That returning from Europe, he brought with him the esteem of the greatest and best friends of America; and hath received from the illustrious monarch of France that reward of warlike virtue which his subjects receive by a long series of faithful services or uncommon merit.

"The Board are of opinion that the conduct of Paul Jones merits particular attention, and some distinguished mark of approbation from the United States in Congress assembled."

Had the reports been drawn up by himself, or his most zealous friends, they could not have been more gratifying. He also received the solemn thanks of Congress, recorded in the following document:—

"BY THE UNITED STATES IN CONGRESS ASSEMBLED.

"Saturday, April 14, 1781.

"On the report of a committee consisting of Mr Varnun, Mr Houston, and Mr Mathews, to which was referred a motion of Mr Varnun:

"The United States, in Congress assembled, having taken into consideration the report of the Board of Admiralty of the 28th March last, respecting the conduct of John Paul Jones, Esq., captain in the navy, do,

"*Resolve*, That the thanks of the United States in Congress assembled be given to Captain John Paul Jones, for the zeal, prudence, and intrepidity with which he hath supported the honour of the American flag, for his bold and successful enterprises to redeem from captivity the citizens of these States who had fallen under the power of the enemy, and in general for the good conduct and eminent services by which he has added a lustre to his character and to the American arms.

"That the thanks of the United States in Congress assembled be also given to the officers and men who have faithfully served under him from time to time, for their steady affection to the cause of their country, and the bravery and perseverance they have manifested therein."

The following letter from Washington, of which the original is preserved among his papers, must have completed the satisfaction Paul Jones experienced in his honourable public acquittal:—

"Head Quarters, New Windsor,
15th May, 1781.

"Sir,

"My partial acquaintance with either our naval or commercial affairs makes it altogether impossible for me to account for the unfortunate delay of those articles of military stores and clothing which have been so long provided in France.

"Had I had any particular reasons to have suspected you of being accessary to that delay, which I assure you has not been the case, my suspicions would have been removed by the very full and satisfactory answers which you have, to the best of my knowledge, made to the questions proposed to you by the Board of Admiralty, and upon which that Board have, in their report to Congress, testified the high sense which they entertain of your merits and services.

"Whether our naval affairs have in general been well or ill conducted would be presumptuous in me to determine. Instances of bravery and good conduct in several of our officers have not, however, been wanting. Delicacy forbids me to mention *that particular one* which has attracted the admiration of all the world, and which has influenced the most illustrious Monarch to confer a mark of his favour which can only be obtained by a long and honourable service, or by the performance of some brilliant action.

"That you may long enjoy the reputation you have so justly acquired is the sincere wish of,

Sir,

Your most obedient servant,

Geo. Washington."

In the investigation respecting the delay of the stores, Franklin had been implicated as well as Jones. He now stood equally clear; and, however reluctant Jones might have been, after Landais had usurped his command, and run away with his ship, to put to sea with a single vessel, and that of inferior force, the paramount and unceasing anxiety of Franklin to forward the stores, does not by any means admit a doubt. In the awkward affair of Landais it was accordingly decided that Franklin had done nothing for which he had not ample discretionary powers; and as an appropriate mark of the entire confidence of Congress, he was appointed by the Marine Committee to the sole management of maritime affairs in Europe. The patron of Landais, the strenuous supporter of constitutional rights, Mr Arthur Lee, now thought proper to abandon his former opinions, together with his unlucky *protegé*, and even to appear among the active friends of Commodore Jones.

On coming thus clearly and honourably out of this investigation, Jones, besides the vote of thanks so gratifying to his feelings, obtained the reward which of all others he valued the highest, a farther opportunity of extending his fame by active service in the cause of America. By an unanimous ballot, (for in this manner it seems officers were chosen,) he was appointed to the command of the America, a fine vessel, still on the stocks. Almost immediately he went to Portsmouth, in New Hampshire, to superintend the building and equipment of this ship.

This seems to have been one of the few intervals of leisure and tranquillity which his chequered life afforded. It was sweetened by the hope of future services to be performed, and future glories to be acquired. He continued for some months in the little town of Portsmouth, and, besides maintaining an extensive correspondence in France and America, found time to mature and arrange his ideas on the subject of the American navy.

We have not sufficient nautical skill to decide how far the belief of Jones in the relative superiority of the French to the English system of naval tactics was even theoretically correct ; it is enough, that almost every succeeding naval engagement has practically demonstrated the futility of his speculations. The ships of England scarcely ever afterwards met those of her rival save to beat them, till the flag of France was literally swept from the seas. But though the opinions of Jones are thus, in all probability, abstractly of no great value as those of a great naval tactician, they are of some consequence, as they discover the state of his own mind, his strong prepossession for whatever was French, and his jealousy of English naval supremacy. It is but fair to let him state his reasons for his singular belief.

"The beginning of our navy," he says, "as navies now rank, was so singularly small, that I am of opinion it has no precedent in history. Was it a proof of madness in the first corps of sea-officers to have, at so critical a period, launched out on the ocean with only two armed merchant ships, two armed brigantines, and one armed sloop, to make war against such a power as Great Britain? To be diffident is not always a proof of ignorance. I had sailed before this revolution in armed ships and frigates, yet, when I came to try my skill, I am not ashamed to own I did not find myself perfect in the duties of a first lieutenant. If midnight study, and the instruction of the greatest and most learned sea-officers, can have given me advantages, I am not without them. I confess, however, I have yet to learn; it is the work of many years' study and experience to acquire the high degree of science necessary for a great sea-officer. Cruising after merchant ships, the service in which our frigates have generally been employed, affords, I may say, no part of the knowledge necessary for conducting fleets and their operations. There is now, perhaps, as much difference between a battle between two ships, and an engagement between two fleets, as there is between a duel and a ranged battle between two armies. The English, who boast so much of their navy, never fought a ranged battle on the ocean before the war that is now ended. The battle off Ushant was, on their part, like their former ones, irregular; and Admiral Keppell could only justify himself by the example of Hawke in our remembrance, and of Russel in the last century. From that moment the English were forced to study and to imitate the French in their evolutions. They never gained any advantage when they had to do with equal force, and the unfortunate defeat of Count de Grasse was owing more to the unfavourable circumstances of the wind coming ahead four points at the beginning of the battle, which put his fleet into the order of *echiquier* when it was too late to tack, and of calm and currents afterwards, which brought on an entire disorder, than to the admiralship, or even the vast superiority of Rodney, who had forty sail of the line against thirty, and five three-deckers against one. By the account of some of the French officers, Rodney might as well have been asleep, not having made a second signal during the battle, so that every captain did as he pleased.

"The English are very deficient in signals as well as in naval tactic. This I know, having in my possession their present fighting and sailing instructions, which comprehend all their signals and evolutions. Lord Howe has, indeed, made some improvements by borrowing from the French. But Kempenfelt, who seems to have been a more promising officer, had made a still greater improvement by the same means. It was said of Kempenfelt, when he was drowned in the Royal George, England has lost her Du Pavillion. That great man, the Chevalier du Pavillion, commanded the Triumphant, and was killed in the last battle of Count de Grasse. France lost in him one of her greatest naval tacticians, and a man who had, besides, the honour (in 1773) to invent the new system of naval signals, by which sixteen hundred orders, questions, answers, and informations, can, without confusion or misconstruction, and with the greatest celerity, be communicated through a great fleet. It was his fixed opinion that a smaller number of signals would be insufficient. A captain of the line at this day must be a tactician. A captain of a cruising frigate may make shift without ever having heard of naval tactics. Until I arrived in France, and became acquainted with that great tactician Count D'Orvilliers, and his judicious assistant the Chevalier du Pavillion, who, each of them, honoured me with instructions respecting the science of governing the operations, &c. of a fleet, I confess I was not sensible how ignorant I had been before that time of naval tactics."*

* Jones forgets once writing Franklin that this illustrious commander chose rather to permit several English

However defective the general views of the Commodore might be as a great tactician, his ideas of the proper formation and internal policy and regulation of a navy for the young republic of America discover a comprehensive mind, and a liberal and generous spirit. On these points he had to contend with no lurking prepossessions. His very prejudices were here all on the right side.

"From the observations I have made," he says, "and what I have read, it is my opinion, that in a navy there ought to be at least as many grades below a captain of the line as there are below a colonel of a regiment. Even the navy of France is deficient in subaltern grades, and has paid dearly for that error in its constitution, joined to another of equal magnitude, which authorises ensigns of the navy to take charge of watch on board ships of the line. One instance may be sufficient to show this. The Zélé, in the night between the 11th and 12th of April, 1782,

---

frigates to escape him, than violate professional etiquette by breaking his line! This was tactics with a vengeance!

ran on board the Ville de Paris, which accident was the principal cause of the unfortunate battle that ensued next day between Count de Grasse and Admiral Rodney. That accident in all probability would not have happened had the deck of the Zélé been at the time commanded by a steady experienced lieutenant of the line instead of a young ensign. The charge of the deck of a ship of the line should, in my judgment, never be intrusted to an officer under twenty-five years of age. At that time of life he may be supposed to have served nine or ten years,—a term not more than sufficient to have furnished him with the necessary knowledge for so great a charge. It is easy to conceive that the minds of officers must become uneasy, when they are continued too long in any one grade, which must happen (if regard be paid to the good of the service) where there are no more subaltern grades than midshipman and lieutenant. Would it not be wiser to raise young men by smaller steps, and to increase the number?

"I have many things to offer respecting the formation of our navy. We are a young people, and need not be ashamed to ask advice from nations older and more experienced in marine affairs than ourselves. This, I conceive, might be done in a manner that would be received as a compliment by several, or perhaps all the marine powers of Europe, and at the same time would enable us to collect such helps as would be of vast use when we come to form a constitution for the creation and government of our marine, the establishment and police of our dock-yards, academies, hospitals, &c. &c., and the general police of our seamen throughout the continent. These considerations induced me, on my return from the fleet of his excellency the Marquis de Vaudreuil, to propose to you to lay my ideas on the subject before Congress, and to propose sending a proper person to Europe in a handsome frigate, to display our flag in the ports of the different marine powers, to offer them the free use of our ports, and propose to them commercial advantages, &c., and then to ask permission to visit their marine arsenals, to be informed how they are furnished both with men, provision, materials, and warlike stores,—by what police and officers they are governed, how and from what resources the officers and men are paid, &c.—the line of conduct drawn between the officers of the fleet and the officers of the ports, &c.—also the armament and equipment of the different ships of war, with their dimensions, the number and qualities of their officers and men, by what police they are governed in port and at sea, how and from what resources they are fed, clothed, and paid, &c., and the general police of their seamen, and academies, hospitals, &c. &c. If you still object to my project on account of the expense of sending a frigate to Europe, and keeping her there till the business can be effected, I think it may be done, though perhaps not with the same dignity, without a frigate. My plan for forming a proper corps of sea-officers is, by teaching them the naval tactics in a fleet of evolution. To lessen the expense as much as possible, I would compose that fleet of frigates instead of ships of the line; on board of each I would have a little academy, where the officers should be taught the principles of mathematics and mechanics, when off duty. When in port, the young officers should be obliged to attend the academies established at each dock-yard, where they should be taught the principles of every art and science that is necessary to form the character of a great sea-officer. And every commission officer of the navy should have free access, and be entitled to receive instruction gratis at those academies. All this would be attended with no very great expense, and the public advantage resulting from it would be immense. I am sensible it cannot be immediately adopted, and that we must first look about for ways and means; but the sooner it is adopted the better. We cannot, like the ancients, build a fleet in a month, and we ought to take example from what has lately befallen Holland. In time of peace it is necessary to prepare, and be always prepared, for war by sea. I have had the honour to be presented with copies of the signals, tactics, and police, that have been adopted under the different admirals of France and Spain during the war, and have in my last campaign seen them put in practice. While I was at Brest, as well as while I was inspecting the building of the America, as I had furnished myself with good authors, I applied much of my leisure time to the study of naval architecture, and other matters that relate to the establishment and police of dock-yards, &c. I, however, feel myself bound to say again, I have yet much need to be instructed."

The ship America, by his exertions, was now nearly completed, and Jones had once more the immediate prospect of active service; but fortune had yet another reverse in store for him; or more properly, at this time commenced that series of disappointments and chagrins which, whether in Europe or America, continued, with brief intermissions, to pursue him through his subsequent life, till they consigned him to a premature grave. It appears to have been the fate of Jones at different epochs of his life, by the energies and activity of his character, and the impetuosity of his temper, to have momentarily strained the instruments of his advancement so far beyond the proper pitch, that they violently recoiled, as if by the counteracting force caused by their over-tension, on the instant that his vigorous hand was removed.

The *Magnifique*, a seventy-four gun ship, belonging to France, had, by accident or mismanagement, been lost in the harbour of Boston. To make up this loss, and keep their powerful ally in good humour, Congress did not scruple to strip Jones of the command so flatteringly bestowed, and this without giving him any equivalent appointment, or any future pledge. This was the second time he had been disappointed in a similar way: the America shared the fate of the *Indien;* it was presented by Congress to the Chevalier de la Luzerne, for the service of his Most Christian Majesty. Fifteen months after his appointment Jones received the following letter from the Minister of Marine:—

"Marine Office, 4th Sept. 1782.

"Dear Sir,

"The enclosed resolution will show you the destination of the ship *America*. Nothing could be more pleasing to me than this disposition, excepting so far as you are affected by it. I know you so well as to be convinced that it must give you great pain, and I sincerely sympathize with you. But although you will undergo much concern at being deprived of this opportunity to reap laurels on your favourite field, yet your regard for France will in some measure alleviate it; and to this your good sense will naturally add the delays which must have happened in fitting the ship for sea. I must entreat you to continue your inspection until she is launched, and to urge forward the business. When that is done, if you will come hither I will explain to you the reasons which led to this measure, and my views of employing you in the service of your country. You will on your route have an opportunity of conferring with the General on the blow you mentioned to me in one of your letters." * * * * *

Whatever might have been the feelings of Jones on this abrupt and painful communication, they were stifled by prudence and patriotism; and the cheerfulness and magnanimity with which he submitted to this stroke elicited the subjoined letter from Morris:—

"Marine Office, 4th October, 1782.

"Sir,

"I have received your letter of the 22d of last month. The sentiments contained in it will always reflect the highest honour upon your character. They have made so strong an impression upon my mind, that I immediately transmitted an extract of your letter to Congress. I doubt not but they will view it in the same manner that I have done."

Jones, on the request of the Minister, continued to superintend the equipment of the ship; but as honourable employment, whether in the sea or land service, was ever his favourite object, he now solicited the leave of Congress to go on board the French fleet, then cruising in the American seas, for improvement in his profession. This was given in the most gracious manner, in the subjoined resolution:—

BY THE UNITED STATES IN CONGRESS ASSEMBLED.

"Wednesday, Dec. 4, 1782.

"*Resolved*, That the agent of marine be informed that Congress, having a high sense of the merit and services of Captain John Paul Jones, and being disposed to favour the zeal manifested by him to acquire improvement in the line of his profession, do grant the permission which he requests, and that the said agent be instructed to recommend him accordingly to the countenance of his Excellency the Marquis de Vaudreuil."

The languor of inactivity, and the disappointment which followed, were also somewhat soothed by the receipt, from time to time, of letters, of which the following from La Fayette and Adams may furnish a sample :—

"Alliance, off Boston, 22d Dec. 1781.

"I have been honoured with your polite favour, my dear Paul Jones; but before it reached me I already was on board the Alliance, and every minute expecting to put to sea. It would have afforded me great satisfaction to pay my respects to the inhabitants of Portsmouth, and the State in which you are for the present. As to the pleasure to take you by the hand, my dear Paul Jones, you know my affectionate sentiments, and my very great regard for you, so that I need not add any thing on that subject.

"Accept my best thanks for the kind expressions in your letter. His Lordship's downfall* is a great event, and the greater, as it was equally and amicably shared by the two allied nations. Your coming to the army I had the honour to command would have been considered as a very flattering compliment to me who love you and know your worth. I am impatient to hear you are ready to sail, and I am of opinion we ought to unite under you every continental ship we can muster, with such a body of well-appointed marines as might cut a good figure ashore; and then give you plenty of provision, and *carte blanche.*

"I am sorry I cannot see you. I also had many things to tell you; write me by good opportunities, but not often in ciphers, unless the matter is very important," &c. &c.

"La Fayette."

---

* Lord Cornwallis.

"Hague, 12th August, 1782.

"Dear Sir,

"I had yesterday the pleasure of receiving your favour of the 10th December last, * * * * * The command of the *America* could not have been more judiciously bestowed; and it is with impatience I wish her at sea, where she will do honour to her name. Nothing gives me so much surprise, or so much regret, as the inattention of my countrymen to their navy. It is to us a bulwark as essential as it is to Great Britain. It is less costly than armies, and more easily removed from one of the United States to the other. * * *

"Every day shows that the Batavians have not wholly lost their ancient character. They are always timid and slow in adopting their political systems; but always firm and able in support of them; and always brave and active in war. They have hitherto been restrained by their chiefs; but if the war continue, they will show that they are possessed of the spirit of liberty, and that they have lost none of their great qualities.

"Rodney's victory has intoxicated Britain

again to such a degree, that I think there will be no peace for some time. Indeed, if I could see a prospect of having a half-dozen line-of-battle ships under the American flag, commanded by Commodore Paul Jones, engaged with an equal British force, I apprehend the event would be so glorious for the United States, and lay so sure a foundation for their prosperity, that it would be a rich compensation for a continuance of the war. However, it does not depend upon us to finish it. There is but one way, and that is *Burgoynizing Carlton* in New York * *

* * * * * * *

"JOHN ADAMS."

Jones went on board the French fleet according to the permission granted by Congress; but peace put a sudden end to his nautical studies in this school; and a few complimentary letters are the sole trophies that remain of his bloodless campaign. These testimonies of his talents and conduct were addressed by the Marquis de Vaudreuil to Mr Morris, the Minister of the American Marine, and to the Chevalier de la Luzerne, the French Ambassador to the United States.

That impatience of inactivity, which appears to have been an inherent quality in the mind of Jones, and considerations of private interest and friendship, now induced him to solicit an appointment in Europe, as agent for prize-money, of which large sums were still due to himself, and to his officers and men, both in France and Denmark. Their claims had indeed never been settled, and the arrangement was no easy matter. Pursuant to a resolution of Congress, he was, on the 1st Nov. 1783, formally appointed "agent for all prizes taken in Europe under his own command." On his arrival in Paris, his mission was sanctioned by Franklin, still minister plenipotentiary at Versailles, and he proceeded in the affair, which had baffled other negotiators, with his characteristic vigour and perseverance. We are well warranted in presuming that Jones would infinitely rather have re-visited Europe at this time, commander of that gallant experimental frigate which he had so earnestly recommended Congress to equip, than in the comparatively tame character he now held. His embassy, for such he loved to consider it, proved tedious, and even vexatious. His old antagonist, M. de Chaumont, had become insolvent; the French finances were already in great disorder, and disinclination existed in every department to an adjustment or liquidation of the claims of the captors. The opposition of Chaumont was peculiarly irritating to Jones, who lost no opportunity of reviling and exposing him in his frequent correspondence with the Marshal de Castries.

While this affair was in progress, Jones renewed and extended his former social connexions in Paris; and for three years, at this time, supported a considerable figure in the fashionable society of that capital, both for the gratification of his personal feelings and the advancement of his mission. In this interval he also formed several projects of commercial speculations, on the scale suited to the enterprising character of his mind, and in concert with different individuals of capital and influence. One of these projects, of which a sketch still remains among his papers, was to establish a fur-trade between the north-west coast of America and China, or Japan. The person fixed on to act as supercargo in this adventurous expedition was the celebrated John Ledyard, with whom it probably originated. It went so far, that Jones was on the point of purchasing a ship; but failed, partly from the jealousy of the Spanish government, and partly from private causes. The Algerines, and the sufferings of their American captives, was another object of his anxious attention, and one of which he never lost sight for the short remainder of his life, though he was not able to effect much in the behalf of this unfortunate portion of his countrymen.

Another of Jones' amusements at this time was having his bust taken, which was afterwards somewhat ostentatiously presented to a favoured few in America. He also handed round the journal of his short and brilliant campaign, and received in return the usual requital of letters of compliment, which, when proceeding from such characters as Malsherbes and D'Estaing, any man may be pardoned for overvaluing. A compliment was never thrown away on the Commodore, and seldom forgotten.

Tedious as the affair of the prize-money proved, an equitable and even liberal adjustment was obtained in France long before any prospect of a settlement of the claims on Denmark, which power had shuffled for eight years with considerable dexterity, and continued to do so still.

With his mission thus far accomplished, Jones, in the summer of 1787, returned to America, giving the following reasons for not at this time proceeding to Copenhagen:—

To His Excellency John Jay, Esq. Minister of Foreign Affairs.

"New York, July 8th, 1787.

"SIR,

"The application I made for a compensation for our prizes through the Danish minister in London not having succeeded, it was determined between Mr Jefferson and myself, that the proper method to obtain satisfaction was for me to go in person to the court of Copenhagen. It was necessary for me to see the Baron de Blome before I could leave France on that business, and he being absent on a tour in Switzerland, did not return to Paris till the beginning of last winter. I left Paris in the spring, and went as far as Brussels on my way to Copenhagen, when an unforeseen circumstance in my private affairs rendered it indispensable for me to turn about and cross the ocean. My private business here being already finished, I shall in a few days re-embark for Europe, in order to proceed to the court of Denmark. It is my intention to go by the way of Paris, in order to obtain a letter to the French minister at Copenhagen, from the Count de Montmorin, as the one I obtained is from the Count de Vergennes. It would be highly flattering to me if I could carry a letter with me from Congress to his Most Christian Majesty, thanking him for the squadron he did us the honour to support under our flag. And on this occasion, Sir, permit me, with becoming diffidence, to recall the attention of my Sovereign to the letter of recommendation I brought with me from the court of France, dated 30th May, 1780. It would be pleasing to me if that letter should be found to merit a place on the journals of Congress. Permit me also to entreat that Congress will be pleased to read the letter I received from the minister of marine, when his Majesty deigned to bestow on me a golden-hilted sword, emblematical of the happy alliance,—an honour which his Majesty never conferred on any other foreign officer. I owed the high favour I enjoyed at the court of France in a great degree to the favourable testimony of my conduct which had been communicated by his Majesty's ambassador, under whose eye I acted in the most critical situation in the Texel, as well as to the public opinion of Europe. And the letter with which I was honoured by the prime minister of France, when I was about to return to America, is a clear proof that we might have drawn still greater advantages from the generous disposition of our ally, if our marine had not been lost whilst I was, under perplexing circumstances, detained in Europe, after I had given the Count de Maurepas my plan for forming a combined squadron of ten or twelve sail of frigates, supported by the America, with a detachment of French troops on board; the whole at the expense of his Majesty.

"It is certain that I am much flattered by receiving a gold sword from the most illustrious monarch now living; but I had refused to accept his commission on two occasions before that time, when some firmness was necessary to resist the temptation. He was not my sovereign; I served the cause of freedom; and honours from my sovereign would be more pleasing. Since the year 1775, when I displayed the American flag for the first time with my own hands, I have been constantly devoted to the interests of America. Foreigners have, perhaps, given me too much credit, and this may have raised my ideas of my services above their real value; but my zeal can never be over-rated.

"I should act inconsistently if I omitted to mention the dreadful situation of our unhappy fellow-citizens in slavery at Algiers. Their almost hopeless fate is a deep reflection on our national character in Europe. I beg leave to influence the humanity of Congress in their behalf, and to propose that some expedient may be adopted for their redemption. A fund might be raised for that purpose by a duty of a shilling per month from seamen's wages throughout the continent, and I am persuaded that no difficulty would be made to that requisition.

I have the honour to be,

Sir, &c. &c.

" PAUL JONES."

The manner in which Jones had divided the quotas, and the magnitude of his private claims for personal expenses while engaged in this service, did not satisfy the Board of Treasury of the United States, and their report highly offended him. He, however, made out what, allowing for a considerable alloy of self-eulogium, inseparable from all his vindicatory writings, may be called a triumphant case. " The settlement," he says, " that I made with the court of France had first Dr Franklin's and afterwards Mr Jefferson's approbation, in every stage and article of the business; and I presume it will be found, at least so far as depended on me, to merit that of the United States. The Board of Treasury have been pleased in their report to treat me as a mere agent, though employed in that delicate national concern. In France I was received and treated by the King and his ministers as a general officer and a special minister from Congress. The credit with which I am honoured as an officer, in the opinion of Europe, and the personal intimacy I have with many great characters at Paris, with my exclusive knowledge of all circumstances relative to the business, ensured me a success which no other man could have obtained. My situation subjected me to considerable expense. I went to Court much oftener, and mixed with the great much more frequently, than our minister plenipotentiary, yet the gentlemen in that situation consider their salary of two thousand a-year as scarcely adequate to their expenses." But the reader is already so familiar with the services of the Commodore to the public cause of America, that we spare them the repetition which follows, and pass to the issue of this altercation, which was a resolution of Congress, passed a few days afterwards, declaring his distribution of the quotas valid, and allowing him the sum claimed as expended by him on this service. This was 47,972 livres, instead of the usual commission on sums recovered, which would not nearly have defrayed his expenses.

To complete his triumph over the Board of Treasury, Congress, in a few days afterwards, unanimously resolved " that a gold medal should be struck, and presented to Chevalier J. Paul Jones, in commemoration of the valour and brilliant services of that officer while in command of a squadron of French and American ships, under the flag and commission of the States of America." It was farther resolved that a letter should be written to his Most Christian Majesty; and accordingly, furnished with the following letter, Jones left the shores of America, which he was destined never again to revisit:—

" *To His Most Christian Majesty, Louis, King of France and Navarre.*

" Great and beloved Friend!

" We, the United States in Congress assembled, in consideration of the distinguished marks of approbation with which your Majesty has been pleased to honour the Chevalier John Paul Jones, as well as from a sense of his merit, have unanimously directed a medal of gold to be struck and presented to him, in commemoration of his valour and brilliant services while commanding a squadron of French and American ships, under our flag and commission, off the coast of Great Britain, in the late war.

"As it is his earnest desire to acquire knowledge in his profession, we cannot forbear requesting of your Majesty to permit him to embark in your fleets of evolution, where only it will be probably in his power to acquire that degree of knowledge which may hereafter render him most extensively useful.

"Permit us to repeat to your Majesty, our sincere assurances, that the various and important benefits for which we are indebted to your friendship will never cease to interest us in whatever may concern the happiness of your Majesty, your family, and people. We pray God to keep you, our great and beloved friend, under his holy protection.

"Done at the city of New York, the 16th day of October, in the year of our Lord 1787, and of our Sovereignty and Independence the 12th."

It is not probable, though just possible, that, before this last departure for Europe, Jones was aware, that, in conversation with M. de Simolin, the Russian ambassador at Paris, Mr Jefferson had proposed him to serve Russia in the Black Sea. This conversation arose in consequence of the disasters which had befallen her Imperial Majesty's fleet in a tempest in the month of September of that year. During the late negotiations about the prize-money, Jones had come in close contact with Mr Jefferson, who immediately succeeded to Franklin as ambassador, and had gained his friendship and esteem. Though he might not be aware thus early of this private treaty concerning him, there is no room to doubt that, with all the indifference and coquettish reluctance he afterwards thought fit to affect, he was from the first moment dazzled and infatuated by the prospects which thus opened so unexpectedly upon him in a new career of glory and distinction. He landed at Dover from stress of weather, and, after spending a few days in London, and making certain arrangements with the American ambassador there, respecting the Danish claims, went to Paris, and was there at least informed by Mr Jefferson of the high destinies which probably awaited him in Russia. He accordingly deferred delivering the letter which he bore from Congress to his Most Christian Majesty, till a more convenient season, and set out for Copenhagen in mid-winter, ostensibly only to solicit indemnification for the prizes so long before delivered up to the English minister, but in reality to draw a step nearer to St Petersburgh. There is no evidence that the court of Russia had ever thought of John Paul Jones as a naval commander till M. de Simolin had written home, "that with the chief command of the fleet, and *carte blanche*, he would undertake that in a year Paul Jones would make Constantinople tremble."

Jones was furnished with letters to the French ambassador at Copenhagen, and other influential persons, and gives this account of his reception in that capital:—

"I have been so much indisposed since my arrival here the 4th, from the fatigue and excessive cold I suffered on the road, that I have been obliged to confine myself almost constantly to my chamber. I have kept my bed for several days; but I now feel myself better, and hope the danger is over. On my arrival I paid my respects to the minister of France. He received me with great kindness; we went, five days ago, to the minister of foreign affairs. I was much flattered with my reception, and our conversation was long and very particular respecting America and the new constitution, of which I presented a copy. He observed, that it had struck him as a very dangerous power to make the president commander-in-chief: in other respects it appeared to please him much, as leading to a near and sure treaty of commerce between America and Denmark. It was a day of public business, and I could not do more than present your letter. I shall follow the business closely. In a few days, when I am re-established in health, I am to be presented to the whole court, and to sup with the King. I shall after that be presented to all the corps diplomatique and other persons of distinction here. I am infinitely indebted to the attentions I receive from the minister of France. I made the inquiry you desired in Holland, and should then have written to you in consequence, had I not been assured, by authority, (*M. Van Stophorst,*) that I could not doubt that letters had been sent you on the subject, that could not fail of giving you satisfaction. M. Van Stophorst was very obliging. At Hamburgh I ordered the smoked beef you desired to be sent to you, to the care of the American agent at Havre de Grace; you have nothing to do but receive it, paying what little charges may be on it. My ill health and fatigue on the road hindered me from preparing the extract of the engagement. When you see M. Littlepage, I pray you to present my kind compliments. It is said here, that the Empress confides the commerce of her fleet, that will pass the Sound, to Admiral Greig; and that he means to call at an English port to take provisions, &c. The Hamburgh papers, I am told, have announced the death of Dr Franklin. I shall be extremely concerned if the account prove true—God forbid!"

A subsequent letter states,—

"Yesterday his excellency the Baron de La Houge, minister plenipotentiary of France at this court, did me the honour to present me publicly to his Majesty, the Royal Family, and chief personages at the royal palace here.

"I had a very polite and distinguished reception. The Queen Dowager conversed with me for some time, and said the most civil things. Her Majesty has a dignity of person and deportment which becomes her well, and which she has the secret to reconcile with great affability and ease. The Princess Royal is a charming person, and the graces are so much her own, that it is impossible to see and converse with her without paying her that homage which artless beauty and good nature will ever command. All the Royal Family spoke to me except the King, who speaks to no person when presented. His Majesty saluted me with great complaisance at first, and as often afterwards as we met in the course of the evening. The Prince Royal is greatly beloved and extremely affable; he asked me a number of pertinent questions respecting America. I had the honour to be invited to sup with his Majesty and the Royal Family. The company at table (consisting of seventy ladies and gentlemen, including the Royal Family, the ministers of state, and foreign ambassadors) was very brilliant."

But this flattering reception, and abundance of diplomatic courtesy, did not long satisfy the negotiator, who was moreover engaged in another game with Baron Krudner, the Russian Envoy at this court, which interested him far more deeply. He was, in short, impatient to reach the goal of his new-sprung hopes, St Petersburgh, and accordingly addressed Count Bernstorf in his best style of diplomacy :—

Captain Paul Jones to Count Bernstorf.

"Copenhagen, 24th March, 1788.

"From the act of Congress, (the act by which I am honoured with a *gold medal*,) I had the honour to show your Excellency the 21st of this month, as well as from the conversation that followed, you must be convinced that circumstances do not permit me to remain here; but that I am under the necessity, either to return to France or to proceed to Russia.—As the minister of the United States of America at Paris gave me the perusal of the packet he wrote by me, and which I had the honour to present to you on my arrival here, it is needless to go into any detail on the object of my mission to this court; which Mr Jefferson has particularly explained. The promise you have given me, of a prompt and explicit decision, from this Court, on the act of Congress of the 25th of October last, inspires me with full confidence. I have been very particular in communicating to the United States all the polite attentions with which I have been honoured at this Court; and they will learn with great pleasure the kind reception I had from you. I felicitated myself on being the instrument to settle the delicate national business in question, with a minister who conciliates the views of the wise statesman with the noble sentiments and cultivated mind of the true philosopher and man of letters."

Paul Jones to Count Bernstorf.

"Copenhagen, March 30, 1788.

"Your silence on the subject of my mission from the United States to this Court leaves me in the most painful suspense; the more so, as I have made your Excellency acquainted with the promise I am under to proceed as soon as possible to St Petersburgh. This being the ninth year since the three prizes reclaimed by the United States were seized upon in the port of Bergen, in Norway, it is to be presumed that this Court has long since taken an ultimate resolution respecting the compensation demand made by Congress. Though I am extremely sensible of the favourable reception with which I have been distinguished at this Court, and am particularly flattered by the polite attentions with which you have honoured me at every conference; yet I have remarked, with great concern, that you have never led the conversation to the object of my mission here. A man of your liberal sentiments will not, therefore, be surprised, or offended at my plain dealing, when I repeat that I impatiently expect a prompt and categorical answer, in writing, from this Court, to the act of Congress of the 25th of October last. Both my duty and the circumstances of my situation constrain me to make this demand in the name of my Sovereign the United States of America; but I beseech you to believe, that though I am extremely tenacious of the *honour* of the *American flag*, yet my personal interest in the decision I now ask would never have induced me to present myself at this Court. You are too just, Sir, to delay my business here; which would put me under the necessity to break the promise I have made to her Imperial Majesty, conformable to your advice."

Count Bernstorf to Paul Jones.

"Copenhagen, April 4, 1788.

"Sir,

"You have requested of me an answer to the

letter you did me the honour to remit me from Mr Jefferson, minister plenipotentiary of the United States of America, near his most Christian Majesty. I do it with so much more pleasure, as you have inspired me with as much interest as confidence, and this occasion appears to me favourable to make known the sentiments of the King my master, on the objects to which we attach so much importance. Nothing can be farther from the plans and the wishes of his majesty than to let fall a negotiation which has only been suspended in consequence of circumstances arising from the necessity of maturing a new situation, so as to enlighten himself on their reciprocal interests, and to avoid the inconvenience of a precipitate and imperfect arrangement. I am authorized, Sir, to give you, and through you to Mr Jefferson, the word of the King, that his majesty will renew the negotiation for a treaty of amity and commerce in the forms already agreed upon, at the instant that the new Constitution (that admirable plan, so worthy of the wisdom of the most enlightened men) will have been adopted by the states, to which nothing more was wanted to assure to itself a perfect consideration. If it has not been possible, Sir, to discuss, definitively with you, neither the principal object nor its accessories, the idea of eluding the question, or of retarding the decision, had not the least part in it. I have already had the honour to express to you, in our conversations, that your want of plenipotentiary powers from Congress was a natural and invincible obstacle. It would be, likewise, contrary to the established custom to change the seat of negotiation, which has not been broken off, but only suspended, thereby to transfer it from Paris to Copenhagen.

"I have only one more favour to ask of you, Sir, that you would be the interpreter of our sentiments in regard to the United States. It would be a source of gratification to me to think that what I have said to you on this subject carries with it that conviction of the truth which it merits. We desire to form with them connexions, solid, useful, and essential; we wish to establish them on bases natural and immoveable. The momentary clouds, the incertitudes, which the misfortunes of the times brought with them, exist no longer. We should no longer recollect it, but to feel in a more lively manner the happiness of a more fortunate period; and to show ourselves more eager to prove the dispositions most proper to effect an union, and to procure reciprocally the advantages which a sincere alliance can afford, and of which the two countries are susceptible. These are the sentiments which I can promise you, Sir, on our part, and we flatter ourselves to find them likewise in America; nothing, then, can retard the conclusion of an arrangement, which I am happy to see so far advanced."

Paul Jones to Count Bernstorf.

"Copenhagen, April 5, 1788.

"I pray your Excellency to inform me when I can have the honour to wait on you, to receive the letter you have been kind enough to promise to write me, in answer to the act of Congress of the 25th October last. As you have told me that my want of plenipotentiary powers to terminate *ultimately* the business now on the carpet, between the Court and the United States, has determined you to authorize the Baron de Blôme to negotiate and settle the same with Mr Jefferson at Paris, and to conclude, at the same time, an advantageous treaty of commerce between Denmark and the United States,—my business here will of course be at an end when I shall have received your letter and paid you my thanks in person for the very polite attentions with which you have honoured me."

From Baron Krudner, shortly after his arrival, Jones received the following letter, which of itself denotes a foregone conclusion, and his acceptance of the invitation of Russia :—

(Translation.)

" Sir,

" I am much disappointed at not meeting you at Court, as I had promised myself, but a slight indisposition prevented me from going abroad; besides, I have been agreeably occupied in writing letters. My Sovereign will learn with pleasure the acquisition which she has made in your great talents. I have her commands for your acceptance of the grade of Captain Commandant, with the rank of Major General, in her service, and that you should proceed as soon as your affairs permit; the intention of her Imperial Majesty being to give you a command in the Black Sea, and under the orders of Prince Potemkin, from the opening of the campaign. The immortal glory by which you have illustrated your name cannot make you indifferent to the fresh laurels you must gather in the new career which opens to you. I have the honour of being on this occasion the interpreter of those sentiments of esteem with which for a long period your brilliant exploits have inspired her Imperial Majesty. Under a Sovereign so magnanimous, in pursuing glory you need not doubt of the most distinguished rewards, and that every advantage of fortune will await you," &c. &c.

This was so far well, but did not entirely come up to the high-raised expectations of Jones. In a letter to Jefferson about this same time, he says, "Before you can receive this, M. de Simolin will have informed you that your proposal to him, and his application on that idea, have been well received. The matter is communicated to me here, in the most flattering terms, by a letter I have received from his Excellency the Baron de Krudner." This is indeed perfectly contradictory of the statement Jones gives in the introduction to his Journal of the Campaign of the Liman, where the proposal of M. de Simolin is represented as quite spontaneous, and treated by himself at first as chimerical; but this is evidently the correct one. " There seems," he continues, " to remain some difficulty respecting the *letter* of M. de Simolin's proposal, though it is accepted in substance;" he then expresses his gratitude to the Russian Ambassador, and to Mr Littlepage, who had contributed so materially to his success in this affair. In a subsequent letter to Jefferson, written immediately before leaving Copenhagen, after enumerating his services, and mentioning what might have been his services had he possessed more ample diplomatic powers, he introduces the subject nearest his heart. Russia had demurred to his demand of the rank of Rear-Admiral. " If Congress," he says, " should think I deserve the promotion that was proposed when I was in America, and should condescend to confer on me the grade of Rear-Admiral, from the day I took the Serapis, (23d September, 1779, exactly nine years before,) I am persuaded it would be very agreeable to the Empress, who now deigns to offer me an equal rank in her service, although I never had the honour to draw my sword in her cause, nor to do any other act that could merit her imperial benevolence." He afterwards continues: "The mark I mentioned of the approbation of that honourable body, (Congress) would be extremely flattering to me in the career I am now to pursue, and would stimulate all my ambition to acquire the necessary talents to merit that, and even greater favours at a future day. I pray you, Sir, to explain the circumstances of my situation; and be the interpreter of my sentiments to the United States in Congress. I ask for nothing, and beg leave to be understood only as having hinted what is natural to conceive, that the mark of approbation I mentioned could not fail to be infinitely serviceable to my views and success in the country where I am going." Serviceable this piece of idle distinction might have been in smoothing the difficulties thrown in the way of his obtaining the rank of Rear-Admiral, for which he stipulated on entering the Russian service, and which, as appears from his former letter to Jefferson, and from the letter of Baron Krudner, given above, was refused at the outset. Though not disposed to break off his engagement, neither was he willing to give up his claims to the desired grade without a strenuous effort. He immediately replied to the Baron, going over the whole ground:—"I am extremely flattered," he says, "by the obliging things expressed in the letter your Excellency has done me the honour to write me yesterday. The very favourable sentiments with which my zeal for the cause of America, rather than my professional skill, has inspired her Imperial Majesty, fills me with an irresistible desire to merit the precious opinion with which her Majesty deigns to honour me. Though I cannot conceive the reason why any difficulty should be made to my being admitted into the marine of her Imperial Majesty as Rear-Admiral, a rank to which I have some claim, and that it should at the same time be proposed to give me the grade of Major-General, to which I have no title, it is not my intention to withdraw from the engagement which you have formed in my name, in the letter you addressed your court on the 23d current. You will be convinced by the papers I have the honour to submit to your inspection, that I am not an adventurer in search of fortune. You will discover, I presume, that my talents have been considerable; but that, loving glory, I am perhaps too much attached to honours, though personal interest is an idol to which I have never bowed the knee. The unbounded admiration and profound respect which I have long felt for the glorious character of her Imperial Majesty, forbids the idea that a sovereign so magnanimous should sanction any arrangement that may give pain at the outset to the man she deigns to honour with her notice, and who wishes to devote himself entirely to her service. A conjoined command is hurtful, and often fatal in military operations. There is no military man who is so entirely master of his passions as to keep free of jealousy and its consequences in such circumstances. Being quite a stranger, I have more to fear from a conjoined command than any other officer in the service of her Imperial Majesty. I cannot imagine why her Majesty should think it best to divide the command on the Black Sea; and if the direction of that department be already confided to an officer of sufficient ability and experience, I do not seek to interfere with his command."

Jones was already aware of the appointment of the Prince of Nassau, and even thus early foresaw many of the probable difficulties of his situation; but he had that confidence in himself which gave him assurance of triumphing over them, and proceeded, if not blindfold, yet determined not to see. We leave to his own narrative the account of his almost romantic journey from Copenhagen to St Petersburgh. In that capital he was received with a distinction which might have turned the soundest head. His very manner of approach had disposed people to gaze on the American hero as a wonder; his door was besieged with carriages, and his table loaded with invitations. In short, he was now in Russia, and the man whom, for the time, the Empress delighted to honour; the expected conqueror of the Turks; and it might be, a future Potemkin.*

At this curiously-timed juncture he received a patent from the King of Denmark, granting him for life an annual pension of 1500 Danish crowns, "for the respect he had shown to the Danish flag while he commanded in the North Seas." To pension the agent whose claims for his constituents are deferred or evaded, is at all times a somewhat suspicious circumstance; though this grant being unexpected and unsolicited, Jones stands clear in what he himself justly calls "an embarrassing situation." It was three years before he even mentioned this grant to his American friends; and had his affairs prospered, it is

* The cards of many of the Russian nobility received at this time, and of the whole host of Members of Legation, Envoys, Residents, &c., in short, all the component parts of a great court, still remain among the papers of Paul Jones, who through life seems to have been peculiarly diligent in the accumulation of such "frail memorials."

probable he never would have looked after it. As it was, when his large expenditure in Russia made it necessary to draw on this fund, which he did with the sanction of certain American gentlemen, whose advice he requested, he never received a single crown of the spontaneous royal grant thus pressed upon him.

For a fortnight Jones remained at St Petersburgh, " feasted at court, and in the first society." " The Empress," he writes to La Fayette, " received me with a distinction the most flattering that perhaps any stranger can boast of on entering the Russian service. Her Majesty conferred on me immediately the grade of Rear-Admiral. I was detained, against my will, a fortnight, and continually feasted at court, and in the first society. This was a cruel grief to the English; and I own their vexation, which I believe was general in and about St Petersburgh, gave me no pain." Before the year elapsed, the Rear-Admiral found some cause to change his opinions in many things; and even respecting the English at St Petersburgh. He was about this time at least three-fourths Russian. We hear no longer of America as his sole country, though he assumes a certain patronizing air towards that young State. "I certainly wish to be useful to a country which I have so long served. I love the people and their cause, and shall always rejoice when I can be useful to promote their happiness." "What are you about, my dear General? are you so absorbed in politics as to be insensible to glory? that is impossible,—quit then your divine Calypso, come here and pay your court to Bellona, who you are sure will receive you as her favourite. You would be charmed with Prince Potemkin. He is a most amiable man, and none can be more noble-minded. For the Empress, fame has never yet done her justice. I am sure that no stranger who has not known that illustrious character, ever conceived how much her Majesty is made to reign over a great empire, to make people happy, and to attach grateful and susceptible minds. Is not the present a happy moment for France to declare for Russia?" Such were the extraordinary lights that had suddenly dawned upon the former champion of liberty and assertor of the "dignity of human nature."

A few weeks before the above letter was despatched to La Fayette, the Empress, with her own hand, had written to the Rear-Admiral, enclosing a letter from M. de Simolin, regarding his affairs. Though disappointed of sole command, as will appear in the subjoined narrative, he still continued to be dazzled with his prospects. The letter of her Imperial Majesty, who spared no pains in carrying a favourite point, as well as its enclosure, deserves to be preserved:—

From the Empress Catherine to Rear-Admiral Paul Jones.

"Sir,—A courier from Paris has just brought from my Envoy in France, M. de Simolin, the enclosed letter to Count Besborodko. As I believe that this letter may help to confirm to you what I have already told you verbally, I have sent it, and beg you to return it, as I have not even made a copy be taken, so anxious am I that you should see it. I hope that it will efface all doubts from your mind, and prove to you that you are to be connected only with those who are most favourably disposed towards you. I have no doubt but that on your side you will fully justify the opinion which we have formed of you, and apply yourself with zeal to support the reputation and the name you have acquired for valour and skill on the element in which you are to serve.

Adieu,

I wish you happiness and health,

CATHERINE."

Extract of the Letter from M. de Simólin to Count de Besborodko, enclosed in the above.

"THE letter with which your Excellency favoured me on the 16th February, was delivered by Mr Poliranoff. By it I was informed of the resolution of her Imperial Majesty, on the subject of the engagement with the Chevalier Paul Jones; and the same day Lieutenant-Colonel de Baner, who was despatched from St Elizabeth by

Prince Potemkin on the 9th March, brought me two letters, the subject of one of which was the said Chevalier Jones, whom he requested me to induce to repair to his head-quarters as quickly as possible, that he might employ his talents at the opening of the campaign ; and to assure him that in entering the service, he, (Potemkin,) would do all that depended on him to make his situation pleasant and advantageous, and certainly procure for him occasions in which he might display his skill and valour." "Has he kept his word ?" says Jones in a note long afterwards affixed to this letter, which at the moment must have given him so much pleasure.

Such were the flattering auspices under which Paul Jones entered the service of Russia. From this point his history will be continued for some time by the most interesting portion of his remaining papers—his Journal of the Campaign of the Liman.

END OF VOLUME I.

OLIVER & BOYD, PRINTERS.

MEMOIRS

OF

REAR-ADMIRAL PAUL JONES.

MEMOIRS

OF

REAR-ADMIRAL PAUL JONES,

CHEVALIER OF THE MILITARY ORDER OF MERIT, AND OF THE RUSSIAN ORDER OF ST ANNE, &c. &c.

NOW FIRST COMPILED FROM HIS ORIGINAL JOURNALS AND CORRESPONDENCE: INCLUDING AN ACCOUNT OF HIS SERVICES UNDER PRINCE POTEMKIN, PREPARED FOR PUBLICATION BY HIMSELF

VOL. II.

PUBLISHED BY OLIVER & BOYD, EDINBURGH;
AND SIMPKIN & MARSHALL, LONDON.

MDCCCXXX.

MEMOIRS OF PAUL JONES.

CHAPTER I.

THIS narrative is now arrived at a period in which it can be for some time continued in the most desirable way, namely, by the Journal of the Rear-Admiral, kept by himself on the scene of action during his memorable campaign against the Turks, afterwards extended at St Petersburgh and Warsaw, and prepared for publication at Paris. Had he acted the part which manliness and sound wisdom dictated, in openly withdrawing from the service which had been to him one of misery and bondage, in which all the better qualities and higher energies of his mind were converted into the means of self-torture, he would unquestionably have published this Journal himself, if not in France, either in England or America. He long contemplated the necessity of both of these steps, and all along felt that his leave of absence for two years was in fact a virtual dismission; but, by the strange fatality, which often appears to enchain a man's will in spite of the suggestions of his reason, he lingered on till death closed the scene.

In a letter written to Mr Jefferson, twenty months after he had been exiled from Russia, and when his last remaining hopes in life began to turn to America, his first country, he says, "As it has been and still is my first wish, and my highest ambition, to show myself worthy of the flattering marks of esteem with which I have been honoured by my country, I think it my duty to lay before you, both as my particular friend and as a public minister, the papers I now enclose relative to my connexion with Russia, viz. three pieces dated St Petersburgh, and signed by the Court de Segur; a letter from me dated at Paris last summer, and sent to the Prince de Potemkin; and a letter from me to the Empress, dated a few days afterwards, enclosing eleven pieces as numbered in the margin. I have selected those testimonies from a great variety of perhaps still stronger proofs in my hands; but, though the Baron de Grimm* has undertaken to transmit to her Imperial Majesty's own hands my last packet, I shall not be surprised if I should find myself obliged to withdraw from the service of Russia, and to publish my Journal of the Campaign (in which) I commanded. In that case I hope to prove to the world that *my operations* not only saved Cherson and the Crimea, but decided the fate of the war."

The Journal is written in disjointed portions, and in a spirit of alternate bitterness and boasting, which the indulgent reader must attribute to the personal feelings from which the work

---

* Baron Grimm was a sort of man-of-all-work for the Empress Catherine II., whose business was to despatch, as frequently as possible, all the scandal, literary gossip, and political intelligence, his peculiar industry could pick up in Paris, for the information or amusement of the Empress and her Court. The German had too much tact to be the means of transmitting any thing disagreeable.

arose. The injustice, mortification, and persecution endured by the man and the officer must plead the apology of the author.

To the historian this Journal is of considerable value. It places in an entirely new aspect one of the most memorable of the campaigns between Russia and the Porte; and affords a clue, were that any longer needed, to the crooked and debasing spirit of intrigue by which the domestic policy of Russia was conducted, even under the auspices of the great Catherine.

"*Introduction to the Journal of Rear-Admiral Paul Jones's Campaign in the Liman in* 1788.

"The United States of America having charged me with a mission of a political nature to the Court of Denmark, and having at the same time given me a letter to deliver personally to his Most Christian Majesty, Louis XVI., I embarked at New York on the 11th November, 1787, in an American vessel bound for Holland, the captain of which agreed to land me in France.

"After a voyage of a month, I landed at Dover, in England, not being able to get ashore in France. From Dover I went to London, where I saw the minister of the United States. I passed some days with my friends there, and went to Covent Garden Theatre. I afterwards set out for Paris, where I arrived on the 20th December.

" Mr Jefferson, the Ambassador of the United States, visited me on the night of my arrival, and informed me that M. de Simolin, minister plenipotentiary of her Imperial Majesty of all the Russias, had often spoken of me while I was in America, and appeared anxious that I should agree to go to Russia, to command the fleet against the Turks in the Black Sea. I regarded this proposal as a castle in the air; and as I did not wish to be employed in foreign service, I avoided meeting M. de Simolin, for whose character I had, at the same time, the highest respect.

" As the letter, of which I was the bearer to the King of France, concerned myself alone, my friends advised me not to seek an interview with his Majesty till after my return from Denmark. In that letter the United States requested his Majesty to permit me to embark in his fleet of evolution, to complete my knowledge of naval tactics, and of military and maritime operations upon the great scale.

"Speaking to a man of very high rank at Paris, I informed him of the proposal communicated to me by Mr Jefferson. He replied, that 'he would advise me to go to Constantinople at once rather than enter the service of Russia.'*

"On the 1st of February, 1788, at the moment of my departure from Paris, I received a note from Mr Littlepage, chamberlain to the King of Poland, earnestly requesting me to breakfast with him next morning, as he had matters of the ut-

* Whether from a magnanimous sense of justice, or dislike to his associates and rivals, or, as is probable, a mixture of these motives, Paul Jones, in the course of the campaign, became somewhat Turkish, and a warm admirer of the Capitan Pacha. In the Journal he does the Turks ample justice; and in a letter to Baron de la Houze, the minister of France at Copenhagen, we find him saying,—"I have much to tell you respecting the 'moustaches of the Capitan Pacha,'" of which the Baron had probably jocularly desired Paul Jones to send him a good account; "he is a very brave man, and the public have been much deceived as to our affairs with him."

most importance to communicate to me. I went to him that same night, and he told me that M. de Simolin had the greatest desire to converse with me before my departure, and that he expected him to breakfast with us next day.

"M. de Simolin said the most polite and obliging things to me,—that, having known me well by reputation whilst he was ambassador in England, and since he had come to France, he had already proposed me to his Sovereign as commander of the fleet in the Black Sea, and that he expected her Imperial Majesty would make me proposals in consequence. I could not yet look upon the affair very seriously; but I was much flattered with the opinion of M. de Simolin, to whom I expressed my gratitude. When he had left the house, Mr Littlepage assured me that he had written to his Court, that 'if her Imperial Majesty confided to me the chief command of her fleet on the Black Sea, with *carte blanche*, he would answer for it that in less than a year I should make Constantinople tremble.'

"In Denmark I put in train a treaty between that power and the United States; but this arrangement was interrupted by the arrival of a courier from St Petersburgh, despatched express by the Empress, to invite me to repair to her Court.

"Though I foresaw many obstacles in the way of my entering the service of Russia, I believed that I could not avoid going to St Petersburgh, to thank the Empress for the favourable opinion she had conceived of me. I transferred the treaty going forward at Copenhagen to Paris, to be concluded there, and set out for St Petersburgh by Sweden. At Stockholm I staid but one night, to see Count Rasaumorsky. Want of time prevented me from appearing at Court.

"At Gresholm I was stopped by the ice, which prevented me from crossing the Gulf of Bothnia, and even from approaching the first of the isles in the passage. After having made several unsuccessful efforts to get to Finland by the isles, I imagined that it might be practicable to effect my object by doubling the ice to the southward, and entering the Baltic Sea.

"This enterprise was very daring, and had never before been attempted. But by the north the roads were impracticable, and, knowing that the Empress expected me from day to day, I could not think of going back by Elsineur.

"I left Gresholm early one morning, in an undecked passage-boat, about thirty feet in length. I made another boat follow, of half that size. This last was for dragging over the ice, and for passing from one piece of ice to another, to gain the coast of Finland. I durst not make my project known to the boatmen, which would have been the sure means of defeating it. After endeavouring, as before, to gain the first isle, I made them steer for the south, and we kept along the coast of Sweden all the day, finding difficulty enough to pass between the ice and the shore. Towards night, being almost opposite Stockholm, pistol in hand I forced the boatmen to enter the Baltic Sea, and steer for the coast. We ran near the coast of Finland. All night the wind was fair, and we hoped to land next day. This we found impossible. The ice did not permit us to approach the shore, which we only saw from a distance. It was impossible to regain the Swedish side, the wind being high and directly contrary. I had nothing left for it but to stand for the Gulf of Finland. There was a small compass in the boat, and I fixed the lamp of my travelling carriage so as to throw a light on it.

"On the same night we lost the small boat; but the men saved themselves in the large one, which with difficulty escaped the same fate. At the end of four days we landed at Revel, where our enterprise was regarded as a kind of miracle. Having satisfied the boatmen for their services and their loss, I gave them a good pilot, with the provisions necessary for making their homeward voyage, when the weather should become more favourable.

"I arrived at St Petersburgh in the evening on the 23d of April, old style, and on the 25th had my first audience of the Empress. Her Majesty gave me so flattering a reception, and up to the period of my departure treated me with so much distinction, that I was overcome by her courtesies (*je me laissai séduire,*) and put myself into her hands without making any stipulation for my personal advantage. I demanded but one favour, 'that I should never be condemned unheard.'

"On the 7th May I set out from the Imperial Palace, carrying with me a letter from her Majesty to his Highness the Prince-Marshal Potemkin at St Elizabeth, where I arrived on the 19th. The Prince-Marshal received me with much kindness, and destined me the command of the fleet of Serastapole against the Capitan Pacha, who, he supposed, intended to make a descent in the Crimea. His Highness was mistaken in this, and the next day he received information that the Capitan Pacha was at anchor within Kinbourn, having come to succour Oczakow with a hundred and twenty armed vessels and other armed craft.

"The Prince-Marshal then requested me to assume command of the naval force stationed in the Liman, (which is at the embouchure of the Dnieper,) to act against the Capitan Pacha till Oczakow should fall. I considered this change of destination as a flattering mark of confidenec; and having received my orders, I set out on the same day for Cherson, in company with the Chevalier de Ribas, Brigadier du Jour of the Prince-Marshal. He was ordered to make all the arrangements necessary to place me in command.

At parting, the Prince-Marshal promised me to bring forward his troops without loss of time, to co-operate with the maritime force he had intrusted to my command; and on the journey M. de Ribas told me, 'that all the force of the Liman, comprehending that of the Prince of Nassau, would be under my orders.'

"I spent but one evening and night at Cherson. But even this short period was enough to show that I had entered on a delicate and disagreeable service. Rear-Admiral Mordwinoff, chief of the Admiralty, did not affect to disguise his displeasure at my arrival; and though he had orders from the Prince-Marshal to communicate to me all the details concerning the force in the Liman, and to put me in possession of the flag belonging to my rank as Rear-Admiral, he spared himself the trouble of compliance.

"We set out early next morning for Glouboca, the armament of the Liman being at anchor very near that place, in the roads of Schiroque, between the bar of the Dnieper and the embouchure of the river Bog. We went on board the Wolodimer before mid-day, where we found that Brigadier Alexiano had assembled all the commanders, to draw them into a cabal against my authority. I may mention here, that this man was a Greek, as ignorant of seamanship as of military affairs, who, under an exterior and manners the most gross, concealed infinite cunning, and, by affected plainness and hardihood of discourse, had the address to pass for a blunt honest man. Though a subject of Turkey, it was alleged that he made war with the Mussulmans by attacking their commerce in the Archipelago on his own authority, and that he had followed this means of enriching himself up to the period that Count D'Orloff arrived with the Russian fleet. Though I do not affirm the fact, several persons of credit have assured me that there are often pirates who infest the coast, and the isles between Constantinople and Egypt, who attack the commerce of all nations, and run down the vessels after having seized the cargoes and cut the throats of the crews. Alexiano had been employed by Count D'Orloff. He had reached the rank of Brigadier. Alexiano was a good deal offended in the first instance, and afterwards made great merit with the Prince-Marshal, of the sacrifice which he affected to make in serving under me. He said, that if he withdrew, all the other officers would follow his example. The Prince-Marshal sent presents to his wife, and wrote him kindly, persuading him to remain in the service. All the difficulty he made was nothing more than a piece of manœuvring to increase his importance; for from what followed I know that, had he left the service, it would have been alone, and that no one would have regretted his absence.

"To give time to those angry spirits to become calm, and to be able to decide on the part I should take, I proposed to Brigadier de Ribas, that we should together make a journey to Kinbourn, to see the entrance of the Dnieper and reconnoitre the position and strength of the Turkish fleet and flotilla. At my return all the officers appeared contented, and I hoisted my flag on board the Wolodimer on the 26th of May, 1788.

"The Prince of Nassau Siegen, whom I had known slightly at Paris, told me, 'that if we gained any advantage over the Turks, it was necessary to exaggerate it to the utmost; and that this was the counsel the Chevalier de Ribas had given him.' I replied, 'that I never had adopted this method of heightening my personal importance.' "

The Journal of the Rear-Admiral, after this introduction, is continued in the third person for some time; and afterwards goes on to the end as a narrative in the first person, which would have been desirable throughout; it is, however, thought best to adhere faithfully to the original.

Journal of the Campaign of the Liman in 1788, *drawn up by Rear-Admiral Paul Jones, for the perusal of her Imperial Majesty of all the Russias, and now first published from his original MS.*

"At the opening of this campaign the squadron of Cherson was obliged to remain for two days in the road of Schiroque, till the troops should embark which were to form part of the crew. The Prince of Nassau, who had been appointed commander of the flotilla, and who had by this time received on board all the troops intended for him, durst not venture to advance even four or five verstes without being escorted by three frigates. The Prince of Nassau was so apprehensive of danger, that on the 28th of May Rear-Admiral Paul Jones, commander of the squadron, reinforced him with a fourth frigate.

"On the 29th, the troops being all on board, the squadron advanced, and led on the flotilla, which lay scattered about at anchor without any observance of order. The squadron drew up opposite the first village, to the left of the Bog, in an obtuse angle, and thus commanded, by a cross-fire, the only passage of the Liman. This lies between two sand-banks, through which the Turks must advance with their heavy vessels. By this position the Rear-Admiral covered Cherson, and the country on both banks of the Liman, made good the free passage of the Bog to the army of the Prince-Marshal, and held the Turks in check in any attempt they might make against Kinbourn.

"The Prince of Nassau at this time talked a great deal of projects of descents, surprises, and attacks, but without any rational plan.

" A battery having been raised upon the point of Stanislaus, the Prince of Nassau expressed himself delighted with it, as in case of necessity he might there find shelter. The Rear-Admiral could not have retreated, as several of his vessels were already within a few inches of getting aground. The Rear-Admiral was aware that the Turks, having a very superior force, would not give any opportunity of attacking them; and that it was therefore necessary to maintain the strong position he had taken, till the advance of Prince Potemkin, in order to concert plans, and combine his operations with those of the land forces.

" In the meanwhile General Swaroff, commandant of Kinbourn, made the Rear-Admiral responsible for the safety of that place; while Brigadier Alexiano and the Prince of Nassau did all that was possible to make him distrustful of the means which he possessed for attack or defence. They alleged, that the vessels forming the flotilla, having been constructed merely to convey the carriages of the Empress in her late progress, might be expected, at the first attack, to sink under the enormous weight of the guns.

"The squadron made a formidable appearance, but had little real strength. The Wolodimer and the Alexander were but half-armed; and both vessels were already within a few inches of touching the bottom, so shallow is the Liman for vessels of war. In this most critical situation, having no orders from his Highness the Prince-Marshal for his guidance, and knowing nothing either of his intentions, or of the actual position of the army, the Rear-Admiral resolved on assembling a council of war, in conformity to the ordonnance of Peter the Great. The council he opened by a speech suited to the occasion, the main object of which was to show the necessity of a perfect understanding between the squadron and the flotilla; and that, uniting heart and hand, and forgetting all personal considerations, they should determine to conquer, as the true glory of a patriot was to be useful to his country."

[The Journal of the Rear-Admiral details at some length the points on which the council, composed of such discordant elements, were agreed, and states that it was to meet again next day, to arrange the best plans of attack and defence, and the signals for the fleet. But the cabals of the Prince of Nassau and of the Greek Brigadier Alexiano prevailed, and this heterogeneous body did not again meet. Something, however, was done; and we again resume the narrative of the Rear-Admiral.]

"On the 6th* of June, at two in the morning, the Prince of Nassau advanced, as had been previously agreed on, with the greater part of the flotilla; but, in place of cutting off the retreat of the vessels forming the enemy's advanced guard, he retired at daybreak before a very inferior force, and without offering the smallest resistance!—The Turks chased him, keeping up a cannonade, into the midst of the squadron, which, as had been arranged, advanced to take a position to support him.

"The precipitate retreat of the Prince of

* The Russians compute time by the old style, which sometimes produces an apparent confusion of dates in the Journal,—Paul Jones sometimes reckoning by the one mode and sometimes by the other.

Nassau inspirited the Turks so much, that, during the night between the 6th and 7th, they drew up their flotilla in two divisions, in a shallow, close by their own shore. The first of these divisions had by day-dawn advanced within cannon-shot of our reserve, which had been posted the previous night on the right wing.

"At sunrise the Turks made sail; and Brigadier Alexiano ran upon the deck of the Wolodimer half-naked, exclaiming, like a frantic man, in French and Russian, that the Turks were going to attack and board us, and that we would be blown to pieces for having been so foolish as to leave our former position. He had, notwithstanding, in the council of war, given his voice in favour of the position we now actually held. Brigadier Ribas, the captain, and all the crew, were witnesses of his extravagant and unjustifiable behaviour.

"This proved a false alarm; the Turkish fleet did not stir.

"The Prince of Nassau came on board the Wolodimer, and the Rear-Admiral proposed to him to reconnoitre the enemy's fleet and flotilla.

As they advanced together, the first division of the Turkish flotilla began to fire from their canoes, and raised their anchors and rowed forward towards our reserve, which they attacked briskly. At the same time several corps of Turkish troops advanced along the opposite bank, as if they intended to establish a post or battery to act on our flank. As our reserve had been posted to cover our right wing, the Prince of Nassau, who knew not what to do, proposed to make it draw up in the form of an arch (*crochet de houlette*,) the better to sustain the assault. The Rear-Admiral told him, that, on the contrary, it was necessary to lift the anchors with the utmost despatch, and to form in line of battle to meet the attack of the Turks. The combat having commenced according to this plan, the Rear-Admiral hastened along the lines, to issue orders to the squadron, and, above all, to make the remainder of the flotilla, posted between the ships and upon the left wing, advance. The wind being adverse, he made these vessels be towed by the ships' boats and other boats attached to the squadron ; and by an oblique movement formed in line of battle, with the intention of cutting off the retreat of the enemy, and galling him by a cross-fire. As soon as the Capitan Pacha perceived the manœuvre of the Rear-Admiral, he came forward himself in his kirlangitch, having a very favourable wind, and made the second division of his flotilla advance.

"At this time our reserve was very critically situated. A double chaloupe quitted the action, and four of our galleys were in danger of being captured. The Prince of Nassau, who did not relish going himself, sent Brigadier Corsacoff, who made these retreat. Instead of remaining with the reserve, which, being without a commander, was in very great disorder, the Prince of Nassau quitted his own post, and stationed himself before the Rear-Admiral, where he could be of no use whatever. The Rear-Admiral went into the same boat with the Prince of Nassau, and again issued his orders along the line. Being now within cannon-shot of the enemy, he opened fire, advancing always in an oblique line to cut off the enemy's retreat. At the same time he despatched Brigadier Alexiano to endeavour to rally the vessels of the reserve, which the Prince of Nassau had deserted; but Alexiano contented himself with waving his hat in the air, and shouting from behind the lines,—'Fire, my lads, on the kirlangitch of the Capitan Pacha!'

"When the line led on by the Rear-Admiral came to close fire with the enemy, their flotilla was thrown into the utmost confusion. Our reserve gave no farther way, and the enemy was placed under a cross-fire. The Capitan Pacha availed himself of the only resource in his power; he set every sail to withdraw his force. Had he remained a half-hour longer, he would have been surrounded. Two of his vessels were burnt in this affair. The flotilla of the enemy was composed of fifty-seven vessels, and we chased into the middle of their fleet. The Rear-Admiral, who had directed the whole affair, gave all the credit of it to the Prince of Nassau.

"An idea may be formed of the capacity of the Prince of Nassau from the following circumstance:—At the beginning of the action he requested the Rear-Admiral to bring forward to the support of the reserve only the vessels posted on the left wing, which consisted of one galley and a double chaloupe. Besides the insufficiency of force, these vessels had a very long way to make, and that against the wind.

"The Turks remained quiet for some time after this. The Prince of Nassau, who had scarce spoken one word during the affair, save to make extravagant professions of regard for the Rear-Admiral, now began to give himself airs. On the 13th June he addressed a writing of an extraordinary character to the Rear-Admiral, the object of which appeared to be, that an advance should be made of three verstes nearer the enemy, who had taken post under the batteries of Oczakow. The Rear-Admiral, who could perceive no advantage to the service in such a movement, refused his concurrence. Had he agreed, the movement would have been fatal to Russia, as will be seen by what follows.

"By the 16th June the patience of the Capitan Pacha was exhausted. He brought from his grand fleet, without Kinbourn, two thousand picked men, to reinforce the body under the walls of Oczakow; and being strengthened still

2

farther by the troops of the garrison, he advanced with his whole fleet and flotilla, and with a fair wind, into the Liman, to attack and board us. The ship, which bore one of the Admiral's flags, steered right towards the Wolodimer from the commencement of the movement. When within three verstes of us, or little more, this ship got aground, and all the vessels which accompanied it immediately dropt anchor. It was then about two in the afternoon.

" The Rear-Admiral summoned a council of war to consult on what should be done. He addressed the council, at which were present all the commanders of the squadron and the flotilla, and concluded by telling them, ' that they must make up their minds to conquer or die for the country.'

" The wind, which was rather fresh, being against us, the only thing proposed by the Rear-Admiral that was found practicable, was to draw up our force in an obtuse angle, by bringing forward the right of the line upon the centre.*

* " The plan of the Capitan Pacha was to bear down

This movement was completed before midnight. The wind had shifted to N.N.E.; and at break of day the Rear-Admiral made signal, and the whole squadron immediately set sail to commence the attack on the Turks.

"The Turks got into confusion the instant this manœuvre was perceived. They raised their anchors or cut their cables in the greatest precipitation, and not the shadow of discipline remained in their fleet. Our squadron advanced in line of battle with a striking and formidable appearance, so that the Turks knew not how weak it really was. As our flotilla had been very slow in weighing anchor, the Rear-Admiral was obliged to make the squadron halt twice to await

---

full sail on the vessels of our flotilla, and run them to the bottom by the shock of the encounter of his large ships. He also proposed to burn our squadron by throwing in fire-balls (*grappins*), and setting fire to certain trading vessels which he had prepared as fire-ships. He had reason to calculate on success, had he not been thwarted by a circumstance which no man could have foreseen."—*Note by* Paul Jones.

it. At length, the flotilla being always last, the squadron opened fire on the enemy, of whom the person second in command, who had flown about like a fool, quickly ran his ship on a sand-bank on the south of the Liman. There was no longer hope for him ; from the moment he grounded he was ours. The enemy still kept flying about, and always in the greatest disorder. The Rear-Admiral made his ship (the Wolodimer) be steered to within pistol-shot of the vessel of the Capitan Pacha, but the latter again ran aground upon a sand-bank ; and a few minutes afterwards the Brigadier Alexiano gave orders in the Russian language, and unknown to the Rear-Admiral, to drop the Wolodimer's anchor. It was pretended that there were but fifteen feet of water a little way in advance of the ship, which was not true. A considerable time before this the squadron had been taken on the right flank by the Turkish flotilla, drawn up on the shallows, approaching the bank to the east of Oczakow, and commanded by the Capitan Pacha himself. The flotilla annoyed the squadron considerably, by incessantly throwing in along our line both bombs and balls of great size. Wanting depth of water, our frigates could not advance far enough to dislodge them, and, besides, they found that their guns were too small. The Capitan Pacha had struck down one of our frigates, named the Little Alexander, by a bomb, at the side of the Wolodimer, and at the very instant Brigadier Alexiano made the anchor be cast. Our flotilla still lagged behind, but it did at last advance. Having passed through the squadron in the greatest disorder, and without the least appearance of plan, instead of pursuing the flying Turks, the flotilla swarmed round the Turkish ships which were aground like a hive of bees.

" The Rear-Admiral commanded Brigadier Alexiano to get together some vessels of our flotilla to dislodge the Turkish flotilla. At the same moment the Rear-Admiral advanced in his boat towards the left wing, where the Prince of Nassau was with his body of reserve, employed to very little purpose, in firing on the Turkish vessels already aground. The Rear-Admiral entreated him to lead or send the reserve to act against the Turkish flotilla upon our right flank, and informed him of the misfortune which had befallen the Little Alexander; but M. de Nassau remained quietly behind his batteries, and made no movement to dislodge the flotilla of the enemy.

"The Rear-Admiral then met Brigadier Corcascoff, to whom he gave orders similar to those he had given to M. Alexiano; and these two officers having got together as many vessels as they could collect, assisted our frigates in dislodging and chasing the Turkish flotilla even till under the walls of Oczakow. M. de Corsacoff was a brave and an intelligent man; he did not affect to have done any thing wonderful. Alexiano was a man of limited talent and of questionable courage, but his vanity was excessive. He pretended to have hauled a battery to within pistol-shot of the enemy's flotilla; but M. Akmatoff, who commanded that battery, declared that neither he nor any one of our people ever were nearer the Turkish flotilla than half cannon-shot.

"The Turkish fleet was now distant. The Prince of Nassau was told that the Admiral's flag, which had been displayed on the vessel of the

Capitan Pacha, was struck down, and he hastily advanced to claim it. The ship of the Capitan Pacha, like all the others of the band, leaned much to one side, and consequently could not fully avail itself of its guns. As the flag of the Capitan Pacha fell into the water from the top of the main-mast, having been struck down by a ball, it is not difficult to discover that the vessel which had fired this ball was in no danger of being touched by case-shot. The saporoses drew the flag from the water, and the Prince of Nassau, a long while afterwards, had the glory (which he turned to good account,) of snatching it from their hands. The Rear-Admiral might have claimed at least the half of this flag, as he had his hands on it at the same moment with the Prince of Nassau; but he regarded it as a thing of very little consequence.

" Brandcougles* had been thrown into the two

---

* A note by Paul Jones describes these incendiary missiles as a kind of bomb-shells, perforated with holes, and filled inside with combustible materials. They were fired from a sort of pieces called *Licornes*.

Turkish vessels, and they were burnt. Was this a good or a bad piece of service ? These two vessels were only ours from the accident of having run aground, and because their crews had been left by their countrymen under the guns of our squadron. Wherefore did the flotilla interfere with them ?—ought it not rather to have pursued the flying Turks, who were not yet under the protection of the guns of Oczakow ? Our flotilla had received no injury, and had nothing to fear from the shallowness of the water.

" Having first sounded, the Rear-Admiral made the squadron advance another verste, and took post in a right line, barely out of shot of Oczakow, and in line with the farthest back of the Turkish ships that had been run aground and taken. Fire soon after broke out in this prize, which had been imprudently fired upon with brandcougles.

" The fleet and flotilla of the Turks now drew up in a line parallel to ours, and under the walls of Oczakow.

" How imbecile does the human mind become under the influence of sudden panic ! The Rear-Admiral, an hour after the affair, advanced in his boat, and took soundings all along the Turkish line, opposite the walls of Oczakow, and within reach of case-shot, and not a single gun was fired upon him.

"Previously to taking command of the squadron, the Rear-Admiral, as has been noticed, had gone to Kinbourn with the Chevalier Ribas, brigadier *du jour*, to the Prince-Marshal, to reconnoitre the position and force of the fleet and flotilla under the Capitan Pacha, and to examine the entrance of the Liman. They arrived at Kinbourn at the very time that the Capitan Pacha had detached twenty-one vessels of war from his fleet, and with that force entered the road of Oczakow, the wind not permitting him to enter the Liman, where his flotilla and some transport ships were already stationed. The Rear-Admiral was so struck at finding the tongue of land at Kinbourn without any battery or block-fort, that he instantly spoke of it to the Commandant, General Swaroff. This tongue of land, from its position, commands the only passage by which large vessels can either enter or come out of the Liman. The fortress of Kinbourn being far too distant to be able to command this passage, the Rear-Admiral proposed to establish one or more strong batteries upon this stripe of land, and M. de Ribas seconded the proposition. After considerable delay, General Swaroff was persuaded to establish a block-fort with heavy cannon upon this tongue or point of land, and a battery farther within. But the Capitan Pacha had already got the twenty-one ships in question into the Liman.

"To resume—On the night between the 17th and 18th of June, the Capitan Pacha attempted to bring the remains of his squadron, which had been defeated on the previous day, out of the Liman; but the newly-erected block-fort and battery fired on his ships, of which nine of the largest were forced aground upon the sand-bank which runs out from Oczakow, till within a little way of cannon-shot from the block-fort.

"The block-fort and battery fired on the enemy's ships the whole night, and at daybreak General Swaroff sent to us, requesting that we would send vessels to take possession of those ships of the enemy which had got aground.

The Rear-Admiral wished to send frigates; but Brigadier Alexiano assured him that he would run the risk of losing them. The current there, he said, 'was like that of a mill-dam, and the bottom was so bad that anchors would not hold.'

"It was, accordingly, resolved to proceed with the flotilla; and Alexiano, who had his private reasons, set out with the Prince of Nassau. The flotilla went pell-mell, and without any sort of order or plan, upon the nine ships aground, and fired brandcougles into them without mercy. It was in vain the wretched Turks made the sign of the cross, and begged for quarter on their knees! Above three thousand of them were burnt with their ships. By some chance two of these vessels, the least and the largest, did not take fire; the one was a corvette, very indifferently armed, carrying one battery and four pieces between decks. The other was a small brigantine, of French construction, armed with forty small guns.

"Neither the Prince of Nassau nor Alexiano was to be seen at this time. They were together, and at some distance, during this frightful carnage; and it was afterwards asked of them if they had not, during this time, been at Kinbourn? As the greatest confusion reigned among the vessels of the flotilla, though our loss was not great, there is no doubt that part of it was owing to Russian bullets.*

"The army of Prince Potemkin having come up on the 27th June, the Prince of Nassau had orders to attack and destroy, or capture, the Turkish flotilla which lay under the walls of Oczakow; and the Rear-Admiral was commanded to give him every assistance that might be useful. In pursuance of these orders, on the first of July, at one in the morning, the flotilla advanced. The Rear-Admiral had sent all the chaloupes and barcasses belonging to the squadron to haul out the vessels of the flotilla. The

* The species of warfare in which he was now daily engaged was new to the Anglo-American. The monstrous and wanton cruelties to which the Turks were subjected by the more barbarous and brutal Russians were accordingly viewed by him with horror and disgust.

Prince-Marshal had taken the trouble to arrange the plan of attack himself, but his plan was not followed.

" At day-dawn, our flotilla having advanced within cannon-shot, opened fire upon the Turkish flotilla, and on the place. The current having carried several of our batteries and double chaloupes rather too far to leeward, the Rear-Admiral made them be hauled up by the boats and barcasses of the squadron, and set the example himself with the chaloupe in which he was. The Turks set fire to a little frigate which they had prepared as a fire-ship, and placed at anchor to the N. E. of Fort Hassan Pacha.

"At six in the morning, the Rear-Admiral went himself considerably in advance of the flotilla to seize five of the enemy's galleys which lay within case-shot of Fort Hassan. The position of these galleys, between the cross-fire of our flotilla on the one side, and that of Fort Hassan, the Turkish flotilla, and Oczakow on the other, rendered this a very dangerous enterprise. The Rear-Admiral boarded the galley which lay farthest out, and made it be hauled in a little way by Lieutenant

Leff Fabrician. He afterwards boarded the galley of the Capitan Pacha, which lay considerably nearer the Fort. From unskilfulness, and excess of zeal, a young officer cut the cable of this galley without waiting the orders of the Rear-Admiral, and before the boats could be got in order to haul it out, the wind drifted the galley towards the shore, and still nearer to the Fort. The Rear-Admiral made the galley be lightened by throwing many things overboard. After much search for ropes that might stretch to the wreck of the burnt frigate, and by fastening the galley there, keep it afloat, the plan failed from the ropes not being long enough. The Rear-Admiral was very unwilling to yield to the obstinate opposition of the Turks, who fired upon him from all their bastions and from their flotilla, and he despatched Lieutenant Fox to the Wolodimer, to fetch an anchor and cable. This was a certain means of securing his object; and in waiting the return of the Lieutenant, he left the galley with his people, and assisted in the flotilla's advance. Before the return of Lieutenant Fox, he had, however, the mortification to see fire break out in the galley of the Capitan Pacha. He at first believed that the slaves chained on board had found means to escape, and had set fire to the vessel; but he had afterwards positive proof that Brigadier Alexiano being in a boat at the time with the Prince of Nassau, on the outside of the flotilla, and being aware of the intention of the Rear-Admiral, swore that it should not succeed, and sent a Greek canoe to set fire to the galley!* The three other Turkish galleys were at once run down and burnt by brandcougles. There were also a two-masted ship and a large bomb-vessel burnt near Fort Hassan Pacha. This includes all that was taken or destroyed by water, save fifty-two prisoners taken by the Rear-Admiral in the two galleys. The wretched beings, who were chained in the galley

---

* The attestation of a Russian officer to this singular fact is among the *Pieces Justificatives* appended to the Journal; and the original of that attestation, written in French, and subscribed Bilicroff, officer of the guard, and dated at Kinbourn the 26th October, 1788, remains among Jones's papers.

of the Capitan Pacha, perished there in the flames!

"The Prince-Marshal having made an important diversion on the land-side, it is to be regretted that advantage was not taken of this movement to seize the remainder of the enemy's flotilla. But our flotilla never came up within reach of grape-shot."

The above extracts from the Rear-Admiral's Journal are verified in the following manner:—

"These extracts have been translated by me into the Russian language, and read before the commanders of the ship Wolodimer, Captain of the Second Rank, Zefaliano; of the frigate Scoroi, Captain of the Second Rank, Aboljanin; of the frigate Nicolai, Captain Lieutenant Daniloff; of the frigate Taheuroc, Lieutenant Makinin; of the frigate the Little Alexander, Lieutenant Savitzsky; and they have found nothing in them contrary to truth.

"On board the Wolodimer, before Ockzakow, the 28th October, 1788.

"Paul Denetreffsky, Honorary Counsellor of the College for Foreign affairs, and by special orders of her Imperial Majesty of all the Russias, Secretary to Rear-Admiral and Chevalier Paul Jones."

Addition of Rear-Admiral Jones to the preceding Journal. Translated from the French of the MS. volume, prepared for Publication by himself.

"The moment the ships began to withdraw from Oczakow, the Prince of Nassau and Brigadier Alexiano hurried straight to the head-quarters of the Prince-Marshal, to relate the deeds which they pretended they had performed. In a few minutes after the flotilla began to retire, the rain fell in torrents, of which Nassau and Alexiano received their own share before reaching head-quarters.

"Two days afterwards, Brigadier Alexiano returned on board the Wolodimer, having caught a malignant fever, of which he died on the 8th

July. The Prince of Nassau, who had made use of him in caballing against me, God knows for what, neither visited him in his sickness, nor assisted at his funeral. At first it was given out, that the service must sustain the loss of every Greek in it on account of his death; but I soon experienced the reverse. Not one asked to be dismissed; they remained under my command the same as the Russians, and were better pleased than before. On the day preceding the death of Alexiano, he had received intelligence of having been promoted two grades; and that her Majesty had bestowed on him a fine estate, and peasants, in White Russia. At the same time the Prince of Nassau had received a very valuable estate, with three or four thousand peasants, also in White Russia, and the Military Order of St George, of the Second Class. Her Majesty likewise gave him liberty to hoist the flag of Vice-Admiral on the taking of Oczakow, to which event it was apparently believed he had greatly contributed. I received the Order of St Anne, an honour with which I am highly flattered, and with which I could have been perfectly satisfied, had others been recompensed only in the same proportion, and according to the merit of their services. All the officers of the flotilla received a step of promotion and the gratuity of a year's pay. The greater part of them also obtained the Order of St George, of the Last Class. Only two of these officers had been bred to the sea; all the others were ignorant of naval affairs. The officers of the squadron under my command were almost wholly marine officers. They had done their duty well when opposed to the enemy; but they obtained no promotion, no mark of distinction, no pecuniary reward. My mortification was excessive.

"My officers at this time gave me a very gratifying proof of their attachment. On promising that I would demand justice for them from the Prince-Marshal at the close of the campaign, they stifled their vexation, and made no complaint.

"It ought to have to have been mentioned in the proper place, that three days after our success in the Liman, Prince Potemkin arrived at Kinbourn, from whence he came on board the

Wolodimer to make me a visit. He was accompanied by General Count de Brandisky of Poland, the Prince de Repuin, the Prince de Ligne, General de Samoilow, and several other officers. His Highness did me the honour to remain to dinner; and as he knew that an altercation had taken place between the Prince of Nassau and myself on the morning of the 18th of June, he had the goodness to employ the Prince de Ligne, and M. Littlepage, Chamberlain to the King of Poland, to persuade the Prince of Nassau to make me an apology. I accepted it with sincere pleasure. We embraced in presence of this honourable company, and I believed him as sincere as myself.*

* Probably the first cause of Potemkin's dislike to Jones was owing to the squabbles between him and the Prince of Nassau. Besides the scene above related, Potemkin had previously endeavoured to establish a good understanding between them. On the 30th of May he himself wrote to the Rear-Admiral:—"It is with great pleasure that I hear that harmony is established between you and the Prince of Nassau. I regard union as the foundation of all the services that your talents and your known

"The Prince-Marshal charged me at this time to make arrangements for raising the cannon,

---

valour give you both the power of rendering to my country; and I cannot strongly enough recommend to you to live in perfect understanding with the Prince of Nassau." On another occasion, he thanks Jones for having acted in concert with Nassau,—"a concert as useful as necessary to the service of the Empress, and, above all, at such a time."

It is to be presumed, that, if it had been possible for Jones to keep on terms with the Prince of Nassau, he would have done so. His own interest, as well as the public service, and the wishes of his best friends, counselled this; but it seems to have been impossible. A letter on this subject, written from the Russian headquarters by Mr Littlepage, is earnest, sensible, and friendly. "I am not ignorant," he says, "of the bad understanding that unfortunately subsisted between you and the Prince of Nassau, before the 7th of June; but both Prince Potemkin and myself were persuaded that was all ended. He has learned that it has again broke out, and I know that trifling circumstances can give him much trouble. I can easily conceive the delicacy of your situation, and I know that your honour can sacrifice nothing; but, for Heaven's sake, my dear friend, be prudent, as much for yourself as your friends. Prince Potemkin anchors, and other stores belonging to the enemy's ships which had been burnt, without loss

---

has conceived a high esteem for you, but he loves Nassau. If ever mutual interest dictated union between two persons, it is between you and the Prince of Nassau at the present moment. The reverse will be to the prejudice of both. In the name of friendship, reflect upon this. Remember that the eyes of all Europe are fixed upon you. Fear no competition, and be indulgent to those who have not the same reason to feel above rivalry. Nassau has been unfortunate. If you see weakness in his character, excuse it; and remember that he was, and I hope still is, your friend." Jones took this letter in good part, and assured the sensible writer, that for the good of the service, and the esteem and attachment he had for Prince Potemkin, he had borne more from Nassau than he could have done "from any other than a madman." Littlepage was appointed to a command in the squadron, and soon found that it is much easier to give good advice at a distance, than to act under such temperate counsels. He did at once what every man of spirit and common sense would have done,—threw up his command and returned to Warsaw. The words in which he bade Jones farewell show that he thoroughly understood the nature of the generally worthless, and of time, and I sent off a transport ship with officers and men on this duty.

"His Highness the Prince-Marshal now made his troops advance. They passed the Bog, and appeared in sight of us, on the banks of the Liman, on the 27th of June; and next morning the Capitan Pacha made his grand fleet, which had always remained at anchor twenty or thirty

---

always discordant persons, whether Greeks, Russians, Cossacks, or other tribes of which this heterogeneous mass was composed. "Farewell, my dear Admiral; take care of yourself, and look to whom you trust. Remember that you have rather to play the part of a politician than a warrior,—more of a courtier than a soldier." "I was not skilled" says Jones, "in playing such a part." "I never neglected my duty," he says again, "when stung with the insolent reproaches, or rather the threats, of Potemkin. On the contrary, I had but too often exposed myself to personal danger to satisfy his caprice." In another place, when Potemkin had addressed an order to him, concluding thus,—"Moreover, if the enemy attempt to pass to Oczakow, prevent him at all hazards, and defend yourself boldly," Jones says, "It is not easy to believe that such words were addressed to Paul Jones."

verstes without Kinbourn, weigh anchor, and directed his course towards the entrance of the Danube, carrying three Admiral's flags, and followed by all the vessels that had escaped us in the Liman. During the whole time that we were exposed to having a serious affair with the Turks, Brigadier Alexiano had carefully kept a Greek felucca of eighteen oars alongside the Wolodimer. This felucca was better built for sailing than any of the other chaloupes or rowing vessels belonging to the whole squadron, so that he had at all times the means of saving himself in case of any disastrous event. Even the Prince of Nassau, since his retreat on the 6th of June, was never seen in any vessel of the flotilla, but always in a chaloupe, which had been built for the especial use of her Imperial Majesty on her late voyage. For myself, I took no such precautions. I saw that I must conquer or die. For me there was no retreat. The instant that Alexiano saw the troops appear, he despatched his felucca to inform the Prince-Marshal that it was he, in his zeal for the service, who had employed people to save the effects of the burnt prizes. Nothing could be less true. He had not taken the smallest concern in the matter. But this shows the character of the man. Next day I was informed that the transport ship I had employed on this service was already too heavily laden, and made a great deal of water. As the wind was fair for Glauboca, I gave orders that she should immediately go thither to unload. Some hours after the departure of the transport, Brigadier Alexiano returned from Kinbourn, where he had dined, and said several impertinent things to me on the subject of the transport. He went afterwards to head-quarters to complain of me to the Prince-Marshal. In consequence of this complaint I received a letter from his brigadier *du jour*, the Chevalier Ribas, which, among other things, mentioned that the Prince-Marshal was "singularly severe and strict in all that related to the orders he gave." I replied, that I was not afraid of the severity of the Prince-Marshal, as I had done nothing save my duty, in pursuance of his own orders.*

* After this affair, Jones seems to have completely lost all self-command. He had no longer any hope of con-

Next day I paid a visit to the Prince of Nassau. I imagined I should be welcomed with open arms;

---

ciliating the Prince of Nassau, and accordingly henceforth waged against him a determined and not very generous hostility. The following letter, addressed to Ribas, was certainly intended for the perusal of Potemkin. It is one of almost open defiance:—

"On board the Wolodimer, before Oczakow, 1st August, 1788.

"SIR,—Having been at Kinbourn this afternoon, to concert operations with the Commandant-General, I received at my return here a kind of note without date, which purports to be from you, but which I do not recognise as your hand-writing. This note adverts to the question of saluting the flag of the Vice-Admiral; but I am not aware if there be an officer of this rank nearer us than St Petersburgh. I highly respect the authority and the power of his Highness the Prince-Marshal. I love good order, and I am devoted with enthusiasm to the welfare of the empire, but the first duty of a man is to guard his own honour.

"I have no wish to speak of myself, but circumstances demand it. I was living in America in the bosom of peace and friendship when his Excellency, M. de Simolin, did me the honour, unknown to myself, to propose me to her Imperial Majesty and the Prince-Marbut he attacked me about the transport-ship, which belonged, he said, to his flotilla. I re-

---

shal as Commander-in-Chief on the Black Sea. I was too much flattered by the reception of her Majesty to stipulate the slightest condition on entering her service. She deigned to receive me. I was to serve only under the command of the Prince-Marshal.

"I imagined myself intended for another command than that which was given me; but I looked on the change as a flattering proof of the confidence of the Prince-Marshal. Never, probably, did any commanding officer commence service under circumstances more painful; but, in spite of the restraints imposed on me by treacherous colleagues, in spite of their unceasing efforts to draw me into error, and their opposition to all my plans, I have extricated myself from the affair with no sacrifice save of my own feelings and interests. I was a true philosopher, and the service has not suffered. My firmness and integrity have supported me against those detestable snares laid by my enemies for my ruin; yet I have served as the cat's paw to draw the chestnuts from the fire for them.

"I am much flattered by the Order of St Anne granted me for my zealous services; but I should have been ashamed to receive brilliant rewards for false, empty boasts.

"As I can never think of having any connexion with

plied, that I had been charged with this duty by the Prince-Marshal; that all the ships of war

---

a man so detestable as M. de Nassau, I can never acknowledge him for my superior. If he has received the rank of Vice-Admiral, I will say in the face of the universe that he is unworthy of it. It is now ten years since he wished to serve under my command. I have known him without fully understanding his character. I knew that he was foolish, (*bête,*) but I was not aware, till it was proved to me, that the only military merit he possesses is a mean effrontery. The only thing he has done, was (after the affair of the 17th June) to snatch the flag of the Capitan Pacha from the hands of the Saporoses, who had got it a long time before he came up. He has never shown either order or intelligence in managing the flotilla. Every Commander of a boat, or other vessel, was his own master, and conducted matters according to his own notions."

The letter goes on to describe the action of the 17th June, and then continues :—

"A single galley, in the hands of a good officer, would, in like circumstances, have been sufficient to conquer a ship of the largest size. But we should be just to the Commander of the flotilla. He always had the prudence to keep behind his men; and in critical moments he always had in his mind, and sometimes on and transports belonged to her Imperial Majesty; and that the vessel in question, being unem-

---

his lips, ways and means of retiring beyond the batteries of Stanislaus. He well knew that for me there was no retreat. In the affair between the flotillas, on the 7th of June, there was something like military combination; but it is not to him this should be attributed. If he had been left to himself, he would have been beaten at least as disgracefully as he had been chased by the Turks on the preceding evening. As to the affair of the 17th June, of the merits of which he so greatly boasts, the Turks got into confusion the moment they saw our squadron under sail and advancing to attack them. They had set sail, and the rout was general even before the whole of our flotilla had raised their anchors. The Turkish squadron had made no arrangement for fight, but fled in the greatest disorder and trepidation at the very commencement. I had given orders to advance near the vessel of the Capitan Pacha, but M. Alexiano thwarted me, and cast anchor without my orders, at the moment when the second Turkish ship (the Admiral) was striking.

"The Turkish flotilla was manœuvred with more skill upon the shallows on the right flank of our squadron, from whence they threw bombs, and sunk the small frigate, the Petit Alexander. The commander of our flotilla had paid no attention to my request to send a ployed at the time when I took it, I could not perceive the smallest cause of complaint. He

---

detachment of the flotilla to dislodge them. The Brigadiers Alexiano and Corsacoff had assembled and brought forward batteries for this purpose, according to my orders, in concert with our frigates on the right wing. The affair of the 18th was the result of panic, and of the batteries which, in concert with you, (Ribas,) I had the credit of establishing at the point of Kinbourn. A very small detachment would have been sufficient to have secured the nine vessels under the cannon of our batteries, and out of the reach of those of the enemy. A good officer, who had commanded such an expedition, would have known how to bring in these nine vessels, without having exposed his people to destruction, and without having the folly to destroy ships of which we stood so much in need, by brandcougles.

"I could not leave my own duties to be present at this affair; but I am told that some who were there inquired if M. de Nassau had not been at Kinbourn during the attack.

"After all, we owe our success to favourable circumstances, to the good disposition, and the imposing appearance of our squadron in advancing to the attack on the 17th June; for the enemy had taken flight before the approach of our flotilla, which was tardy in weighing an-was beside himself with anger; but, as the good of the service no longer required our combined

---

chor, and got into confusion from the beginning of the movement. It has been seen meanwhile that M. de Nassau, who did nothing, and who had not a single man wounded near him, has been rewarded as if he had performed the most heroic actions. Marshal Saxe said to his troops,—'I am not one of those ——— generals who cry to their soldiers, FALL ON! I say to mine,—My soldiers, behold the enemy,—LET US FALL ON.' M. de Nassau has not shown that he is of the opinion of the Marshal. Never was bravado more impudent than that of M. de Nassau. To depart from truth costs him nothing. He had the effrontery to deceive the Prince-Marshal (to whom he owes the bread that he eats) in saying he had burnt six ships of the line and had taken two. These pretended ships of the line were nothing other than the merchant vessels called caravellas. In time of peace they trade between Constantinople and Egypt; in time of war such ships are armed, but always badly. In place of eight but four entered the Liman. I have made Lieutenant Fox measure the length of two of the largest; the one was 135 feet, the other 130 feet English measure," &c. &c. &c. The Rear-Admiral proceeds,—"In place of two there was but one three-masted ship that escaped burning. It is true, that there was likewise operations, I thought this quarrel too childish to give myself uneasiness about it. I took leave of him, begging him to reflect, that I had given him no cause of displeasure. I did not wish to come to a rupture with him; but, on the 1st of July, seeing the day dawn, and that the flotilla was still far too distant to make the necessary attack, meeting him in his chaloupe, I asked 'If he did not think it time to begin the attack?'—'Is it of me you thus inquire?' he replied; 'I have nothing to say to you on the

---

spared, in the barbarous conflagration of the 18th June, a small brigantine. We must then consider this small brigantine as a ship of the line taken by M. de Nassau. This prize remained, and has been totally wrecked. Humanity recoils with indignation and horror from seeing so many wretched creatures perish in the flames without any necessity. But these are trifling marks of goodness of heart and of gratitude which M. de Nassau has been pleased to show, to prove that he is worthy of the benefits he has lately received from Constantinople. Now he is with Russia, and in that he finds his advantage. The same motives, however, which have induced him to come here may lead him back to Constantinople."

subject.' After a reply so uncivil, and so publicly made, it was impossible I could have any farther intercourse with the Prince of Nassau.

"On the 18th June, in giving an account to the Prince-Marshal of the fate of the nine vessels run aground in coming out of the Liman, upon the shallows opposite the battery and block-fort on the tongue of land of Kinbourn, I took the liberty to propose to him to get the Wolodimer, which had port-holes for seventy pieces of cannon, and the large frigate Alexander, which might have carried fifty pieces, completely armed, that at the first opportunity the squadron of Cherson might join that of Sevastopole; but his Highness gave no orders for this purpose till the month of September; and the Admiralty was so slow in acting, that the vessels were not equipped by the 18th October, when I was recalled to St Petersburgh by an order from her Imperial Majesty.

"The fleet of the Capitan Pacha having sailed on the 28th of June, had a rencounter with that of Sevastopole, which had come out some days before; but the Turkish fleet being much stronger than that of Russia, the latter fled, and had the good fortune to get back to Sevastopole without loss, having no more than six or seven men killed and wounded, which shows that the affair was neither close nor warm.

"After the affair of the 18th of June, the greater part of our flotilla remained several days at anchor between Kinbourn and the block-fort upon the tongue of land. It is surprising that the Russian seamen and pilots could be so profoundly ignorant respecting the anchorage, currents, and depth of the Liman, and, above all, of the channel and the road between Oczakow and Beresane. At first not a single commander in the flotilla durst venture to cast an anchor.

"Being at Kinbourn on the 28th June, General Suwaroff spoke to me of the unpleasant circumstance of not being able to cut off the communication between Oczakow and Beresane. Having sounded myself, I informed him that this was quite as practicable as it was useful to the service, and I would place the frigates there instantly if he would only require me to do so. He did not hesitate, and the same day I placed three frigates there. M. Alexiano did all he could to prevent me; and when he saw the frigates set off, prophesied that I would never see them return. He carried his intrigues so far, that the Prince-Marshal wrote me a warning letter on the 29th, and on the 1st July a peremptory order to withdraw them. During the short time they were there they took two Turkish armed chaloupes and a batteau laden with powder and shot; and cut off the enemy's communication between Oczakow and Beresane.

"The Prince-Marshal had not been satisfied with the conduct of the flotilla in the affair of attacking Oczakow on the 1st July, which was conducted in a very irregular manner, and at too great a distance. The most advanced charge was that of the battery commanded by M. Akmatoff, who was never less than 900 toises distant from the enemy.

"On the 10th of July the Prince-Marshal sent the Prince of Nassau to Sevastopole, to learn if the squadron had been much damaged in the rencounter with the Turkish fleet. Immediately after the departure of the Prince of Nassau, the Prince-Marshal gave the Chevalier Ribas the command of the flotilla, with orders to go to Kinbourn, to receive on board the troops he destined to make a descent on the island of Beresane. At the same time he ordered me to establish a line of blockade between that island and Oczakow. I stationed five frigates, carrying eighteen-pounders, in the roads for this purpose.

"On the 14th I was ordered to inspect the entrance of the Liman. I immediately went to Kinbourn to have an understanding with General Suwaroff and the Brigadier de Ribas. Though the Brigadier had been incessantly occupied since the departure of the Prince of Nassau in bringing the crews of the flotilla to some sort of order, he had not yet completed this task. So great was the confusion that reigned, that he could not find in any vessel five soldiers belonging to the same company; and the officers knew not where to look for their men. This retarded the embarkation of the troops destined for the descent on Beresane till the 16th. The Prince-Marshal was so much displeased with this delay, that on the 17th he gave orders to land the troops, that they might join his army before Oczakow, and that the flotilla should again pass into the Liman, as well as the frigates I had posted for the blockade.

"From the commencement of the projected expedition against Beresane, M. Ribas had requested me to conduct the flotilla and the descent of the troops. Though a man of much talent, he had not the misplaced conceit of some persons who readily take upon them things far beyond their capacity. I told him, 'He well knew I ought to have commanded the flotilla as well as the squadron, from the beginning of the campaign, but that my gratitude for the gracious reception accorded me by her Imperial Majesty, together with the very delicate state in which I had found affairs, had induced me to sacrifice my feelings, and even greatly to hazard my reputation, for the good of the empire; that I could never so far humble myself as to request the command of the flotilla, but if it were given me by the Prince-Marshal, I would do my best to make the most of it possible.'

"On the afternoon of the 17th the Prince-Marshal fairly proposed to give me the command of the flotilla. His Highness informed me his intention was to have Oczakow attacked a second time. I replied, that I was disposed to execute with zeal whatever he might think proper for the good of the service; but that to attack with advantage it was necessary to come to close quarters, and to advance in better order than on the 1st July. He was of the same opinion, and requested me to come ashore next day, that we might concert together the plan of attack.

" I did not fail to comply with the orders of the Prince-Marshal, but his Highness spoke no more of the flotilla. I remained to dinner and supper, and afterwards returned on board of my ship.

" The Prince of Nassau having returned some days before, had intrigued with the Prince de Ligne; and the Prince-Marshal restored him to the command of the flotilla.

" On the 18th June I had been ordered to despatch the five frigates which had returned into the Liman, to be refitted at Glouboca, *en batterie*. I sent them off at daybreak on the 19th, having drawn the greater part of their crews from the gun-boats and bomb-vessels which the

Prince-Marshal had placed under my command. On the 20th I received twenty-one gun-boats, each carrying a single piece, from eighteen to thirty-two pounders; and five bomb-vessels, each carrying a mortar, of which four were of three *poods*, and one of five *poods*.* The same day the Prince-Marshal having established his head-quarters to the right of his army upon the shores of the Black Sea, (he had hitherto been on the shores of the Liman, on the left wing,) pointed out to me two of the enemy's gun-boats, stationed close by the fort of Hassan Pacha, and the Turkish lines on the side of Beresane. He was persuaded that they would attempt to come out during the night with despatches, and inquired of me if it were not possible to capture them. As his Highness appeared to attach great importance to this service, I undertook it.

"I returned on board the Wolodimer, from whence, at eight in the evening, I set off with five armed chaloupes. I made five gun-boats follow, as a measure of precaution in case the

---

* A *pood*, or *poud*, is a Russian weight, equal to 36 lbs. English weight.

Turks had attempted to make a sortie, as their chaloupes sailed much faster than ours.

"I found one of the Turkish gun-boats aground, hauled up, and almost dry on the sands adjoining the battery, and on an intrenchment the enemy had cast up on the water's edge. It was impossible to get it afloat under the terrible fire which we sustained from all the lines and batteries on the shore. The other gun-boat lay hard by the fort of Hassan Pacha, to the south. Lieutenant Edwards boarded this vessel, and cut her cables; but having had several of his men wounded, and being deserted by one of the chaloupes, he was obliged to give up the attempt, lest he should be left by the other chaloupe also. During this time I had made some efforts to get the other Turkish boat afloat. I now rowed quickly to the assistance of Mr Edwards, but the night being dark, he was already out of sight. I boarded the vessel in which he had been. I had several men wounded around me; but, in defiance of the enemy, I hauled the vessel out, and stationed it right opposite the head-quarters of the Prince-Marshal.

"On the 21st, at daybreak, I sailed with the Wolodimer, followed by all the vessels of the squadron that yet remained with me, and twenty-five armed boats and bomb-vessels that had been placed under my command. The object of this movement was again to blockade Oczakow by sea, and to cut off the communication between that place and Beresane. To accomplish this object, I stationed the Wolodimer and the Alexander to blockade the channel at the entrance of the Liman, and I continued the same line of blockade into the road, by placing the smaller vessels there. As the bomb-vessels and gun-boats had not water-casks, the Prince-Marshal, who wished to see these craft opposite his head-quarters, made wells be dug on shore for the accommodation of the crews; and on the 24th ordered my officer *du jour* to have three vessels stationed near the shore. I knew nothing of this change, for I had placed them the previous night, in line, and far enough off to be in safety. On the 25th the wind was from the south, but was not violent. After dinner I went to head-quarters to make a visit to the Prince-Marshal, and found, to my great astonishment, that half the boats were cast ashore, and the other half in the greatest danger. I set to work instantly, with my chaloupe, to haul off, and bring to anchor all the vessels possible; and by means of anchors and cables, for which I sent to the squadron, we saved them all, except six gun-boats, which went to pieces, and filled with sand. On the 26th the Prince-Marshal wrote me by his Brigadier *du jour*, requiring to know, since I was master of the vessels saved, what I meant to do with them? I placed them near the tongue of land of Kinbourn, where they had a sheltered haven, and also wells for the accommodation of the men. They sustained no farther injury during the time they remained under my command. After this, two chaloupes or small cutters were placed under my orders, of which each carried two licornes, forty-eight pounders, in the fore-part, and six falconets on the sides. Shortly afterwards I got two larger cutters, carrying each two mortars, of five poods.

"On the 31st July, the Capitan Pacha again made his appearance with his fleet, followed by several vessels which he had not when he went off. His advanced guard, composed of his frigates, bomb-vessels, and small craft, cast anchor near Beresane, whilst his large squadron of ships of the line resumed their old position. The Prince-Marshal ordered me to bring back my small vessels to assist in blocking up the passage of the Liman; and the Prince of Nassau was ordered to block up the road with his flotilla, and thus cut off the communication of the Turkish small vessels by the shallows to the south of Fort Hassan Pacha.

"The Prince of Nassau hoisted a Vice-Admiral's flag on one of the galleys in coming out of the Liman, and that galley having passed under the stern of the Wolodimer on the 1st of August, he assumed that I ought to have saluted him as Vice-Admiral!"

[The Rear-Admiral here enumerates six different special reasons for not saluting the said flag; and we fear somewhat tediously, for which reason we spare the reader this concatenation; the only important fact being, that the Prince of Nassau endeavoured to make the Court of Russia believe that the denial of this piece of courtesy was the only subject of dispute between himself and Paul Jones. We again resume the narrative.]

“ The Capitan Pacha came out from day to day, to sound and reconnoitre, in his kirlangitz, which sailed like the wind, and always displayed an Admiral's flag. As the block-fort and battery on the tongue of land at Kinbourn were only constructed of bags of sand, and were neither protected by ditch nor palisade, I was afraid that the Capitan Pacha might try to carry them by a sudden descent, which he could have done by landing five hundred men.

“ General Suwaroff had been dangerously wounded in a sortie made by the garrison of Oczakow, and had come to Kinbourn. I convinced him that the block-fort and battery were menaced, and as he had a greater quantity of chevaux de frize than he required, I suggested that he should employ what was superfluous in surrounding the block-fort and battery. The General gave orders accordingly, and I ranged all my gun-boats and bomb-vessels right by the strip of ground between the block-fort and the battery. The sand served them as a parapet, so that there was a line of fire continued from the point on to the battery. The small craft were, besides, always ready to change their position at the first movement of the enemy, and I placed the squadron so advantageously as to communicate with the block-fort and the battery, without confining their fire, and to keep back the enemy by a cross-fire, on entering the channel of the Liman; so that, though we were very weak compared with the Turkish fleet, the Capitan Pacha never either attempted to make a descent, or to force the passage of the entrance of the Liman.

"The Prince-Marshal having ordered Rear-Admiral Wognowitch to sail from Sevastopole with the fleet under his command, and that officer having raised obstacles because his force was not, he conceived, powerful enough to attack that under the command of the Capitan Pacha, his Highness sent me a letter, written by his chief secretary, Brigadier Popoff, on the 19th August, (old style,) proposing that I should go to Sevastopole to take command of the fleet. It may be remembered that I was brought to Russia to command *all* the naval force in the Black Sea, consequently this proposition did not surprise me. Had the Prince-Marshal ordered me to go, I would have proceeded immediately, but I could not seem as if I sought to be sent. In the *first* place, the naval signals used in that fleet were imperfect and very limited. *2dly*, My naval signals had not yet been translated into the Russian language, as no attention had been given to my request for a person capable of translating them. *3dly*, I was acquainted with no one in the fleet, and I was aware that the Prince-Marshal wished that it should come out the very day after my arrival at Sevastopole. *4thly*, The fleet had been compelled to fly before that of the Capitan Pacha, at a time when he had two thousand fewer good seamen. *5thly*, The fleet at Sevastopole was much as before, but that of the Capitan Pacha was stronger in craft, and had all the men replaced that had been lost in the affair of the Liman. *6thly*, I had just received preparatory orders from the Prince-Marshal to attack Fort Hassan Pacha; and I hoped to show him the difference between my fashion of attack and that of the 1st of July. I replied, in answer to his letter, that being entirely devoted to the good of the state, his Highness would find me eager to fulfil his orders. It was said, that some days afterwards the Prince-Marshal sent positive orders to Admiral Wognowitch to come out, but that he always found means for not coming to close quarters with the Capitan Pacha.

"On the 30th August the Turks took a small lodka, freighted with water-melons, belonging to the merchants of Kinbourn. In coming down the Liman the people on board had been foolish enough to pass too close to Oczakow.

"To '*punish the Turks*' for this, the Prince of Nassau, at evening, made his flotilla advance to assault Oczakow!

"I sent my secretary to head-quarters, and in the meanwhile assembled the commanders of divisions of my gun-boats and bomb-vessels, and ordered them to bring forward their divisions, and form in line of battle between the squadron and Oczakow, ready to attack the Fort of Hassan Pacha the moment orders should arrive.

"Upon the return of the Capitan Pacha, M. Littlepage, Chamberlain to the King of Poland, being then with the Prince-Marshal, had solicited and obtained leave to command a division of my gun-boats.

"Night being come on, the chiefs of division wishing to bring forward their boats, found that thirteen of them had quitted their posts, against the most positive orders to make no movement without their commanders of division. This movement had been occasioned by the rashness of a Greek Lieutenant belonging to the division of M. Littlepage. The boat of this officer had fired eight shots against the place, and another boat six shots, but no one else had fired. As this Lieutenant was the most to blame, I deprived him of his command, and sent him to head-quarters, which was required by the Prince-Marshal.

"The Prince of Nassau, who had very idly wasted a great deal of ammunition, pretended that my boats had prevented him from taking the whole Turkish flotilla!

"The Greek Lieutenant whom I had disgraced, instead of being punished, was promoted to the command of a double chaloupe, heavily armed. M. Littlepage gave a particular account of the whole affair in a letter to the Grand General of Poland.

"A few days after this, the Prince-Marshal sent Rear-Admiral Mordwinoff on board the Wolodimer, to assemble all the captains and master pilots of the squadron to hold a council on the means of effecting a junction between the squadron of Cherson and the fleet of Sevastopole. It has been said that the Prince-Marshal had earnestly entreated this officer to take the affair upon himself, and that he had positively declined it. I can say nothing on this head; I only know that it was a delicate step in relation to me, to send another officer on board my ship to hold a council; and, above all, without having apprized me either by speech or writing. If I had been stickling, I would have put this officer under arrest, as he could show no authority nor precedent for holding a council where I commanded. But as I was influenced by the good of the service above every personal consideration, I received Admiral Mordwinoff most amicably, and after dinner assembled the officers for the necessary consultation. Many difficulties presented themselves to their minds against the proposed junction; but as it was known that the Prince-Marshal was determined on the measure, it was agreed that it could not be effected but at Hagdge-bay, upon the coast, between Beresane and the Danube, at the distance of fifty verstes* from the point of Kinbourn. I raised no obstacle. I only observed, that since it was pressingly necessary to beat the advanced guard of the enemy before we could effect the proposed junction, it was indispensable to station the squadron previously in the road of Oczakow, and to sail from thence with the wind from N. to N.N.W., to avoid being attacked on the way by the grand fleet of the Turks, and also to keep to the leeward till the junction was effected.

"It was only a few days previously that preparations had been begun to complete the arming of the Wolodimer and Alexander.

"During this time her Imperial Majesty had

* A verste is equal to 3500 English feet.

sent twenty-four gold swords to head-quarters, to be distributed among the officers on account of the battle of the Liman. The Prince-Marshal himself received a gold sword, enriched with diamonds and emeralds; and the Prince of Nassau got one ornamented with a row of diamonds. There were a number of silver medals sent at the same time to be distributed among the soldiers and seamen. The swords had not yet been distributed, but the medals were all given to the men of the flotilla, and not one to any man in the squadron. It is usual to give subalterns the more merit the more they are exposed to personal danger. The crews of the squadron had often hauled the flotilla totally uncovered, and exposed to the fire of the enemy, whilst the people of the flotilla were screened by parapets made of bags of wool, by which the vessels were surrounded.

"On the 18th September I received a secret order from the Prince-Marshal to attack the advanced-guard of the enemy, anchored under Beresane. His Highness proposed to make the attack with the five frigates which had been sent to Glouboca to be mounted as batteries; and the frigates were to be supported by all the other vessels of the squadron, save the Wolodimer and the Alexander, the arming of which went on very slowly on account of difficulties on the part of the Admiralty. Two of the frigates, the Scoroi and the Boristhenes, had already rejoined the squadron. Before the equipments of those frigates were altered, they carried more guns than are ever put, either by the French or English, into ships of the same kind. The Scoroi, for example, carried forty guns, and in England they would not have put more than thirty-two into her. She now carried sixteen 36-pounders, and four licornes, 18-pounders."

[Here follows a detailed account of the armament of this frigate, and the Rear-Admiral's opinion of the best way of arming ships, which he appears himself to think not much to the point, for he returns to the narrative of the campaign by saying as much.]

" The five frigates, of which I have perhaps spoken too much, appeared to me very fit to place behind a stoccado, or bar. But I never would make choice of ships of this kind for the sea-service. The first broadside is all that is to be feared from them.

"I replied in writing to the proposition of the Prince-Marshal for attacking the advanced guard of the Turks near Beresane, and afterwards made a plan of attack be drawn out for his inspection. He was much pleased with it. As it was necessary to take advantage of a northerly wind to effect the enterprise, I proposed to the Prince-Marshal to place the frigates in the road as soon as they arrived from Glouboca, to serve, while waiting the attack on the line, as a permanent outer blockade between Oczakow and the enemy. His Highness said it was not yet time for this, and ordered me to place them in a line with the other vessels of my squadron, so as to make an imposing figure in the channel of the Liman.

"In the end of the month, the Turkish fleet set sail in the night, followed by all the vessels that had lain under Beresane; nor did we perceive it till late in the next morning. The Capitan Pacha returned in about thirty-six hours, and resumed the position he had left. The only difference was, that he brought in some additional small vessels, and that he considerably reinforced his advanced guard under Beresane. As our flotilla, which ought to have blockaded the road, and cut off the communication with the small vessels on that side, were only there occasionally, as if by caprice, it was quite natural for the Turks to profit by its absence, and go out and in when they found the way clear.

"The flotilla being to leeward, between my squadron and Kinbourn, on the 8th October, the Capitan Pacha sent off in the evening three vessels of his advanced guard, which entered Oczakow unmolested, by an open passage. Our flotilla made no movement. I made an attempt to intercept the enemy's progress with my gunboats, which I caused to be hauled to windward by the ship's boats of the squadron. But the wind being high, they could not bring them to attack. Our batteries nearest to Oczakow fired on the three Turkish vessels, but without being able to arrest their progress. It was now dark; and, moreover, the distance between these batteries and the block-fort, on the side of Kinbourn, being seven verstes, the land-batteries never could have prevented either the entrance or exit of small vessels.

"One of the Turkish ships had the folly to cast anchor in the shallows of Fort Hassan Pacha; and at daybreak on the ninth, being within shot of our most advanced land-battery, was struck between wind and water, and run down; the other two vessels got in without difficulty. I have already mentioned, that on the 18th of August I received an order to be in readiness to attack the fortress of Hassan Pacha with my bomb-vessels, and the chaloupes armed with licornes and mortars. I expected from day to day an order for action, and had in consequence bestowed much pains in training my men to the necessary evolutions; but the final orders never arrived.

"The Prince of Nassau having run down my plan of attack, it was set aside; and by a new arrangement, which I was commanded to form with General Muller, Commander-in-chief of Artillery, I was destined to assault the intrenchment, and the Turkish battery on the shore of the road.

"On the 9th of October the flotilla advanced from the shores of Kinbourn, and attacked Oczakow; but this attack was conducted and ended in the very same manner as that of the 30th August, save that a small vessel of the Turkish flotilla, which lay farther out than any of the others, ran aground on the shallows of Fort Hassan Pacha.

"On the 10th of October I received another preparatory order; and soon afterwards was ordered to give up all my gun-boats to the flotilla. Towards evening I went to head-quarters to ascertain what was to be done regarding these boats. The Prince-Marshal at this time told me he had the strongest desire to see pitched overboard a large piece of artillery placed on the fore-part of the vessel of the Turkish flotilla that stood farthest out, and which had run aground. I imagined at the time that there was no other vessel run aground save the one in the road, at the distance of a verste from the fortress of Hassan Pacha; so I said the thing was quite easy; for although the Turks should come up in force to defend the vessel, there would always be time to spike the piece of cannon.

"It was night when I undertook this little enterprise. As I did not imagine the Prince-Marshal attached so much importance to it as to wish that I should conduct it in person, I confided it to Lieutenant Edwards, a brave and an intelligent man, whom I wished to requite for past services. On the 1st of July he had followed me throughout, and was a long time with me in the galley of the Capitan Pacha. He had followed me on the night of the 20th of July, and had boarded, and cut the cable of the vessel which I took opposite the fortress of Hassan Pacha. He had assisted me some days afterwards, when, by orders of the Prince-Marshal, we made trial of bombarding the fort from one of the bomb-vessels; from which service we had some difficulty in withdrawing, as the wind, which rose in a moment, kept us for a long while under the fire of the enemy's musketry, which wounded some of our men.

"Mr Edwards returned before daybreak, without having succeeded. He said there were a great many men in the ship, who fired on him, and that he durst not board her, he was so ill supported. I was vexed that he had failed; and in my report to the Prince-Marshal I said that I would conduct the enterprise myself next night, if that would satisfy him.

"The Prince-Marshal held me at my word; but it was eleven at night when Mr Edwards returned with the order. The wind, which was high, was quite against me, as well as a strong tide; and I would have deferred the attempt, if I had not conceived my honour pledged. I was led to hope, that after midnight the wind might fall, and the strength of the tide lessen, if it did not change. The night was very dark, and the rain fell in torrents. I waited till two o'clock, when the moon rose. I had with me five armed boats, and I calculated on being followed by four *batteaux saporoses*, and by one of the armed vessels I had taken from the Turks; but it was impossible to haul them against the wind, and I was compelled to go on as I best could, with only my five boats. I have noticed that our flotilla had run down a small Turkish vessel in the shallows of the fortress of Hassan Pacha, but I did not perceive this till the moment after I had despatched Mr Edwards to head-quarters, because the vessel lay so near the fortress, where the water is of little depth, that it had only sunk a foot or fifteen inches, and consequently appeared as if still afloat. As the Prince-Marshal had only spoken to me of the farthest out of the Turkish flotilla, I now believed he meant the one nearest the fortress, in which idea I was confirmed by Mr Edwards, at his return from head-quarters, telling me he had heard ashore that the vessel run down in the road had been visited, but that nothing had been found there. I rowed for the vessel nearest the fortress, which carried a large cannon in her bow; but, after having fatigued my rowers, I was vexed to see daylight appear, whilst I had still more than a verste to go before I could reach the vessel. I returned on board my own ship, to prevent a useless alarm, intending to renew the attempt next night.

"Without waiting to receive my report, the Prince-Marshal sent me orders 'to abandon the enterprise, for he had intrusted it to other ships.' There was fine weather on the night between the 12th and 13th, but the 'other ships' did nothing; and the Turks availed themselves of an open way to bring out all their flotilla, which rejoined the ships of the advanced guard under Beresane.

"Some days afterwards, a Colonel of Cossacks boarded the vessel run down in the road, and set fire to it, for which he received public thanks.

"On the 13th the Prince-Marshal wished to establish a permanent line of blockade in the road, by placing my frigates there, and some other small vessels. He wrote me a letter on this subject, which strongly affected me, and to which I replied next day, with perhaps rather too much freedom and warmth.* This occasion-

---

* This letter, taken in connexion with the circumstances which preceded it, was the ultimate cause of the dismissal of Paul Jones before the campaign ended. His recall to St Petersburgh, under pretence of being employed in the North Sea, in name of the Empress, but really ordered by Potemkin, was a mere piece of

ed an interchange of letters, which was only terminated on the 18th by the arrival of Admiral

---

jugglery to get rid of him, of which he was not even the dupe. The following is an extract of his letter, and a copy of Potemkin's order, which provoked it:—

"*Order to Rear-Admiral Chevalier Paul Jones.*

"As it is seen that the Capitan Pacha comes in his kirlangich from the grand fleet to the smaller vessels, and as before quitting this he may attempt something, I request your Excellence, the Capitan Pacha having actually a greater number of vessels, to hold yourself in readiness to receive him courageously, and drive him back. I require that this be done without loss of time; if not, you will be made answerable for every neglect.

"PRINCE POTEMKIN TAURICIEN.

"13th October, 1788."

To this truly Russian order Jones has affixed the following characteristic note:—"A warrior is always ready, and I had not come there an apprentice." His reply to this order led to his instant dismissal. Potemkin was a person in no shape to be trifled with; and though Jones at first attributed his want of favour in this powerful quarter to the ill offices of those around Potemkin, he

Mordwinoff, to take command of the squadron and the flotilla; for the Prince of Nassau had set

---

came to see that much of what he suffered emanated directly from the impatience, jealousy, and caprice of this spoiled tyrant. When the Rear-Admiral went to head-quarters to take leave, Potemkin disdained and disclaimed the insinuation of being influenced by those around him. "Do not imagine any one leads me,—leads me!"—he swore, and stamping with his foot, added, "Not even the Empress!" Fatal as the reply to the above order proved to Jones, and deeply as he regretted it, the reader must be pleased to see that he retained so much of his original spirit as appears in this singular document. "I have always," he says, "conformed myself immediately, without murmuring, and most exactly, to the commands of your Highness; and on occasions when you have deigned to leave any thing to my own discretion, I have been exceedingly flattered, and believe you have had no occasion to repent. At present, in case the Capitan Pacha does resolve on attempting any thing before his departure, I can give assurance beforehand, that the brave officers and crews I have the honour to command will do their duty 'courageously,' though they have not yet been rewarded for the important services they have performed for the empire under my eyes. I off for Warsaw some days after his affair of the 9th, with which the Prince-Marshal had been much dissatisfied. I at the same time received orders from her Imperial Majesty to go to St Petersburgh to be employed in the North Sea. Sweden had declared war against Russia at the commencement of the campaign, and Admiral Greig, who had commanded the Russian fleet, having died, I was assured her Majesty had very important views in recalling me. Yet I could not but feel grieved to be deprived of my command when the campaign, so far as regarded maritime operations, was so nearly concluded.

"As soon as the Prince of Nassau went off, all the gold swords were distributed among the officers of the flotilla. It may easily be imagined that this transaction, as well as several things

---

answer for this with my honour, and will explain myself fairly on this delicate point at the end of the campaign. In the meanwhile, I may merely say, that it is upon the sacred promise I have given them of demanding justice from your Highness in their behalf, that they have consented to stifle their grievances and keep silent."

which preceded it, were not calculated to give me much pleasure. The capture of the Turkish galley, and the boarding the galley of the Capitan Pacha on the 1st of July, were without dispute the most brilliant actions of the campaign of the Liman. The credit of them was most unjustly given to the flotilla, and my officers remained without any reward for the important services which they had rendered in these affairs, laying aside those of the 18th June, the 30th of August, and the 9th of October, from which they reaped no advantage. After the gold swords had been distributed, I myself heard several of the officers who got them express their astonishment, not being able to guess for what they had been so highly rewarded.

"It is worthy of notice, that all the large vessels which the flotilla attacked were previously aground. In this case, they might be compared to men with their feet nailed to planks, and their hands tied behind their backs. This is the only instance in history of ships aground, and out of the possibility of being re-captured, being attacked and destroyed, with their crews, by combustibles. It may be recollected, that during the whole campaign the flotilla had not taken even one small vessel afloat. Since a very mistaken notion has been formed of the vessels taken in the Liman on the 17th and 18th of June, which have been called " ships of the line," it is but right to say that I made Lieutenant Fox measure the hulls of the two largest, and we found that the size of the one was 130, and of the other 135 feet English in total length, in the line of their first battery. Apply this to naval architecture. Yet the Prince of Nassau had been rewarded in a brilliant manner for " having destroyed six, and captured two *ships of the line*." The only three-masted vessel which escaped burning upon the 18th June was a corvette of one battery, and four pieces between decks. I had almost forgot that there was one small brigantine of fourteen three-pounders. Such were the two *vessels of the line* that were captured, and the latter was wrecked next day by the carelessness of those who had the charge of her. In place of eight *vessels of the line*, the Capitan Pacha had come into the Liman with only a detachment of corvettes, or large merchantmen, frigates, bomb-ships, and other craft. Only four of the corvettes carried guns between decks. Of this number was the vessel saved. On one of these four vessels was displayed a square flag; but there was the same on the galley and the kirlangich of the Capitan Pacha. It has been already said that the grand fleet without Kinbourn displayed three Admirals' flags. From the account of the campaign given by the Prince of Nassau, it appears that the Capitan Pacha had lost his best ship, manned with the picked men of his fleet, and his only flag as Grand Admiral, while it is well known that at the end of the campaign he went back to Constantinople with all the ships of the line he had at the commencement of it.

As it had been told me that some ill-intentioned persons in the army had said that I had been deprived of my command because the officers were unwilling to serve under me, I endeavoured to procure testimonials to the contrary, and have seen with regret that the mind is not always free; and that it sometimes dare not render homage to truth.*

"The last of the five frigates, called 'Sea Batteries,' did not join the squadron till the 19th of October, and the same day Admiral Mordwinoff placed the line of blockade in the road much farther out than it ever had been, so that the vessels masked the fire of all the guns on shore on both sides." [Here the Rear-Admiral enters into certain professional criticisms on his successor's arrangements, which are neither pe-

---

* In the service in which Paul Jones was engaged that was impossible, which in any service requires considerable moral courage. His Russian Secretary drew up for the signature of the officers a testimony in favour of "Rear-Admiral Paul Jones, Chevalier of the Military Order of Merit, the Order of St Anne, and of Cincinnatus;" which, says the Secretary, they, for *powerful reasons*, declined to subscribe, though they at the same time owned there was nothing in it contrary to *pure truth*. It was drawn up on the very eve of Paul Jones's departure for St Petersburgh. The Captain of his late ship, the Wolodimer, subscribed it, and also one of the other officers.

culiarly interesting, nor yet very good-natured, but which may, nevertheless, be very just. We pass them, and again take up the personal narrative.]

"Having reflected that the season was too far advanced to render my services necessary in the North Sea before the following year, I wrote to the Prince-Marshal, offering to continue my services till the end of the campaign. I was indebted to him for the Order of St Anne, and I have a heart naturally grateful.* He made his Secretary, M. Popoff, write me, that since I was recalled by the order of the Empress, it was necessary I should obey.

"I was, however, invited to head-quarters to take leave, and to receive a letter from the Prince-Marshal for her Imperial Majesty. As I was much interested personally, and still more so in

---

* Paul Jones never appears to have had a true idea of the whole character of Potemkin till long afterwards. Potemkin was, indeed, one of the most extraordinary monsters that ever lived,—a jumble of every moral contradiction.

relation to my officers, I after dinner spoke freely, and told M. Popoff all that was on my mind. This gentleman repeated all I said to the Prince-Marshal. He was offended at first, but afterwards he sent for me to talk with him. Without failing in the respect due to him, I spoke very freely. I told him he had played an unfair game at the opening of the campaign in dividing the command in the Liman in the existing circumstances of the country; and that, if I had not resolved to sacrifice my own feelings in order to manage the persons he had given me for colleagues, the campaign would have taken a very different turn. He confessed it, but said it was too late to think of this now. He then said he would be glad to see me fixed in Russia, and that he was disposed to give me *solid proofs of his esteem*, both now and in future. I showed him the testimonial of the Captain of the Wolodimer, and some other papers, to convince him that he had neither done justice to me nor to the squadron. He said the Prince of Nassau pretended all was done by himself; 'but I have never,' said he, 'been deceived in him. I have always known him for what he is.' He proposed that I should go to Tagenroc to equip and command a squadron he was building there; but, as I had been brought to Russia to take the chief command in the Black Sea, and had received orders from the Empress to repair to St Petersburgh, I declined the offer. I only entreated that he would consider the services of my officers, and give them the seniority they had lost by the promotion of those officers of the flotilla who did not belong to the naval service. Admiral Mordwinoff made the same request, and the Prince promised to do them justice.

"Two days afterwards I received a letter from the Prince-Marshal for the Empress, in which he noticed the zeal and anxiety I had ever shown for her service, and to render myself worthy of her favour.*

---

* We give this letter. It is a good specimen of the sort of thing; nor is it possible to believe that a man so acute as Paul Jones was duped or hoodwinked by this fashion of speaking and writing, though for political reasons he suffered himself to appear so:—

"On the 4th November, the Capitan Pacha having withdrawn his advanced guard in the night, set sail in the morning with his whole force, entering first Varna, and afterwards Constantinople, with every ship of the line he had at the opening of the campaign. It is singular that this enterprising commander did not attempt to force the entrance of the Liman; for Admiral Mordwinoff had placed the squadron in so exposed and disadvantageous a situation, that the fire of the land-batteries, which should have flanked him without, was entirely covered. But it may be presumed that the Turkish Admiral believed he

---

"MADAM,—In sending to the high throne of your Imperial Majesty Rear-Admiral M. Paul Jones, I take, with submission, the liberty of certifying the eagerness and zeal which he has ever shown for the service of your Imperial Majesty, and to render himself worthy of the high favour of your Imperial Majesty.

"From the most faithful subject of your Imperial Majesty,

"PRINCE POTEMKIN TAURICIEN.

"31st October, 1788."

had done enough for the safety of Oczakow by the succours he had thrown in.

"On the morning of the 7th, agreeably to a secret order from the Prince-Marshal, the *Saporoses* landed, to the number of 2000, on the Island of Beresane. The Turkish garrison being only 300 strong, fired a few random shots, and then surrendered at discretion.

"Having given the officers under me such testimonials as they merited, I embarked on the morning of the 9th November in a small open galley for Cherson. I was three days and three nights on the way, and suffered a great deal from the excessive cold. The day after my arrival the river was frozen in, and I was taken dangerously ill. My health was not sufficiently re-established to enable me to proceed before the 6th of December. Having arrived at St Elizabeth, I received intelligence that Oczakow had been taken by storm on the 6th. The garrison was eleven thousand strong, including the three thousand that the Capitan Pacha had thrown into the place before he sailed. But the cold had become extreme, and the Russian army being formed in six columns to attack the place at day-dawn, the Turks were completely taken by surprise, and, becoming panic-struck, suffered themselves to be throttled like as many sheep. In the fury of the assault the Russian soldiers spared nothing. I have been assured, that from eighteen to nineteen thousand Turks perished on that day!

"As I wished to delay my return to court till the arrival of the Prince-Marshal, I stopt some days at Skloff, where General Soritsch loaded me with civilities. I arrived at St Petersburgh on the 28th December, and was ordered to appear at court on the 31st, when her Imperial Majesty did me the honour of granting me a private audience. I presented the letter the Prince-Marshal had given me. A few days afterwards the Empress sent me word, through Count de Dmitrijew-Mamonow, that she must wait the arrival of Prince Potemkin before deciding on what was to be done regarding me. In the meanwhile Count Besborodko told me, that a command of greater importance was intended for me than that of the Black Sea.

"On the 1st February, the Prince-Marshal not having yet arrived, I gave in to the Vice-Chancellor, Count d'Osterman, a project for forming an alliance, political and commercial, between Russia and the United States. As the object of this project was reciprocal advantages, and, above all, to encourage the commerce of the Black Sea, and of the new settlements in the Crimea, I had long intended to transmit it to the Prince-Marshal; and on his arrival at court, about the middle of February, I sent him a copy. Some time afterwards he took me into his cabinet, and said that my plan contained some good ideas; but that he did not think it expedient to adopt it at this time, as this might still further irritate the English against Russia, and that it was necessary first to make peace with the Turks.

"I might say a great deal more about the fleet and flotilla of Cherson, but for the present I have said enough." [The Rear-Admiral does, however, say a good deal about the construction and equipment of the Russian ships, and the internal regulations of the Russian navy, which shows much professional acuteness, but must have small interest now that all is changed. The speculations of a clever and a practical man forty years ago, on the opening prospects of the Russian empire, compared with its actual state, are, however, both curious and important.] "The commerce of the Black Sea," he says, "is an object of very great importance; but this commerce will always be annoyed and often interrupted by the Turks, till Russia has a stronger fleet in the Black Sea to hold them at bay, and to place the keys of Constantinople in the hands of the Empress. Russia having all the requisite materials, in making the necessary arrangements with order and economy (without speaking of war, to avoid exciting suspicion in powers jealous of her glory,) this deficiency might be supplied in a few years. The means of obtaining good seamen is to create a merchant-trade,—to form an alliance with the United States,—and to have a squadron of evolution on the Black Sea, directed by an admiral and a properly-instructed staff.

"I have always believed that Russia requires a port on the Asiatic side, opposite the Crimea, to protect the fleet in winds and currents, and to be as it were a sentinel-post on the Turks. I have thought of Sinople for this purpose, and I spoke of it to the Empress and Prince Potemkin; but, being afterwards better informed, I found a more suitable situation, where I am certain such a post could be securely established at small cost, and beard the whole Ottoman empire.

"I must be permitted to conclude my journal with some reflections naturally suggested by matters affecting my personal honour. I have never been able to conjecture the reason which made Prince Potemkin order Admiral Mordwinoff to give up to him the official account of our operations, which I had drawn up in conformity to the orders of the Admiralty of the Black Sea, as I was assured he had done, both by Admiral Mordwinoff and his brother-in-law. No more could I guess why Prince Potemkin had given orders that no notice should be taken of the little frigate Alexander, which had been run down in the battle of the 17th June. This information also I had from Admiral Mordwinoff after I had given up to him the command of the squadron. I have been assured that this frigate was always retained in the list of the marine. When I found that I received no testimony of the favour of the Empress in this affair, and on other occasions very interesting to the state, I was compelled to think that she had been ill-informed, for her ambition is to be esteemed the most magnanimous and the most generous of all sovereigns.*

---

* It is no new incident in any service for one man to gain the victory for which another is rewarded. This must sometimes occur from due regard to rank and subordination, even where there is the strongest desire to do strict justice to all the commanders. To the counsels of Varage, Captain Winter, and a Milanese officer, De Litta, the subsequent victory of the Cronstadt fleet over the Swedes, for which Nassau was so highly rewarded, were universally ascribed. The most brilliant and decisive sea-battle ever gained by the Russians, that of Tschesme, where the whole Turkish fleet, a town and castle, were taken or destroyed in one morning, was fought by the English officers, Elphinstone, Greig, and especially Dugdale, who performed prodigies of reckless valour at the greatest personal hazard. Yet the Empress thought fit to attribute the victory to Alexy Orloff, either from po-

"I received a letter from the Minister of the United States (to the Court of Versailles,) dated Paris the 23d March, 1789, which began by telling me, that a letter he had received from me, dated at St Petersburgh, the 31st January, *was the only proof my friends had of my existence since I had left Copenhagen.** If I had played

---

licy or want of information. Potemkin himself was never more munificently rewarded for what he had actually accomplished, than was Orloff for a victory of which he obtained the credit. There were great public rejoicings; pillars and palaces were erected, and titles, estates, orders, or whatever the imagination of the Empress could devise to do him honour, were heaped on the murderer of her husband, to whom she had formerly owed a considerable share of her usurped crown.

* In Russia, letters were systematically intercepted. This was part of the policy of the government; and such things have been heard of in that country, even of later date than the reign of Catherine II. When the Archduke Paul was permitted to travel through Europe with the Archdutchess, he was so well aware of the jealousy of his mother and her government, that he arranged a private correspondence to be forwarded to the Swedish post-offices by couriers. His correspondent was a

the part of a cipher in the campaign of the Liman it was for the first time. I either deserved to lose my head, or the history of the operations on the Liman, which had been got up in St Petersburgh during the winter, and which I saw with astonishment in the office of M. Popoff, merited to be burnt. I assert, that it was falsified even to the most trifling circumstances.

"I have acted a public and distinguished part for fifteen years among an enlightened people, where the press is free, and where the conduct of every man is open to discussion, and subjected to the judgment of his fellow-citizens. No man can play the hypocrite during so long a period in a career so trying as was mine. It was natural for the Prince of Nassau and Brigadier Alexiano to be my enemies, for they only sought their

---

young aid-de-camp, Bibikoff, who sometimes permitted himself to describe persons about the court without sufficient regard to decorum. Among those honoured with his notice was *One Eye,* as he termed Potemkin. The courier was intercepted at Riga, and Paul's witty correspondent was exiled to Astracan, where he shortly died.

own advantage; and Prince Potemkin, who knew better, did wrong to place me in competition with them; but I cannot conceive how it happened that I had around Prince Potemkin other enemies as powerful as they were malicious. I ought to have found only friends in Russia, for I have served that empire faithfully and well. The manner in which Prince Potemkin has changed in regard to me, since the commencement of the war, exceeds all imagination. While he supposed that my services would be an acquisition in directing the maritime operations against the Turks, the Admirals Mordwinoff and Woinowitch entirely lost his confidence as officers; and it is evident that Woinowitch had not regained it on the 19th of August, when it was proposed that I should go to Sevastopole to take command of the fleet. When I had the misfortune to offend Prince Potemkin by the freedom of my letter of the 14th October, he sent several couriers, one after another, entreating that Admiral Mordwinoff would take command of the squadron, which the latter only at last accepted on condition of receiving *carte blanche*, and insisted that the Prince should not interfere in any arrangements he thought fit to make.

"I have mentioned that the Dnieper was frozen over the day after my arrival at Cherson, in consequence of which the squadron and flotilla were placed in danger, from not having been properly secured (for the season) after the departure of the Capitan Pacha. I understood that some of the vessels were lost in the Liman, and that the Wolodimer, to save herself, was obliged to risk the passage to Sevastopole without a good part of her ballast.

"Briefly—in a few days after my departure from Cherson, Admiral Mordwinoff was disgraced and sent from the service, whilst Admiral Woinowitch, who had married the daughter of Alexiano, was placed at the head of the Admiralty, with the chief command of the fleet, and the entire confidence of Prince Potemkin.

"It is said that Russia has no longer need of foreign naval officers. No one is more desirous than myself that this may be so, for I cannot be jealous of any one, and I must ever desire the prosperity of a country I have served. I may, however, be allowed to notice, that this opinion is not of very ancient date. If this had been believed before the last campaign, why were my services so anxiously sought after?—It assuredly could not have been in compliment to me, nor in order afterwards to make use of me in promoting certain political designs. I have frequently heard, that, since the war broke out with Sweden, measures have been taken to induce Rear-Admiral Kinsbergen to quit Holland, and re-enter the service of Russia. His countrymen allege that he had been offered the rank of vice-admiral, the Order of Alexander Nevsky, and a fixed revenue of 20,000 roubles a-year; and that he had refused all these advantages, as he had lately married a wife with a fortune which enabled him to live in independence in his own country.

"It is known that the King of Sweden made advantageous offers to Admiral Curtis of the English navy, to induce him to take command of the fleet against Russia; and that this officer declined them, not wishing to hazard his professional reputation in command of a fleet which was not in so good a condition as that of England.

"The Empress will do me the justice to remember, that when I entered her service I did not say one word regarding my personal interests. I have a soul too noble for that; and if my heart had not been devoted to her Majesty, I would never have drawn my sword in her cause. I have now nothing for it but, like Admiral Kinsbergen, to marry a rich wife; but I have sufficient to support me wherever I choose, and I have seen enough of the world to be a philosopher. When I arrived at the Black Sea, if reasons much stronger than those which withheld Admiral Curtis had not influenced my mind and heart, which were devoted to the Empress, I would never have hoisted my flag on board the Wolodimer. I would have refused the poor command offered me, and which was not worthy of me. I have never puffed off my own actions, nor given any piece to the press containing my own panegyric.*

---

* The pettish tone of some of these remarks affords an

" I respect the names of Kinsbergen and Curtis; but the first duty of a gentleman is to respect his own character; and I believe, without vanity, that the name of Paul Jones is of as much value as theirs. It is thirty years since I entered the navy, and I have had for friends and instructors a d'Orvilliers and a Pavilon. Unfortunately Prince Potemkin never gave himself the trouble to know me.

" I had the happiness to be loved by my officers and men, because I treated them justly, and set them a good example in fight. After I ceased to command, though the campaign only lasted a few days, the seamen soon found the difference. They said they had lost their father: they were immediately served with bad provisions.

---

amusing contrast to the affected coolness and indifference of the sentiments they express; but it should be remembered, that, just before this Journal was extended, the man who suffered all the neglect, injustice, and insult which it records, had been irritated to the verge of despair and madness by persecution and injury of a viler and yet more despicable nature. Under the feeling of these wrongs he writes.

"I have already noticed, that Prince Potemkin had promised, in presence of Admiral Mordwinoff, to advance the officers under my command, and to restore to them the seniority they had lost by the promotion of the officers of the flotilla; but I have learnt with much pain that he has not kept his word, and that in consequence my officers, to the number of fifty, have demanded their dismission. Not one of them offered to resign while I held command. Admiral Woinowitch having represented to Prince Potemkin that without these officers the fleet was useless, he was compelled to advance them all. I have been told that they were not yet satisfied, as they were not restored to their seniority, and that they proposed to quit the service at the end of the year. I hope justice will be done them, for they are brave men. For myself I have been marked out from every other officer that served in the Liman; I alone have obtained no promotion, though I commanded and was alone responsible! I may be told that I ought to be satisfied with having received the rank of Rear-admiral on entering the service. I reply, that I could not have been offered an inferior grade. One officer may deserve as much in a day as another in a lifetime, and every officer ought to be advanced according to his merits. I was not favoured in rank on entering the Russian service. I had a full right to obtain that which I accepted. A man, only twenty-four years of age, has since been received into the service with the rank of major-general. I wish to say nothing against this officer; it is not always years that give skill, much less genius, but he must do a great deal before he has my experience.

"It is painful, for the honour of human nature, to reflect on how many malevolent and deceitful persons surround the great, and particularly crowned heads. I speak from my own unhappy experience. Some persons had the malice to make Prince Potemkin believe that I made unhandsome strictures on his military conduct, and ridiculed his manner of conducting the siege of Oczakow. I have heard a great deal said on this subject, and I am aware that it excited considerable discontent in the army. I was told, during my illness at Cherson, that a thousand of his officers had demanded their dismission; but I defy any one to say to my face that I ever allowed myself to criticise his operations. I have been strongly attached to him, of which I have given proofs during my command, and even after he unjustly superseded me. There is evidence of this in my letter of the 7th November, at a time when I certainly had reason to complain of his conduct.

"I have been deeply injured by those secret machinations in the opinion of the Empress. My enemies have had the wickedness to make her believe that I was a *cruel* and *brutal* man; and that I had, during the American war, *even killed my own nephew!*

"It is well known, that, from motives of revenge, the English have invented and propagated a thousand fictions and atrocities to stain, wound, and injure the celebrated men who effected the American revolution:—a Washington and a Franklin, two of the most illustrious and virtuous men that have ever adorned humanity, have not been spared by these calumniators. Are they now the less respected on this account by their fellow-citizens?—On the contrary, they are universally revered, even in Europe, as the fathers of their country, and as examples of all that is great and noble in the human character.

"In civil wars it is not wonderful that opposite factions should mutually endeavour to make it be believed that each is in the right; and it is obvious that the party most in the wrong will always be the most calumnious. If there had really been any thing against my character, the English would not have failed to furnish convincing proofs of it. I was known, with very slender means, to have given more alarm to their three kingdoms during the war than any other individual had done.

"I have heard, that, at the period of my entering the Russian service, the English in St Petersburgh cried out against me, and asserted that I had been a contraband trader. All the world knows that men of this description are actuated entirely by avarice; and every one to whom I have the honour to be known is aware that I am one of the least selfish of mankind. This is known to the whole American people. I have given proofs of it not easily shown, of which I possess very flattering testimonies. In a letter written on the 29th November, 1782, to Congress, by Mr Morris, minister of the marine and finance departments, after having made my eulogium with the warmth of a true patriot, who thoroughly knew me, he says, that 'I had certainly merited the favour of Congress by services and sacrifices the most signal.' Men do not change their characters in these respects.

"If my heart has bled for the Americans,—above all, for those shut up as victims in English prisons by an act of Parliament as sanguinary as unjust,—if I have exposed my health and my life to the greatest dangers, if I have sacrificed my personal tranquillity and my domestic happiness, with a portion of my fortune and my blood, to set at liberty these virtuous and innocent men,—have I not given proofs sufficiently striking that I have a heart the most tender, a soul the most elevated?—I have done more than all this. So far from being *harsh* and *cruel*, nature has given me the mildest disposition. I was formed for love and friendship, and not to be a seaman or a soldier, to which I have sacrificed my natural inclination.

"As an officer I love good discipline, which I consider indispensable to the success of operations, particularly at sea, where men are brought into such close contact. In the English navy it is known that captains of ships are often tyrants, who order the lash for the poor seamen very frequently for nothing. In the American navy we have almost the same regulations; but I look on my crew as my children, and I have always found means to manage them without flogging.

"I never had a nephew, nor any other relation, under my command. Happily these facts are known in America, and they prove how cruel and harsh I am. I have one dear nephew,* who is still too young for service, but who now pursues his studies. Since I came to Russia I have intended him for the Imperial marine. Instead of imbruing my hands in his blood he will be cherished as my son.

---

* The only son of the Rear-Admiral's eldest sister, the late Mrs Taylor of Dumfries.

"In short, my conduct has obtained for me the returns most grateful to my heart. I have had the happiness to give universal satisfaction to two great and enlightened nations which I have served. Of this I have received singular proofs. I am the only man in the world that possesses a sword given by the King of France. It is to me a glorious distinction to wear it; and, above all, to have received it as a proof of the particular esteem of a monarch so august,—a monarch who has declared himself the Protector of the rights of the human race, and who adds to this glorious title that of citizen! I have indelible proofs of the high consideration of the United States; but what completes my happiness is the esteem and friendship of the most virtuous of men, whose fame will be immortal; and that a Washington, a Franklin, a D'Estaing, a La Fayette, think the bust of Paul Jones worthy of being placed side by side with their own. It is then certain that this is not the bust of one *
* * * * * *

* In the mysterious and now perhaps inexplicable in-

"Since I am found too frank and too sincere to make my way at the Court of Russia without creating powerful enemies, I have philosophy enough to withdraw into the peaceful bosom of friendship; but, as I love virtue better than reward, and as my greatest ambition is to preserve,

---

trigue set on foot at the return of Paul Jones from the Liman, to ruin him personally in the good opinion of the Empress, for he had been professionally sacrificed before, it appears, by a passage following the above extravagant self-eulogium, (which we can only pardon in an indignant and persecuted man,) that accusations had been insinuated against him of a yet darker and more revolting character than the alleged murder of his nephew and the violation of a girl. Had not the latter calumny already been made public, as Paul Jones takes no notice of it in his Journal, we would scarce have polluted our pages by reference to it. The circumstance, however, has been noticed by Count Segur, and adverted to by the American biographer; and as we possess ample means from his papers, and the testimony of Segur and Littlepage, of establishing his innocence in this affair, it is noticed. Indeed this absurd charge died away before he left Russia, though stated by the historian of Catherine II. as the cause of his being driven from that country!

even in the shades of retreat, the precious favour of the Empress, I may tell her Majesty, that, even in the midst of my persecutions, my mind was occupied by plans for the essential advancement of her service, of which I gave some idea to her minister in June last (1789.) I have not entered into details, for there are politicians who before now have robbed me of my military plans. I have other projects in view from which the flag of Russia might derive new lustre, and which would cause but little expense to her Majesty at the outset, and perhaps nothing in the end, if I had the direction; for I would be able to make war support war. Whatever be the issue, I have the satisfaction of having done my duty in Russia, and that without any views of self-interest. It is affirmed, that, in general, strangers who come to Russia are adventurers in search of fortune, not having the means of living in their own country. I cannot say as to this; but I at least hope that the Empress will not class me with those.

"Briefly, I am satisfied with myself; and I have the happiness to know, that, though my enemies may not be converted into friends, my name will nevertheless be always respected by worthy men who know me; and it is to me a satisfaction and a signal triumph at the moment of my leaving Russia, that the public, and even the English in St Petersburgh, with whom I had no connexion, have now changed their sentiments in regard to me, give me their esteem, and regret my departure.

"St Petersburgh, 29th July, 1789."

END OF THE JOURNAL OF THE CAMPAIGN OF THE LIMAN.

CHAPTER II.

A BRIEF notice of Russian affairs is perhaps necessary to enable the reader to form a correct opinion of the conduct of Paul Jones during this period.

The whole history of the campaign, so far as it regards Paul Jones, is comprehended in the character of Potemkin. He had provoked the war with Turkey from motives that his extraordinary character render credible, though in relation to any other individual they would remain unworthy of belief. Already loaded with titles, honours, dignities, and crosses of almost all the European orders, he still secretly longed for the grand ribbon of the Order of St George, an order instituted by the Empress. To dismember the Ottoman empire still farther, and procure this distinction, a war was to be provoked by intrigues, bribery, and the promotion of intestine divisions in the Turkish dominions; and when all was prepared, by the insolence of the Russian envoys and consuls, and the barefaced violation of existing treaties, the discredit of actual aggression was artfully thrown on the Porte. Russia had already virtually made war, but the Turks first declared hostilities. The person to whom the conduct of the war on the part of Russia was confided,—Field-Marshal Prince Potemkin,—was one of the most extraordinary men of his own or of any age. If ever great genius be allied to madness it was so in the wildly-organized mind of Potemkin. The Prince de Ligne, who had closely examined his character, and Count de Segur, who long knew him intimately, and watched him strictly, have both left portraits of this singular personage, which, though French in their tone and colouring, give a tolerable idea of the *exterior* of the man on whose interests and caprices the fate of the Russian empire as well as of Paul Jones depended. Neither the acute Austrian, de Ligne, nor the manners-seizing Frenchman, de Segur, held, however, a plummet-line of sufficient length to sound all the depths of Potemkin's character.

The Prince de Ligne saw a great deal of "the Prince," as he was called, during the stately progress of the Empress in 1787, and afterwards at head-quarters during the campaign of 1788. His sketch of an unparalleled original, which was written exactly at the time when Potemkin was in daily contact with Paul Jones, commences thus:—"I here behold a commander-in-chief who looks idle and is always busy; who has no other desk than his knees, no other comb than his fingers; constantly reclining on his couch, yet sleeping neither in the night nor in day-time. His zeal for the Empress he adores keeps him incessantly awake and uneasy; and a cannon-shot, to which he himself is not exposed, disturbs him with the idea, that it costs the life of some of his soldiers; trembling for others, brave for himself; stopping under the hottest fire of a battery to give orders, yet more an *Ulysses* than an *Achilles*; alarmed at the approach of danger, frolicksome when it surrounds him; dull in the midst of pleasure; unhappy in being too fortunate; surfeited with every thing; easily disgusted, morose, inconstant; a profound philosopher, an able minister, a sublime politician, or like a child of ten years of age; not revengeful; asking pardon for a pain he has inflicted; quickly repairing an injustice; thinking he loves God when he fears the devil, whom he fancies still greater and bigger than himself; waving one hand to the females that please him, and with the other making the sign of the cross; embracing the feet of a statue of the Virgin, or the alabaster neck of his mistress; receiving numberless presents from his sovereign, and distributing them immediately to others; accepting estates of the Empress and returning them, or paying her debts without her knowledge."* The

* This is pure fiction. Potemkin would never, if possible, pay his own debts. When any one came to demand payment, Popoff his secretary was asked why that man was not paid? but, by a preconcerted signal, (the Prince closing his hand,) the secretary was given to understand that no payment was intended to be made: when, on the contrary, he opened his hand, which was more rarely, the debt was to be discharged. The Empress had often paid his debts. His rapacity exceeded his profusion.

Prince de Ligne proceeds in the same strain of antithesis:—“ Gambling from morn to night, or not at all; preferring prodigality in giving to regularity in paying; prodigiously rich, and not worth a farthing; abandoning himself to distrust or to confidence, to jealousy or to gratitude, to ill-humour or to pleasantry; talking divinity to his generals and tactics to his bishops; never reading, but sifting every one with whom he converses, and contradicting to be better informed; uncommonly affable or extremely savage; affecting the most attractive or the most repulsive manners; appearing by turns the proudest satrap of the East, or the most polished courtier of Louis XIV.; concealing under the appearance of harshness the greatest benevolence of heart; whimsical with regard to time, repasts, rest, and inclinations; like a child, wanting to have every thing, or like a great man, knowing how to do without many things; sober, though seemingly a glutton; gnawing his fingers, or apples and turnips; scolding or laughing; mimicking or swearing; engaged in wantonness or prayers; singing or meditating; calling or dismissing; sending for twenty aides-de-camp, and saying nothing to any of them; bearing heat better than any man, while he seems to think of nothing but the most voluptuous baths; not caring for cold, though he appears unable to exist without furs; always in his shirt without drawers, or in rich regimentals embroidered on all the seams; barefoot, or in slippers embroidered with spangles; wearing neither hat nor cap; it is thus I saw him once in the midst of a musket-fire. Sometimes in a night-gown; sometimes in a splendid tunic, with his three stars, his orders, and diamonds as large as a thumb round the portrait of the Empress,—they seemed placed there to attract the balls;—crooked and almost bent double when he is at home; and tall, erect, proud, handsome, noble, majestic, or fascinating, when he shows himself to the army, like *Agamemnon* in the midst of the monarchs of Greece. What, then, is his magic?—Genius, natural abilities, an excellent memory, and much elevation of soul; malice without the design of injuring; artifice without craft; a happy mixture of caprices; the art of conquering every heart in his good moments; much generosity, graciousness, and justice in his rewards; a refined or correct taste; the talent of guessing what he is ignorant of; and a consummate knowledge of mankind.'

This sketch is rather the eulogium than the true character of Potemkin. He had originally been the favourite of the Empress, from which thraldom he alone, of her numerous lovers, passed into the possession of greater political power than was enjoyed by any other man in Russia. Till his death he remained master of the destinies of the empire, and retained a paramount influence over the mind of Catharine. He held every office of importance in the state. It was even whispered, that, after the death of her favourite, Lanskoi, Catharine gave her hand in secret to Potemkin. This was doubted at the time, and, at all events, made no change in the mode of life of the Empress or the Prince. It was he, in general, who either chose or recommended the favourites that appeared in rapid succession. A part of his revenue was a hundred thousand roubles from the Empress, and the same sum from the new favourite, as often as this office was changed.

The portrait left of this extraordinary person by Count Segur, if not exact, approaches more nearly to a true likeness than the epigrammatic sketch of De Ligne :—" Prince Gregory Alexandrovitch Potemkin was," says Segur, " one of the most extraordinary men of his times; but, in order to have played so conspicuous a part, he must have been in Russia, and have lived in the reign of Catharine II. In any other country, in any other times, with any other sovereign, he would have been misplaced; and it was a singular stroke of chance that created this man for the period that tallied with him, and brought together and combined all the circumstances with which he could tally.

" In his person were collected the most opposite defects and advantages of every kind. He was avaricious and ostentatious, despotic and popular, inflexible and beneficent, haughty and obliging, politic and confiding, licentious and superstitious, bold and timid, ambitious and indiscreet. Lavish of his bounties to his relations, his mistresses, and his favourites, yet frequently paying neither his household nor his creditors. His consequence always depended on a woman; and he was always unfaithful to her. Nothing could equal the activity of his mind, nor the indolence of his body. No dangers could appal his courage; no difficulties force him to abandon his projects. But the success of an enterprise always brought on disgust.

"He wearied the empire by the number of his posts and the extent of his power. He was himself fatigued with the burthen of his existence; envious of all that he did not do, and sick of all that he did. Rest was not grateful to him, nor occupation pleasing. Every thing with him was desultory; business, pleasure, temper, carriage. In every company he had an embarrassed air, and his presence was a restraint on every company. He was morose to all that stood in awe of him, and caressed all such as accosted him with familiarity.

"Ever promising, seldom keeping his word, and never forgetting any thing. None had read less than he; few people were better informed.

He had talked with the skilful in all professions, in all the sciences, in every art. None better knew how to draw forth and appropriate to himself the knowledge of others. In conversation he would have astonished a scholar, an artist, an artisan, and a divine. His information was not deep, but it was very extensive. He never dived into a subject, but he spoke well on all subjects.

"The inequality of his temper was productive of an inconceivable oddity in his desires, in his conduct, and in his manner of life. One while he formed the project of becoming Duke of Courland; at another he thought of bestowing on himself the crown of Poland. He frequently gave intimations of an intention to make himself a bishop or even a simple monk. He built a superb palace, and wanted to sell it before it was finished. One day he would dream of nothing but war; and only officers, Tartars, and Cossacks, were admitted to him; the next day he was busied only with politics; he would partition the Ottoman empire, and put in agitation all the cabinets of Europe. At other times, with nothing in his head but the court, dressed in a magnificent suit, covered with ribbons presented him by every potentate, displaying diamonds of extraordinary magnitude and brilliance, he was giving superb entertainments without any occasion.

"He was sometimes known for a month, and in the face of all the town, to pass whole evenings at the apartments of a young female, seeming to have alike forgot all business and all decorum. Sometimes also, for several weeks successively, shut up in his room with his nieces and several men of his intimates, he would lounge on a sofa, without speaking, playing at chess, or at cards, with his legs bare, his shirt-collar unbuttoned, in a morning-gown, with a thoughful front, his eyebrows knit, and presenting to the view of strangers who came to see him the figure of a rough and squalid Cossack.

"All these singularities often put the Empress out of humour, but rendered him more interesting to her. In his youth he had pleased her by the ardour of his passion, by his valour, and by his masculine beauty. Being arrived at maturity, he charmed her still by flattering her pride, by calming her apprehensions, by confirming her power, by cherishing her fancies of oriental empire, the expulsion of the barbarians, and the restoration of the Grecian republics.

" At eighteen, an under officer in the horse-guards, on the day of the revolution, he persuaded his corps to take arms, and presented to Catharine his cockade as an ornament for her sword. Soon after, become the rival of Orloff, he performed for his sovereign whatever the most romantic passion could inspire. He put out his eye to free it from a blemish which diminished his beauty. Banished by his rival, he ran to meet death in battle, and returned with glory. A successful lover, he quickly shook off the hypocritical farce, whose catastrophe held out to him the prospect of an obscure destiny. He himself gave favourites to his mistress, and became her confidant, her friend, her general, and her minister.

" Panin was president of the council, and was a stickler for the alliance of Prussia. Potemkin persuaded his mistress that the friendship of the Emperor would be of more use to her in realizing her plans against the Turks. He connected her with Joseph II., and thereby furnished himself with the means of conquering the Crimea and the country of the Nogay Tartars, which depended upon it. Restoring to these regions their sonorous and ancient names, creating a maritime force at Cherson and Sevastopole, he persuaded Catharine to come and admire herself this new scene of his glory. Nothing was spared for rendering this journey renowned to the latest posterity. Thither were conveyed, from all parts of the empire, money, provisions, and horses. The highways were illuminated. The Borysthenes was covered with magnificent galleys. A hundred and fifty thousand soldiers were newly equipped. The Cossacks were brought together; the Tartars were disciplined. Deserts were peopled for the occasion; and palaces were raised in the trackless wild. The nakedness of the plains of the Crimea was disguised by villages built on purpose, and enlivened by fireworks. Chains of mountains were illuminated. Fine roads were opened by the army. Howling wildernesses were transformed into English gardens. The King of Poland came to pay homage to her who had crowned him, and who afterwards struck him from the throne. The Emperor Joseph II. came himself to attend the triumphal progress of the Empress Catharine; and the result of this brilliant journey was another war, which the English and the Prussians impolitically instigated the Turks to undertake, and which was only a fresh instrument to the ambition of Potemkin, by affording him an occasion to conquer Oczakow, which remained to Russia, and to obtain the grand ribbon of St George, the only decoration that was wanting to his vanity. But these latter triumphs were the term of his life. He died in Moldavia, almost by a sudden stroke; and his death, lamented by his nieces and by a small number of friends, concerned only his rivals, who were eager to divide his spoils, and was very soon followed by a total oblivion.

" Like the rapid passage of those shining meteors which astonish us by their lustre, but are empty as air, Potemkin began every thing, completed nothing, disordered the finances, disorganized the army, depopulated his country, and enriched it with other deserts. The fame of the

Empress was increased by his conquests. The admiration they excited was for her; and the hatred they raised for her minister. Posterity, more equitable, will perhaps divide between them both the glory of the successes and the severity of the reproaches. It will not bestow on Potemkin the title of a great man; but it will mention him as an extraordinary person: and, to draw his picture with accuracy, he might be represented as a real emblem, as the living image of the Russian empire.

"For, in fact, he was colossal like Russia. In his mind, as in that country, were cultivated districts and desert plains. It also partook of the Asiatic, of the European, of the Tartarian, and the Cossack; the rudeness of the eleventh century, and the corruption of the eighteenth; the polish of the arts, and the ignorance of the cloisters; an outside of civilization, and many traces of barbarism. In a word, if we might hazard so bold a metaphor, even his two eyes, the one open, and the other closed, reminded us of the Euxine always open, and the Northern ocean, so long shut up with ice.

"This portrait may appear gigantic; but those who knew Potemkin will bear witness to its truth. That man had great defects; but without them, perhaps, he would neither have got the mastery of his sovereign, nor that of his country. He was made by chance precisely such as he ought to be for preserving so long his power over so extraordinary a woman."*

Segur might have added, that this Russian hero was as artful as his impetuous passions permitted; vindictive, rapacious, and self-willed, to a degree which denoted actual frenzy. When young, and though a favourite not yet quite established in the good graces of the Empress, he was, after a quarrel with her favourites, the Orloffs, in which he lost an eye, sent to serve under Field-Marshal Romantzoff. This distinguished commander treated him with civility, praised his military conduct to the Empress, but gave him neither his confidence nor esteem. The haughty Potemkin felt the

---

* Life of Catharine II., Empress of Russia, vol. iii. p. 326—333.

humiliation, and never forgave the man, of whom he really had nothing to complain. He engaged in a despicable intrigue to ruin the Countess Bruce, for no other reason than that she had the misfortune to be the sister of the man he hated, and who disdained to cringe before him. Paul Jones complains that his officers were not promoted during one campaign. The officers of Romantzoff were kept from advancement for fourteen successive years, and the Field-Marshal himself retired at last in chagrin and disgust. It was no unfrequent thing for Potemkin to strike the Russian officers that were about him, though he did not venture to display the same vivacity of temper to foreigners. He sometimes, in the headlong impulse of rage, struck even the native nobility. Field-officers were frequently sent by him from the Crimea, and from places as distant, for a dish of a particular kind of fish-soup, which cost him three hundred roubles; or to St Petersburgh or Riga for a few oysters or oranges. He at one period compelled the Empress to dismiss one of her favourites, (recommended by himself some time before,) at the same instant that she ventured to expostulate with him for having struck the uncle of this young man. He ordered her to "dismiss that white negro, (the favourite Yermoloff,) or he would never again set his foot within the palace,"—and the Empress obeyed! Yermoloff was at the same moment sent on his travels. To Paul Jones he had emphatically said, "None led him—not even the Empress!" He was exceedingly indignant at the Swedish war, which interfered with his views on the Ottoman empire. He termed it an old woman's war. When Catharine wrote him an account of the hasty preparations she had made to repel the Swedes who were approaching her frontier, she inquires, with the good humour which never deserted her, "Have I done right, my master?" This was less a jesting expression than her Majesty probably imagined. The end of this semi-barbarian is not a little edifying. Satiated and disgusted with wealth, honours, conquest, and luxury, in the latter years of his life he would sit, throughout a long winter evening, alone, spreading out his diamonds on a black velvet cloth kept for this purpose, and arranging them in different figures, as crosses, stars, &c., weighing them, or passing them from hand to hand, like a child playing with cherry-stones, though certainly with not half the enjoyment. He would often pass a couple of hours gnawing his nails in gloomy silence, while he paced a saloon filled with mute company, his presence carrying dismay and blighting wherever he appeared. When attacked by the lingering fever which terminated his days in his fifty-second year, he disdained the advice of the court physicians despatched to him by the Empress, and continued to eat and drink with his ordinary intemperance. His usual breakfast at this time was a smoked goose, with a large quantity of wine and spirits. He dined in the same manner. His appetites were all extravagant and irregular, and indulged to excess. With fever raging in his blood, he determined to leave Yassy, whither he had gone to attend a congress with the agents of the Porte. He fancied the air of this place disagreed with him, and determined to go to Nicolayef, one of the towns he had built. He had not proceeded many miles, when he became so ill that his attendants lifted him from his carriage.

He threw himself on the grass, and died under a tree! This was in October 1791. The wonders told of his riches, his estates, his gold, his diamonds, the splendour of his Tauridan Palace, and the magnificence of his fetes, resemble the enchantments of an oriental tale. Like his coadjutor, Suwarrow, Prince Potemkin was what they were pleased to think, or call, religious. Suwarrow never massacred ten or twenty thousand of his fellow-creatures in cold blood without returning thanks to Heaven, and giving glory for the achievement. Potemkin, for a Russian, could not be called cruel, but he was as superstitious as the meanest of his soldiers. At one time he affected extreme sanctity and mortification of life, and even threatened to turn monk. This was for a political purpose, and the grossest hypocrisy. But his superstition was unaffected. He regarded himself as the peculiar favourite of Heaven, and had great faith in his own good fortune. The first success over the Turkish fleet in the campaign of 1788 was gained, as he boasted to the Prince de Ligne, on the festival day of his patron, St Gregory,—" Heaven had not forgotten him." Oczakow was stormed and carried on some other saint's day. The Prince of Nassau, the person with whom Paul Jones was in immediate competition, was a man of much feebler character. A sketch of his career in Russia is the strongest corroboration that the Journal of Rear-Admiral Jones can receive.

The Prince of Nassau Siegen was fickle, arrogant, and of mean capacity. Paul Jones frequently throws doubts on his personal courage; but a man whose whole life was spent in search of wild military adventures, and who continually exposed himself to personal danger, could scarcely have been a coward. Nassau proposed to accompany Jones in the secret expedition against England in 1779, and had abruptly abandoned the scheme without explanation or apology, and without even deigning to reply to the frequent letters which the disappointed Commodore addressed to him. He had served in the unfortunate attempt of the French on the island of Jersey, and in the futile attack of the combined powers of France and Spain at Gibraltar. On the breaking out of the war with Turkey he entered the Russian service. He had previously joined the Empress, along with Potemkin, on her celebrated progress to the Crimea, and was rather a favourite with both of those personages. He obtained the command in the Black Sea, and on the arrival of Jones, there is little doubt that the rival commanders viewed each other with mutual jealousy. In an affair which took place on the 29th July, which Paul Jones has not mentioned, the Prince of Nassau, waiting in vain for orders, and at last acting without them, had the good fortune to support Prince Anhalt in a very pressing emergency, and to save a Russian battery. In his report to Potemkin, he boastingly apologizes "for having advanced with three gun-boats, and forced the Turks to retire, without orders."

The reason of his withdrawing from the Liman before the end of the campaign is thus related: —The supineness of Potemkin in conducting the siege of Oczakow was the subject of much animadversion, and at last of great discontent in the army. For months he lay as if spell-bound in his camp, surrounded by the females and others, ministers of his luxury and pleasure, that accompanied him everywhere, displaying all the eccentricity and caprice of his character more extravagantly than he had ever done before. It is alleged that he was employed all this while in private intrigues to corrupt the Turkish garrison, which he expected to capitulate without bloodshed. In the meanwhile many lives had been lost in sorties and abortive assaults, as well as in the amphibious warfare of the Liman. In a council of war held to concert a decisive plan of attack, Nassau offered, "if he might be intrusted with the operation, to effect a breach in a weak part of the fortress which he had discovered, and which should be large enough to admit a whole regiment." Potemkin, offended by this vain boast, and never, as he afterwards said to Paul Jones, "deceived by Nassau," sarcastically asked him "how many breaches he had made at Gibraltar?" Nassau, offended in his turn, solicited the Empress for his recall. He was accordingly employed in the North Seas, with little honour to himself and great loss to the arms of Russia. In the following year he presented the

Empress with a plan of driving the British from India drawn up by a Frenchman, M. St Genie, whom he patronized. The Empress was at first quite captivated with a scheme, doubly welcome from being brought forward at the very time England was fitting out an armament which was to act in the Baltic, and thus force her to make peace with the Porte. Potemkin, who had been enraged with the Swedish, or, as he called it, "the old woman's war," which interfered with his operations on the Euxine, treated this wild plan of marching a Russian army to Bengal with the derision and contempt it merited. Nassau, however, still maintained a certain degree of favour with the Empress. This was shown in a remarkable instance. By an injudicious and very ill-managed attack of the galley-fleet, which he commanded, on that which was commanded by Gustavus III., his fleet, though twice as large, was completely defeated, with the loss of the one-half of his vessels. His excessive arrogance was not quelled even by witnessing the disastrous consequences of his own ignorance and temerity. His vanity led him to imagine that the Russians had yielded to this very inferior Swedish force merely to " tarnish his glory." He accordingly thus insolently announced his disgraceful reverse to the Empress:—" Madam, I have had the misfortune to fight against the Swedes, the elements, and the Russians. I hope your Majesty will do me justice." To this extraordinary note the Empress replied, " You are in the right, because I am resolved you shall be so. This is highly aristocratic, but it is therefore suitable to the country in which we live. Depend always on your affectionate Catharine."

Assisted by the counsels of several able naval officers of different countries, Nassau, before this time, had gained a victory over the Swedish fleet. This signal defeat, which soon produced peace, was deeply felt by the Empress, however bravely she carried it; and the Prince of Nassau, though loaded with honours, presented with a town-palace in St Petersburgh, an estate, numerous peasants, and a pension of twelve thousand roubles, saw his favour decline, and afterwards entered the service of Prussia. His conduct in the Swedish campaigns affords, as was said, a strong corroboration of the statements of Paul Jones:—guided by abler men, he succeeded,—left to himself, he rushed on destruction.

It is now time to resume the regular course of the memoir, which left Paul Jones re-entering St Petersburgh.

CHAPTER III.

It was under very different circumstances from those which attended his first triumphal entry about eight months before, that Jones returned to the Russian capital. He, however, had still sufficient credit at court to obtain an audience of the Empress, at which he delivered the letter of Potemkin. A few flattering promises were made to him by Count de Besborodko, and he immediately began his ordinary practice of transmitting plans and projects, both diplomatic and military.

While he hung on thus, vainly soliciting employment, the infamous conspiracy alluded to at page 114 was formed against his character and fortune, and threatening even his life, the object of which is easily traced, though the precise motives in which it originated, and the persons who imagined an interest in devising it, were never clearly ascertained, even by the persecuted individual himself. The information on this subject which he procured long afterwards, and which will be laid before the reader in the proper place, though plausible, is neither satisfactory nor supported by much evidence. In his future correspondence, Jones hints that he has reason to impute this most infamous proceeding, if not directly to English influence, at least to the desire of propitiating the English by the sacrifice of an individual so obnoxious as he, somewhat gratuitously, supposed himself to be to that nation. His self-complacence had, on former occasions, seduced him into the belief that the whole British nation were his active enemies, and that his prowess was never to be forgotten nor forgiven. More recently he imagined that his reception at the northern courts had been the subject of deep mortification to such of the English as happened to be at Copenhagen or St Petersburgh. At the court of Denmark he had driven Mr Elliot into despair and solitude; and with the English at St Petersburgh it fared little better.* A few English

* Had the truth of the statement regarding Mr Elliot

naval officers in Russia did indeed raise some obstacle to serving with the celebrated Paul Jones, from a sense of honour and a spirit of professional

---

not been tacitly admitted by the biographer of Jones, it would scarcely be worth notice here. It is but one instance of thousands, of men otherwise very acute, becoming the dupes of their own self-esteem. Jones was well received at the Danish Court, and was even soothed by a promised pension; but the ministers of England had carried their point regarding the prizes during eight years; while the government of Denmark, to flatter England, had contrived to elude every American negotiator, Jones and Franklin included. The chagrin of Mr Elliot at the distinguished reception of the American agent could not probably be very deep, while he saw that the American business was not one jot advanced. The conduct of the Court of Denmark in relation to Paul Jones, the pension included, was exactly what is understood by the vulgar phrase, "too civil by half." It is thus he writes of Mr Elliot's distress:—"I must tell you (La Fayette) that Mr Elliot was furious when he found my business at Copenhagen, and that I was received with great distinction at court, and in all the best societies in Denmark. Every time I was invited to sup with the King, Elliot made an apology; he shut himself up for more than a month, and then left town. This occasioned much laughter: and, as he had shunned society from the time of my arrival, etiquette; but as their destination was the Cronstadt fleet, where Admiral Greig commanded, and as Jones was sent to the Black Sea, this soon passed away.*

---

people said he had gone off in a fright!" He adds, "Elliot had influenced the English to put difficulties in the way of my passage by the Baltic," meaning on his voyage to Russia.

* The Life of the Empress Catharine II., (a book that has long been popular, and which is esteemed authentic,) is full of inaccuracies as far as regards Paul Jones, and indeed in many other particulars. It is stated that he was appointed to a command in the Cronstadt fleet, but that this was withdrawn, as the British officers, to the number of thirty, and without a single exception, remonstrated, "considering this appointment as the highest affront that could be offered them, and a submission to it an act of degradation, that no time nor circumstances could wipe away." They accordingly agreed to "lay down their commissions, declaring it was impossible for them to serve under or to act in any manner or capacity whatever, with a pirate or a renegade." It is to be remembered, that this was six years after the peace with the colonies. The whole passage may as well be given at once. It will then require but one refutation. "The

To Russia, and Russians alone, belong the entire infamy of a conspiracy to ruin a stranger who, it is enough to say, had incurred the dis-

---

appointment of Paul Jones to a command in the Cronstadt fleet," says this work, " was recalled, and that adventurer, whose character for an impetuous courage had made an impression on the court far beyond its value, was ordered to the armament in the Euxine, as second to the Prince of Nassau. In the meantime a report was raised of a scandalous adventure with a girl, which, making a noise in the town, (St Petersburgh,) occasioned him to quit the country entirely." The same work goes on to state that Paul Jones, though " brave at sea, was a coward on shore,—that he more than once refused to accept a challenge, and was handsomely caned on the Exchange of Philadelphia." Moreover, that " he was extremely ignorant, and that his desperate courage only served to render his atrociousness more conspicuous." Now all this is contained in a well-known work, generally esteemed authentic, and of which the fourth edition, printed only eight years after the death of Paul Jones, lies before us. Where then shall we look for truth? According to this writer, Paul Jones never actually served in Russia at all, but was driven from the country by the shame of his vices, before he had joined pleasure of Potemkin. In every despotic court, but especially in that of St Petersburgh, political intriguers will never want servile instruments to forward their basest and darkest purposes. In the present case these instruments were found of all ranks, though but of one nation.

The nature of this disgraceful affair, of which, but for the interference of Count Segur, and it

---

the fleet on the Black Sea. The reader is aware, that, however apprehensive the British officers might be, Jones never was intended to command in the Cronstadt fleet, then so ably conducted by Admiral Greig, supported by other English officers, and also by Danes and Italians. The courier of Potemkin was despatched to forward him at once to the Liman, as appears by M. Simolin's letter at page 330, vol. I. In the Life of Potemkin, his appearance in the important campaign of 1788, and the support he afforded to the Prince of Nassau, are distinctly stated. It was well known to all Europe. How a man possessed "of desperate courage at sea," finds his courage ooze out at his finger-ends on shore, is a phenomenon beyond ordinary comprehension. As we have extenuated no act of Paul Jones which merited reprehension, we must be excused for noticing what is here set down either in wilful malice or unpardonable ignorance.

might be from some latent dread of public opinion in France and America, Jones must have become the victim, will be sufficiently explained by the following letter, addressed to Prince Potemkin, after the unhappy writer had been forbidden to appear at court, and also by an extract which we shall give from the Memoirs of Count Segur :—

Rear-Admiral Paul Jones to Prince Potemkin.

"St Petersburgh, 13th April, 1789.

"My Lord,—Having had the advantage to serve under your orders, and in your sight, I remember, with particular satisfaction, the kind promises and testimonies of your friendship with which you have honoured me. As I have served all my life for honour, I had no other motive for accepting the flattering invitation of her Imperial Majesty, than a laudable ambition to distinguish myself in the service of a sovereign so magnanimous and illustrious; for I never yet have bent the knee to self-interest, nor drawn my sword for hire. A few days ago I thought myself one of the happiest men in the empire!

Your Highness had renewed to me your promise of friendship, and the Empress had assigned me a command of a nature to occupy the most active and enterprising genius.

"A bad woman has accused me of violating her daughter! If she had told the truth, I should have candour enough to own it, and would trust my honour, which is a thousand times dearer to me than my life, to the mercy of the Empress. I declare, with an assurance becoming a military character, that I am innocent. Till that unhappy moment, I have enjoyed the public esteem, and the affection of all who knew me. Shall it be said that in Russia a wretched woman, who *eloped* from her *husband* and *family* in the country, *stole away her daughter*, lives here in a house of bad fame, and leads a debauched and adulterous life, has found credit enough on a simple complaint, unsupported *by any proof*, to affect the honour of a General Officer of reputation, who has merited and received the decorations of America, of France, and of this empire!

"If I had been favoured with the least intimation of a complaint of that nature having found its way to the Sovereign, I know too well what belongs to delicacy to have presented myself in the presence of the Empress before my justification.

"My servant was kept prisoner by the officers of police for several hours, two days successively, and threatened with the knout.

"After the examination of my people before the police, I sent for and employed Monsieur Crimpin as my advocate. As the mother had addressed herself to him before to plead her cause, she naturally spoke to him without reserve, and he learned from her a number of important facts, among others, that she was counselled and supported by a distinguished man of the court.

"By the certificate of the father, attested by the pastor of the colony, the daughter is several years older than is expressed in the complaint. And the complaint contains various other points equally false and easy to be refuted. For instance there is a conversation I am said to have held with the daughter in the Russian language, of which no person ever heard me pronounce two words together,—it is unknown to me.

"I thought that in every country a man accused had a right to employ advocates, and to avail himself of his friends for his justification. Judge, my Prince, of my astonishment and distress of mind, when I yesterday was informed that the day before, the Governor of the city had sent for my advocate, and forbidden *him*, at his peril, or *any other person*, to meddle with *my cause!*

"I am innocent before God! and my conscience knows no reproach. The complaint brought against me is an infamous lie, and there is no circumstance that gives it even an air of probability.

"I address myself to you with confidence, my Prince, and am assured that the friendship you have so kindly promised me will be immediately exerted in my favour; and that you will not suffer the illustrious Sovereign of this great empire to be misled by the false insinuations and secret cabals of my hidden enemies. Your mind will find more true pleasure in pleading the cause of an innocent man whom you honour with your friendship, than can result from other victories equally glorious with that of Oczakow, which will always rank among the most brilliant of military achievements. If your Highness will condescend to question Monsieur Crimpin, (for he dare not now *even speak to me*,) he can tell you many circumstances which will elucidate my innocence. I am, with profound respect, my Lord, your Highness's devoted and most obedient servant," &c. &c.

The document referred to in this letter appears quite satisfactory. It is a declaration by the husband of the woman.

"I certify, that my wife, Fredrica Sophia Koltzwarthen, has left me without any reason; that she has been living in the city with a young man; and that she has clandestinely, and against my will, taken away my daughter Catherine Charlotte, who is now living with her.

"STEPHEN KOLTZWARTHEN.

"Saratowka, 7th April, 1789."

"I certify, that this is the free and voluntary declaration of Stephen Koltzwarthen, and that it is he who has signed it. "G. BRAUN, *Pastor*.

"Saratowka, 7th April, 1789."

"I certify, that my daughter is twelve years of age. STEPHEN KOLTZWARTHEN.

"Saratowka, 7th April, 1789."

"I certify, that Stephen Koltzwarthen has signed what is above written.

"G. BRAUN, *Pastor*."

"*Declaration of the Pastor Lamp of St Petersburgh.*

"I certify, that the name of Koltzwarthen does not at present appear in the roll of those in the communion of the church, and that, previous to the day when she came to my house about the affair of her daughter, I had never seen her.

"J. LAMP, *Pastor*."

The result of this letter to Potemkin does not appear; and any further information concerning this affair must be sought in the Memoirs of Count Segur. It was peculiarly fortunate for Jones that this nobleman, a high-minded and generous individual, of an honourable and a gallant nation, was at this time in Petersburgh. He at once came forward with warmth and intrepidity in defence of the persecuted stranger.

"Paul Jones," he says, "a sharer in the victories of the Prince of Nassau, had returned to Petersburgh; his enemies, unable to bear the triumph of a man whom they treated as a vagabond, a rebel, and a corsair, resolved to destroy him.

"This atrocity, which ought to be imputed to some envious cowards, was, I think, very unjustly attributed to the English officers in the Russian navy, and to the merchants who were their countrymen. These, in truth, did not disguise their animosity against Paul Jones; but it would be unjust to affix upon all a base intrigue, which was, perhaps, but the work of two or three persons, who have continued unknown.

"The American Rear-Admiral was favourably welcomed at Court; often invited to dinner by the Empress, and received with distinction into the best society in the city; on a sudden, Catharine commanded him to appear no more in her presence.

"He was informed that he was accused of an

infamous crime; of assaulting a young girl of fourteen, of grossly violating her; and that probably, after some preliminary information, he would be tried by the Courts of Admiralty, in which there were many English officers, who were strongly prejudiced against him.

"As soon as this order was known, every one abandoned the unhappy American; no one spoke to him, people avoided saluting him, and every door was shut against him. All those by whom but yesterday he had been eagerly welcomed, now fled from him as if he had been infected with a plague; besides, no advocate would take charge of his cause, and no public man would consent to listen to him; at last even his servants would not continue in his service; and Paul Jones, whose exploits every one had so recently been ready to proclaim, and whose friendship had been sought after, found himself alone in the midst of an immense population: Petersburgh, a great capital, became to him a desert.

"I went to see him; he was moved even to tears by my visit. 'I was unwilling,' he said to me, shaking me by the hand, 'to knock at your door, and to expose myself to a fresh affront, which would have been more cutting than all the rest. I have braved death a thousand times, now I wish for it.' His appearance, his arms being laid upon the table, made me suspect some desperate intention.

" 'Resume,' I said to him, 'your composure and your courage. Do you not know that human life, like the sea, has its storms, and that fortune is even more capricious than the winds? If, as I hope, you are innocent, brave this sudden tempest; if, unhappily, you are guilty, confess it to me with unreserved frankness, and I will do every thing I can to snatch you, by a sudden flight, from the danger which threatens you.'

" 'I swear to you upon my honour,' said he, 'that I am innocent, and a victim of the most infamous calumny. This is the truth.—Some days since a young girl came to me in the morning, to ask me if I could give her some linen or lace to mend. She then indulged in some rather earnest and indecent allurements. Astonished at so much boldness in one of such few years, I felt compassion for her; I advised her not to enter upon so vile a career, gave her some money, and dismissed her; but she was determined to remain.

" 'Impatient at this resistance, I took her by the hand and led her to the door; but, at the instant when the door was opened, the little profligate tore her sleeves and her neck-kerchief, raised great cries, complained that I had assaulted her, and threw herself into the arms of an old woman, whom she called her mother, and who, certainly, was not brought there by chance. The mother and the daughter raised the house with their cries, went out and denounced me; and now you know all.'

" 'Very well,' I said, 'but cannot you learn the names of those adventurers?' 'The porter knows them,' he replied. 'Here are their names written down, but I do not know where they live. I was desirous of immediately presenting a memorial about this ridiculous affair, first to the minister, and then to the Empress; but I have been interdicted from access to both of them.' 'Give me the paper,' I said; 'resume your accustomed firmness;—be comforted;—let me undertake it;—in a short time we shall meet again.'

"As soon as I had returned home, I directed some sharp and intelligent agents, who were devoted to me, to get information respecting these suspected females, and to find out what was their mode of life. I was not long in learning that the old woman was in the habit of carrying on a vile traffic in young girls, whom she passed off as her daughters.

"When I was furnished with all the documents and attestations for which I had occasion, I hastened to show them to Paul Jones. 'You have nothing more to fear,' said I; 'the wretches are unmasked. It is only necessary to open the eyes of the Empress, and let her see how unworthily she has been deceived; but this is not so very easy: truth encounters a multitude of people at the doors of a palace, who are very clever in arresting its progress; and sealed letters are, of all others, those which are intercepted with the greatest art and care.

"'Nevertheless, I know that the Empress, who is not ignorant of this, has directed, under very heavy penalties, that no one shall detain on the way any letters which are addressed to her personally, and which may be sent to her by post; therefore, here is a very long letter which I have written to her in your name; nothing of the detail is omitted, although it contains some rough expressions. I am sorry for the Empress; but since she heard and gave credit to a calumny, it is but right that she should read the justification with patience. Copy this letter, sign it, and I will take charge of it; I will send some one to put it in the post at the nearest town. Take courage; believe me, your triumph is not doubtful.'

"In fact, the letter was sent and put in the post; the Empress received it; and, after having read this memorial, which was fully explanatory, and accompanied by undeniable attestations, she inveighed bitterly against the informers, revoked her rigorous orders, recalled Paul Jones to court, and received him with her usual kindness.

"That brave seaman enjoyed with a becoming pride a reparation which was due to him; but he trusted very little to the compliments that were unblushingly heaped upon him by the many persons who had fled from him in his disgrace; and, shortly afterwards, disgusted with a country where the fortune of a man may be exposed to such humiliations, under the pretence of ill health, he asked leave of the Empress to retire, which she granted him, as well as an honourable order and a suitable pension.

"He took leave, after having expressed to me his gratitude for the service which I had rendered him; and his respect for the Sovereign, who, although she might be led into an error, knew at least how to make an honourable reparation for a fault and an act of injustice."

This account is substantially correct. There are some petty errors of detail, but nothing whatever to detract from the noble spirit of generosity in which Count Segur acted to an unfortunate and ill-treated man.

A letter to the Empress, which is still among those papers of Paul Jones which he so carefully collected and preserved, cannot be that alluded to by Count Segur; it has every internal mark of his own authorship; and as it is one of his *pièces justificatives*, we are inclined to believe it the letter really sent to the Empress:—

(Translation.)

"*Letter of Rear-Admiral Paul Jones to the Empress of all the Russias.*

"St Petersburgh, 17th May, 1789.

"MADAM,—I have never served but for honour, I have never sought but glory, and I believed I was in the way of obtaining both, when, accepting the offers made me on the part of your Majesty, I entered your service. I was in America when M. de Simolin, through Mr Jefferson, Minister of the United States at Paris, proposed to me, in name of your Majesty, to take the chief command of the forces in the Black Sea, which were intended to act against the Turks. I abandoned my dearest interests to accept an invitation so flattering, and I would have reached you instantly if the United States had not intrusted me with a special commission to Denmark. Of this I acquitted myself faithfully and promptly." Here follows a detail of that singular voyage performed by the Chevalier in his haste and zeal to reach St Petersburgh, with the particulars of which the reader is already acquainted. We pass this, and resume:—"The distinguished reception which your Majesty deigned to grant me, the kindness with which you loaded me, indemnified me for the dangers to which I had exposed myself for your service, and inspired me with the most ardent desire to encounter more. But knowing mankind, and aware that those persons whom their superiors distinguish and protect are ever the objects of jealousy and envy to the worthless, I entreated your Majesty never to condemn me unheard. You condescended to give me that promise, and I set out with a mind as tranquil as my heart was satisfied.

"In the ports of the Black Sea I found affairs in a very critical condition. The most imminent danger threatened us, and our means were feeble. Neverthless, supported by the love which all your subjects bear to your Majesty, by their courage, by the ability and foresight of the chief who led us, and by the Providence which has always favoured the arms of your Majesty, we beat your enemies, and your flag was covered with fresh laurels.

"I would not notice, Madam, what I then achieved, if Prince Potemkin had not distinguished my services by reiterated thanks, both in speech and writing; and if your Majesty, informed by the Prince-Marshal of my conduct in the first affair which took place on the Liman, had not invested me with the honourable badge of the Order of St Anne. Since that period, though I have been hampered by limited orders, I have committed no professional error; I have often exposed myself to personal danger, and I have even stooped to sacrifice my personal feelings and interests to my devotion for the good of the service.

"At the close of the campaign I received orders to return to court, as your Majesty intended to employ me in the North Seas, and I brought with me a letter from Prince Potemkin for your Majesty, in which he mentioned my zeal and the importance of my services. I had the honour to present it, and M. le Comte de Besborodko acquainted me that a command of greater importance than that of the Black Sea, and affording full scope for the display of talent and intelligence, was intended for me. Such was my situation, when, upon the mere accusation of a crime, the very idea of which wounds my delicacy, I was driven from court, deprived of the good opinion of your Majesty, and forced to employ the time which I wish to devote to the defence of your empire in clearing myself from the stains with which calumny had covered me.

"Condescend to believe, Madam, that if I had got the slightest hint that a complaint of such a nature had been made against me, and still more that it had reached your Majesty, I know too well what is owing to delicacy to have ventured to appear before you till I was completely exculpated.

"Knowing neither the laws, the language, nor the forms of justice of this country, I needed an advocate, and obtained one; but, whether from terror or intimidation, he stopt short all at once, and durst not undertake my defence, though convinced of the justice of my cause. But truth may always venture to show itself alone and unsupported at the foot of the throne of your Majesty. I have not hesitated to labour unaided for my own vindication ; I have attested proofs ; and if such details may appear under the eyes of your Majesty, I present them, and if your Majesty will deign to order some person to examine them, it will be seen by the report which will be made, that my crime is a fiction, invented by the avarice of a wretched woman, who has been countenanced, perhaps incited, by the malice of my numerous enemies. Her husband has given evidence of her infamous conduct. His signature is in my hands, and the pastor of the district has assured me, that if the college of justice will give him an order to this effect, he will obtain an attestation from the country people that the mother of the girl referred to is a wretch absolutely unworthy of belief.

" Take a soldier's word, Madam ; believe an officer whom two great nations esteem, and who has been honoured with flattering marks of their approbation, (of which your Majesty will soon receive a direct proof from the United States,*) I am innocent! and if I were guilty, I would not hesitate to make a candid avowal of my fault, and to commit my honour, which is a thousand times dearer to me than my life, to the hands of your Majesty.

"If you deign, Madam, to give heed to this declaration, proceeding from a heart the most frank and loyal, I venture from your justice to expect that my zeal will not remain longer in shameful and humiliating inaction. It has been useful to your Majesty, and may again be so, especially in the Mediterranean, where, with insignificant means, I will undertake to execute most important operations, the plans for which I have meditated long and deeply. But if circumstances, of which I am ignorant, do not admit the possibility of my being employed during the campaign, I hope your Majesty will give me permission to return to France or America, granting, as the sole reward of the services I have render-

* Referring to the medal ordered to be struck by Congress.

ed, the hope of renewing them at some future day.

"Nothing can ever change or efface in my heart the deep feelings of devotedness with which your Majesty has inspired me.

"To you, Madam, I am personally devoted. I would rather have my head struck off than see those ties broken asunder which bind me to your service. At the feet of your Majesty I swear to be ever faithful to you, as well as to the empire, of which you form the happiness, the ornament, and the glory.—I am,

With the most profound respect,

Madam," &c.

There are, as was said, several important mistakes, though no wilful misrepresentation whatever, in the details given by Count Segur. Though Jones was so far exculpated as to be permitted to appear again at court, it was merely for the ceremony of taking leave of the Empress and royal family, when he had, as will appear, been virtually dismissed from Russia. The Order of St Anne, to which Segur refers, he had obtained long before. So far was he from receiving any pension from Russia, that his small appointments were tardily paid, and not till after repeated solicitation. Instead of being loaded "with compliments," he was treated while he continued to hang on in the hope of employment, first with the most chilling neglect, and afterwards with repulsive rudeness. Besborodko, the favourite minister of Catharine, who, on his coming to Russia, had overwhelmed the Rear-Admiral with kindness, shut his doors in the face of the supernumerary officer, and did not affect to disguise his weariness and disgust of the applausive recapitulations of past services and projects for future maritime achievements with which he continued to be annoyed by the man whose day was gone by. The alleged crime of the Rear-Admiral, had his guilt even been established, would, we are apt to think, have been no insurmountable barrier to his success in Russia, had a continuance of his services been wished for; nor was his innocence found any recommendation. The Empress may have expressed herself in the terms stated by Count Segur, but this as certainly produced no favourable change in the position of the party so grossly injured. His correspondence with Besborodko, after this affair had been closed up, shows the real nature of his situation, and affords a painful and humiliating picture of the dying struggles of ambition.

To strengthen or bolster up his interests in Russia, Paul Jones at this time endeavoured to bring into play a little diplomatic influence, knowing the avidity with which that grasping and ambitious power caught at every appearance of advantage. He had written thus to Mr Jefferson soon after his return from the Liman:—" I can only inform you that I returned here by the special desire of the Empress, but I know not as yet how or where I am to be employed for the next campaign. I mentioned in my last, as my opinion, that if the new government of America determines to chastise the Algerines, I think it now a favourable moment to conclude a treaty with Russia. The Turks and Algerines were combined against us on the Black Sea. The United States could grant leave for Russia to enlist American seamen, and, making a common cause with

Russia in the Mediterranean, might at the peace obtain a free navigation from and to the Black Sea. Such a connexion might lead to various advantages in the commerce between the two nations."

Whether Mr Jefferson thought the Admiral too desirous of cutting out work for himself, or that he rather stepped out of his department in interfering in such affairs, his hints appear to have met with the return to which he was well accustomed—neglect,—neglect which might have repelled a haughtier spirit, and which, in many instances, was keenly felt by him, without, however, deterring him from renewed attempts to bring himself by every possible means into notice.

He waited for some weeks after his character was cleared at court before he sent the minister the following letters, which were formerly alluded to:—

"*To his Excellency Count Besborodko from Rear-Admiral Paul Jones.*

"St Petersburgh, 24th June, 1789.

"SIR,—When I had the honour to see your

Excellency last week, I ventured to promise myself that in two days I would be made acquainted with the ulterior intention of her Majesty, whether this was to give me a command, or a temporary leave of absence. No doubt important affairs have occasioned the delay. You will, I hope, have the goodness to permit me to present myself at your hotel to-morrow afternoon; for if it is thought fit to employ my services, there is no time to lose, seeing the advance of the season.

"The detachment of vessels of which your Excellency spoke to me might probably be most useful in the operations which I have projected; but, at the same time, I regard the plan mentioned in the private note which I have sent you as very useful. I would then wish (if circumstances permitted) to combine these plans; and then I think there would be reason to be satisfied with the result.

"I have mentioned to your Excellency that I am *the only officer* who made the campaign of the Liman without being promoted; but I beseech you to believe that I have not accepted of service in Russia to occasion embarrassment;

and since the Empress had given me her esteem and her confidence, I wish for nothing save new opportunities to prove my devotion by fresh services."

This letter elicited no reply, and produced no improvement in the situation of the applicant, save that the leave of absence at which he hinted, though it was the last thing he wished for, was at once accorded, there being evidently an anxious wish to be rid of himself, his projects, and importunities. The subjoined letter, written soon afterwards, may teach a lesson of contentment, and even of cheerful gratitude, to those persons, if such there be, who, in their ignorance of public life, may envy the brilliant fortunes of a lucky adventurer, raised by circumstances far above the level of those of his original rank in society.

" *Rear-Admiral Paul Jones to Count de Besborodko.*

" St Petersburgh, 14th July, 1789.

" Sir,—I presented myself at your hotel the day before yesterday, to take leave, and, at the same time, to entreat of you to expedite my commission, my passport, and the leave of absence which her Majesty has thought fit to grant me. Though I have perceived on several former occasions that you have shunned giving me any opportunity to speak with you, I made myself certain that this could not occur at a last interview; and I confess I was very much surprised to see you go out by another door, and depart without a single expression of ordinary civility addressed to me at the moment of my leaving Russia, to console me for all the bitter mortifications I have endured in this empire. Before coming to Russia I had been connected with several governments, and no minister ever either refused me an audience, or failed to reply to my letters.

" After the eagerness with which my services were sought, and the fair promises that were made me, I had reason to believe that I would find in Russia every thing pleasant and agreeable. I was confirmed in this belief from the essential services which I had the good fortune to render the empire. I am aware that your Excellency is sometimes teased by importunate persons, but, as I am a man of delicacy in every thing, I deserve to be distinguished from the common herd.

" On the 6th of June, the last time you gave me an opportunity of speaking with you, I gave you a confidential note,* containing the details

---

* *Secret Note addressed to the Minister Besborodko by Rear-Admiral Paul Jones.*

" June 6, 1789.

" The great object of a Russian fleet in the Mediterranean is to endeavour to cut off the communication between Egypt and the coast of Syria with Constantinople, from whence they procure their corn, rice, coffee, &c. This operation will oblige them to withdraw a very considerable part of their fleet from the Black Sea. To encompass this end, I ask a *carte blanche,* and only, exclusive of small boats, five large vessels, like the East-Indiamen which are purchased in London after they have made three voyages, and which carry from forty to fifty guns. They are strong vessels and good sailers. They are sent from London to Naples under the English flag, under pretext of being engaged in mercantile enterprises. No person can have any thing to say against it. The of a plan by which, without interfering with any other project, and with the utmost economy, great service might be done to Russia. You promised to submit it to the Empress; and you yourself proposed to place a detachment of vessels under my command, to serve during the existing campaign in the Black Sea, and afterwards in the Mediterranean. I could not have imagined that these plans were so carelessly to be thrown aside; and, in place of discussing and arranging them with you, I was very much asto-

---

crew of those vessels being arrived in Italy, would engage in the service of Russia. For the rest we would easily find good sailors at Malta and at Naples. I would employ two small French vessels between Malta and Naples, trading to Smyrna, to procure continual news from Constantinople, and of the force and position of the Turkish fleet. There are some very important blows to be made; but in order to succeed we must not speak of this matter beforehand. We are informed that the want of provisions at Constantinople has occasioned a rebellion, discouraged the people, and caused a great desertion of the troops. It is the policy of the vizier to render himself popular by providing sufficiently for them."

nished when his Excellency the Count de Bruce announced to me that the Empress had granted me a leave of two years.

"On the 1st of February I gave in, by order of his Excellency, Count Ostermann, the plan of a treaty, political and commercial, between Russia and the United States. As the Vice-Chancellor spoke to me of going to America about this purpose, and as I shall soon again be connected with my old friends who constitute the present government of the United States, I would be extremely happy to learn, through your Excellency, the intentions of her Imperial Majesty in this respect, and to be appointed to forward an alliance by which Russia must gain.

"The United States having concluded a treaty of friendship and commerce with the Emperor of Morocco, are about to propose to the different powers of Europe a war with the other Barbary states, and to form a confederation against these pirates, till they shall be annihilated as maritime powers. It is proposed, that even the event of a war between the contracting parties shall not disturb the confederation. It would be worthy of the august Sovereign of this empire to place herself at the head of an alliance so honourable, and of which the consequences must be so useful to Russia. It would give me peculiar satisfaction if your Excellency thought fit to appoint me to make known the intentions of the Empress to the United States on these two points, and I trust I should be able to acquit myself of so honourable a duty to your contentment.

"I have the honour to be, with sincere attachment and high consideration," &c. &c.

His Excellency did not "think fit" to make the solicited appointment.

The Rear-Admiral, as unfortunate in his attempts to obtain a diplomatic mission as a naval command, was now obliged to turn his back on Russia, and devour his chagrin and disappointment as he best could. He had, however, the honour of an audience of leave, though he found considerable difficulty in obtaining his pay and arrears. "When," he says in a letter to M. Genet, "the Count de Bruce sent for me on the 27th June," (two days only after his letter to Besborodko,) " he told me, on the part of the Empress, that her Imperial Majesty had granted me a leave for two years, with the appointments belonging to my military rank during my absence. The Count de Besborodko wrote me 30th July, informing me that M. Strekalow had received her Majesty's orders with respect to my appointments and arrearages. I have not been able to see M. de Strekalow, though I have called frequently at the cabinet. I have only received my appointments from the time of my entry into the service to the 1st of July, at the rate of 1800 roubles* a-year; and I was told yesterday at the cabinet, that her Majesty likewise mentions nothing but the appointments then due. If I could believe that this was her Majesty's intention I should remain silent; for I certainly did not accept the service her Majesty offered me on account of my appointments or the usual emoluments of my grade."

---

* A rouble was in 1789 worth about four shillings English money.

He was satisfied in this respect, and thus left St Petersburgh.

In the Memoir of Paul Jones published in London, no occasion is lost of implicating the English and England as the cause, if not the direct instruments, of his persecution in Russia. "Notwithstanding," it is said, "his regaining the favour of the Empress, the Russian ministers were unwilling to offend England by a refusal to drive him from the service; and their intrigues to accomplish this end were unceasing." Now there is not a vestige of evidence that England or the English in Russia ever interfered with his affairs, save to give him their pity as an ill-used man. To this he himself bears testimony, both in his Journal, and, as will afterwards appear, in his correspondence. Nor does it seem that the Russian ministers found it necessary to give themselves much trouble to accomplish their object. Nothing, it has been seen, could be more cool and contemptuous than the whole tenor of their conduct.

The reader, in possession of the real circumstances attending the departure of Paul Jones from Russia, will be able to estimate aright the following letter and paragraph, put forth from the kindest motives by Count de Segur, immediately before the Rear-Admiral left that country:—

"Count de Segur to Count Montmorin.

"St Petersburgh, 21st July, 1789.

"The enemies of the Vice-Admiral Paul Jones having caused to be circulated reports entirely destitute of foundation, concerning the journey which this general officer is about to undertake, I would wish the enclosed article, the authenticity of which I guarantee, should be inserted in the Gazette of France, and in the other public papers which are submitted to the inspection of your department. This article will undeceive those who have believed the calumny, and will prove to the friends and to the compatriots of the Vice-Admiral, that he has sustained the reputation acquired by his bravery and his talents during the last war; that the Empress desires to retain him in her service; and that if he absents himself at this moment, it is with his own free-will, and for particular reasons, which cannot leave any stain on his honour.

"The glorious marks of the satisfaction and bounty of the King towards M. Paul Jones, his attachment to France, which he has served so usefully in the common cause, his rights as a subject, and as an admiral of the United States, the protection of the ministers of the King, and my personal friendship for this distinguished officer, with whom I made a campaign in America, are so many reasons which appear to me to justify the interest which I took in all that concerned him during his stay in Russia.

"THE COUNT DE SEGUR."

"*Article to be inserted in the Public Prints, and particularly in the Gazette of France.*

"St Petersburgh, 21st July, 1789.—The Vice-Admiral Paul Jones, being on the point of returning to France, where private affairs require his presence, had the honour to take leave of the Empress the 7th of this month, and to be admitted to kiss the hand of her Imperial Majesty,* who confided to him the command of her vessels of war stationed on the Liman during the campaign of 1788. As a mark of favour for his conduct during this campaign, the Empress has decorated him with the insignia of the order of St Anne; and her Imperial Majesty, satisfied with his services, only grants him permission to absent himself for a limited time, and still preserves for him his emoluments and his rank."

This was putting the best face on the affair; and the paragraph appeared in the Gazette of France, and in many other journals.

Early in September Jones left St Petersburgh for Warsaw, furnished with letters of introduction, explanation, and vindication from the Count de Segur to different individuals, all written in the same generous spirit as the above. The kindness of Count Segur to a man placed in a situation generally so fatal to court-friendships

* "This general officer, so celebrated by his brilliant actions during the course of the American war, was called, in 1787, to the service of her Imperial Majesty."—*Note to the Newspaper Paragraph.*

does him great honour. His original letters still remain among the papers of the Rear-Admiral, who, however, transmitted copies of them to many of his friends. Count Segur was not the only Frenchman who sustained the calumniated stranger under the base attempts of his enemies. M. de Genet, the younger, was at this time the secretary of legation at St Petersburgh. Paul Jones, at a former period, had been intimate with the father and family of this gentleman at Versailles, and the young Frenchman did not now forget his father's former friend. M. de Genet undertook the arrangement of his pecuniary affairs with the Russian government, and gave him a letter to his sister, the celebrated Madame Campan, explaining the atrocious slanders propagated in St Petersburgh, and placing the innocence of the calumniated individual beyond all suspicion. This original letter also remains among the papers of the Rear-Admiral. It was some months before he returned to Paris, and he might then have felt reluctant to revive the recollection of a charge so disgusting as to make the task of vindication both humiliating and painful to a mind of any delicacy.

Before quitting this subject, it may be proper again to notice that Jones, though occasionally betrayed by self-complacence into the belief that the English were all his enemies, lived to retract much of this absurd notion. He fairly acquits them of having any share in that conspiracy, of which the capital of Russia formed the appropriate scene, and in this shows far more candour than his American or London historian.

In 1791, in writing from Paris to Mr Jefferson, then in America, he gives the following clue to the mystery of his treatment in Russia. "Chevalier Littlepage, now here on his way from Spain to the north, has promised me a letter to you on my subject, which I presume will show you the meanness and absurdity of the intrigues that were practised for my persecution at St Petersburgh. I did not myself comprehend all the blackness of that business till he came here, and related to me the information he received from a gentleman of high rank in the diplomatic department, with whom he had travelled in company from Madrid to Paris. That gentleman had long resided in a public character at St Petersburgh, and was there all the time of the pitiful complot against me, which was conducted by a little great man behind the curtain. The unequalled reception with which I had at first been honoured by the Empress had been extremely mortifying and painful to the English at St Petersburgh; and the courtier just mentioned, (finding that politics had taken a turn far more alarming than he had expected at the beginning of the war,) wishing to sooth the Court of London into a pacific humour, found no first step so expedient as that of sacrificing me. But, instead of producing the effect he wished, this base conduct, on which he pretended to ground a conciliation, rather tended to widen the political breach, and made him despised by the English minister, by the English cabinet, and by the gentleman who related the secret to Mr Littlepage." The letter of Mr Littlepage, transmitted to Mr Jefferson along with the above, in part confirms this solution of an intrigue, so essentially Russian. Yet there remains some secret cause and movement which it is impossible to fathom. "The campaign upon the Liman," says Chevalier Littlepage, "added lustre to the arms of Russia, and ought to have established for ever the reputation and fortune of the gallant officer to whose conduct those successes were owing." (Littlepage attributes to the Rear-Admiral the entire success of the campaign of 1788; not, like Count Segur, dividing his laurels with Nassau; and it is to be remembered, that Littlepage was an eye-witness of an important part of it). "Unfortunately," he continues, "in Russia, more perhaps than elsewhere, every thing is governed by *intrigue*. Some political motives, I have reason to think, concurred in depriving Rear-Admiral Paul Jones of the fruits of his services; he was thought to be particularly obnoxious to the English nation, and the idea of paying a servile compliment to a power whose enmity occasions all the present embarrassments of Russia induced some leading persons to ruin him, in the opinion of the Empress, by an accusation too ridiculous to be mentioned."

On leaving Warsaw, it was the intention of Paul Jones to return to France by Copenhagen and Berlin; but, as it was known that he had left Russia dissatisfied, he deemed it best to avoid all farther occasion of giving his enemies any handle against him, and accordingly kept away from places where it might be presumed that he was tempted to tell tales, or utter complaints.

Disgrace at Petersburgh did not at this juncture imply a cold reception at Warsaw; and in this capital—soon to be a capital no more—Jones was well received, and remained for two months. From Warsaw he despatched the Journal of his American Campaigns for the perusal of the Empress, and also an abridgment of the Journal of his Campaign on the Liman. Her Imperial Majesty had, it seems, at some former period, civilly expressed a desire to see his Journal of the American war. The old spirit was not yet quite subdued. "I have added," he says, "some testimonies of the high and *unanimous* consideration of the United States, and of the private esteem with which I was honoured by several great men *to whom I am perfectly known*, such as M. Malsherbes and the Count d'Estaing* of

* This evidently refers to the complimentary letters with which these gentlemen returned the Journal; in which letters the author of the Journal naturally sees perhaps more than is visible to any eyes less interested. We give them here.

"*Letter from Count d'Estaing to Paul Jones, on reading his Journal.*

"It is impossible, Sir, not to abuse your kindness: never lend me your Journal again, for I give you my honour that I shall every time read it throughout, and always with new delight. It is among the number of things that one wishes to have by heart. In it the lesson of military and naval heroism becomes identified with that of generosity, by your conduct towards Lord and Lady Selkirk.

"I am far from regretting the tribute of admiration I have paid to the fight between the Bon Homme Richard and the Serapis; and though in writing it I did not imagine it could lead to any thing beyond an admission into the society of the Cincinnati,* I cannot but be

* The Count had recommended Captain Edward Stack for admission into this society.

France, and Mr Morris, minister of the American marine. I owe to my own reputation and to

---

flattered to find that you have inserted it among the pieces appended to your Journal.

"I have the honour to be, with the most perfect attachment,

"ESTAING.

"Paris, 18th December, 1785."

"*Letter of M. Malsherbes to Captain Paul Jones, on perusing his Journal.*

"Paris, 27th February, 1786.

"SIR,—I have received this mark of your confidence with much gratitude, and have with great eagerness and pleasure read this interesting relation.

"My first idea was, that you should give it to the press; but since I have perused it, I perceive that it is not for the public you have drawn it up, as it contains matters written only for the King, for whom the narrative was intended. In the meanwhile it is highly necessary that deeds so memorable as yours should be made known to the public in an authentic Journal published in your own name.

"I exhort you to set about this as soon as your affairs permit you, and in the meanwhile I hope the King will truth, to accompany this Journal with an abridgment of that of the campaign of the Liman. If

---

read this work with the attention he owes to the relation of services performed by a man so celebrated as you.

"MALSHERBES."

We may here give the dedication of this Journal to the King of France, as a fair specimen of the elaborate composition of the writer, whose abilities, merely in a literary point of view, are, his narrow education and modes of life considered, not a little remarkable. As is not singular, however, his fine and careful writing is by no means his best style:—

"SIRE,—History gives the world no example of such generosity as that of your Majesty towards the young Republic of America; and I believe that never was a compliment more flattering shown by a Sovereign to his allies, than when your Majesty determined to arm and support a squadron under the flag of the United States.

"Words cannot express my sense of the preference I obtained when your Majesty deigned to make choice of me to command that squadron.

"Your Majesty has as much reputation for know-you, Madam, read it with attention, you will see how little I have deserved the mortifications I have suffered,—mortifications which the justice

---

ledge, and the desire of information, as you have for wisdom and justice; but, besides that consideration, I conceive it to be my duty to lay before your Majesty an account of my conduct as an officer, particularly from the date of the alliance between your Majesty and the United States. As your Majesty understands English, I have perhaps judged ill in presenting the extract of my Journals in French. My motive was to give your Majesty as little trouble as possible. Accept, Sire, with indulgence, this confidential offering of my gratitude, which is an original, written for your particular information.

"It has been and will be the ambition of my life to merit the singular honour conferred on me by your Majesty's brevet, dated at Versailles the 28th June, 1780, which says, 'Sa Majesté voulant marquer au J. Paul Jones, Commodore de la Marine des Etâts-Unis de l'Amérique, *l'estime particulière qu'elle fait de sa personne,* pour les preuves de bravoure et d'intrépidité qu'il a données, et qui sont connus de sa Majesté, elle a jugé à propos de l'associer à l'institution du Merite Militaire,' &c.

"The Congress of the United States has, with great

and goodness of your Majesty can alone make me forget.

"As I never offended in *word* or *thought* against the laws of the strictest delicacy, it would assuredly be most desirable to me to have the

---

justice, styled your Majesty 'The Protector of the Rights of Human Nature.'

"With the order of Military Merit, your Majesty conferred on me a gold sword,—an honour which, I presume, no other officer has received; and 'The Protector of the Rights of Human Nature' will always find me ready to draw that sword, and expose my life for his service.

"I am, Sire,
"With the truest gratitude,
"Your Majesty's most obliged
"And devoted servant,
"J. Paul Jones.

"Paris, January 1st, 1786."

"Protector of fair Freedom's rights,
Louis, thy virtues suit a god;
The good man in thy praise delights,
And tyrants tremble at thy nod.

"Thy people's father, loved so well,
May time respect!—when thou art gone
May each new year of history tell
Thy sons with lustre fill thy throne."

happiness of regaining, in spite of the malice of my enemies, the precious esteem of your Majesty. I would have taken leave with a heart fully satisfied, had I been sent to fight the enemies of the Empress, instead of occupying myself with my own private affairs.

"Trusting entirely on the gracious promise that your Majesty gave me, 'never to condemn me without a hearing,' and being devoted to you, heart and soul,

"I am with profound respect," &c. &c.

To ensure the Journal reaching the hands of the Empress, this postscript is added to the above loyal effusion:—"I shall have the honour of sending the Journal by the courier of Wednesday next, with the proofs of every separate article. It will be sealed with my arms, and addressed to your Majesty, and sent under a second cover, to the address of M. de Chrapowitzky." With all these precautions he feared that his Journal was intercepted, as it contained such "damning proofs against his enemies."

CHAPTER IV.

During his stay in Warsaw, Paul Jones became known to the celebrated Kosciusko. On leaving Poland he sent a farewell note to this noble patriot and determined hater of Russia, which was followed by a rather singular correspondence. Sweden was at this time in the heat of war, and it had been rumoured that the discontented American, who had for a brief space prided himself on being a Russian officer, was now ready to take service with Gustavus III. This report was one reason for Jones avoiding the route of Copenhagen on his way to Holland, and choosing rather to go by Vienna.

" *Rear-Admiral Paul Jones to Major General Kosciusko.*

" Warsaw, November 2d, 1789.

" My dear General,—I intend to set out

this day for Vienna, where I shall only stop a few days. I shall then go to Strasburgh, and from thence to Holland, where I expect to arrive before the 1st of December. My address in Holland is under cover to Messieurs Nic. and Jacob Stophorst, Amsterdam.

"As I shall be in relation with our friends in America, I shall not fail to mention on all occasions the honourable employment and the respect you have attained in your own country, and the great regard you retain for the natives of America, where your character is esteemed, and your name justly beloved for your services.—I am," &c.

The letter of General Kosciusko* is written in English, a language which he wrote but

---

* THADDEUS KOSCIUSKO was a native of Poland, and of good birth. He was educated at the Cadet-School of Warsaw, and was one of four pupils annually chosen by the king, and sent to complete their military studies in France or Germany. He was instructed at the Military Academy of Versailles, and acquired a thorough knowledge of every department of military science, par-

imperfectly. The original orthography is retained.

---

ticularly engineering. It is related, that on returning home he fell desperately in love with a young lady, who eloped with him. The lovers were pursued and overtaken before they could pass the frontiers of Poland; and as Kosciusko could only retain his mistress by killing her father, he resigned her. In consequence, it is said, of this adventure, but more probably from the love of employment and distinction, the young Pole went to America, and was appointed by General Washington one of his aides-de-camp. He continued there till the end of the war. The part he afterwards acted in his native country is well known. In the battle in which he was made prisoner, he had three horses killed under him, and was captured as he fell wounded from the last. He was kept in a Russian dungeon till the death of the Empress Catharine, and only liberated by Paul at his accession. He afterwards visited America and England, and was received with the highest distinction. When Bonaparte entered Poland, he tried to move the nation by a proclamation issued in the name of the patriot chief; but Kosciusko disowned it, and refused to have any alliance either with the French conqueror or with the Russian Emperor, Alexander. " He lived," says his biographer,

" *General Kosciusko to Rear-Admiral Paul Jones, Amsterdam.*

" Warsaw, 15th February, 1790.

" MY DEAR SIR,—I had the honour to write you the 1st or 3d of February. I do not recollect; but I gave you the information to apply to the minister of Sweden at the Hague, for the propositions (according to what M. D'Engestrom told me) they both had order to communicate you. I wish with all my heart that could answer your expectation. I am totaly ignorant what they are; but I could see you to fight against the opression and tyranny. Give me news of every thing.—I am, dear Sir,

" Your most humble and most
" obedient servant,
" J. KOSCIUSKO, G. M."

" in proud independence, superior to fortune and to kings." His latter years were passed at Soleure, where he distinguished himself by generosity to the poor. He possessed a highly-cultivated mind, and was passionately fond of poetry, particularly the works of the English poets, with which he became well acquainted. He died in October 1817, in the 65th year of his age.

"Write me, if you please, who is minister from America at Paris: I want to know his name."

In answer to this letter, Jones wrote from Amsterdam in the following month:—

"My dear Sir,—The letter you did me the honour to write me the 2d February, was delivered to my bankers here, by a man who demanded from them a receipt. I was then at the Hague, and your letter was transmitted to me. On my return here, some days ago, I found another letter from you of the 15th February. This letter had, by the same man, been put into the hands of my bankers. You propose, if I am not mistaken, that I should apply to a gentleman at the Hague, who has something to communicate to me. But a moment's reflection will convince you that considerations of what I owe to myself, as well as the delicacy of my situation, do not permit me to take such a step. If that gentleman has any thing to communicate to me, he can either do it by writing, by desiring a personal conference, or by the mediation of a third person.

I have shown your letter to my bankers, and they have said this much to the gentleman from whom they received it; but this message, they say, he received with an air of indifference."

Thus terminated the enigmatical correspondence between Paul Jones and the illustrious Pole. Reckoning a little on the disinterested love of freedom, once so loudly boasted by all Americans, and somewhat more, probably, on the avowed discontent of the Rear-Admiral, Kosciusko may have wished to draw him into some of those daring schemes with which his own mind, on the highest and purest motives, was now anxiously occupied. But the lingering hope and ardent desire of being again recalled to serve in Russia, cherished in spite of all he had seen and suffered, had not yet left the mind of Jones. To this delusive hope he indeed clung, with an almost abject pertinacity, to the very close of his life. Prudence, besides, forbade a negotiation of so mysterious and suspicious a kind; and there was both honesty and discretion in avoiding it.

While in Holland, Jones wrote many letters to different quarters, desirous to re-establish himself in the good opinion of some old friends, and to revive himself in the memory of others from whom he had been estranged during his Russian bondage, or splendid exile,—for it may be called indifferently by either name. His letters about this time exhibit a curious struggle between the desire of domestic peace and the ambition of again launching into the heady current of public life. He appears at a loss what plan to pursue, whether to purchase a small estate in America, and seek the enjoyments of that tranquil life which in reality possessed no charms for him; to marry a *rich* wife, or to drag on an existence in the longing, lingering hope of being recalled to Russia. His letters reflect the exact complexion of his thoughts, disturbed, broken, and changeful.

He, however, once more felt in security, and gave his pen such scope, that innumerable letters bear date at the Hague or Amsterdam, between December, 1789, and March, 1790.

A selection from the important part of his copious correspondence at this period must be more satisfactory to the reader than any detail we can give: his letters of a private kind written at this time are reserved for the limited portion of this memoir devoted to the domestic history of its subject.

"Rear-Admiral Paul Jones to General Washington, President of the United States.

"Amsterdam, December 20, 1789.

"SIR,—I avail myself of the departure of the Philadelphia packet, Captain Earle, to transmit to your Excellency a letter I received for you on leaving Russia in August last, from my friend, the Count de Segur, minister of France at St Petersburgh. That gentleman and myself have frequently conversed on subjects that regard America; and the most pleasing reflection of all has been, the happy establishment of the new constitution, and that you are so deservedly placed at the head of the government by the unanimous voice of America. Your name alone, Sir, has established in Europe a confidence that was for some time before entirely wanting in American concerns; and I am assured, that the happy effects of your administration are still more sensibly felt throughout the United States. This is more glorious for you than all the laurels that your sword so nobly won in support of the rights of human nature. In war your fame is immortal as the hero of Liberty! In peace you are her patron, and the firmest supporter of her rights! Your greatest admirers, and even your best friends, have now but one wish left for you,—that you may long enjoy health and your present happiness.

"Mr Jefferson can inform you respecting my mission to the court of Denmark. I was received and treated there with marked politeness; and if the *fine words* I received are true, the business will soon be settled. I own, however, that I should have stronger hopes if America had created a respectable marine; for that argument would give weight to every transaction with Europe. I acquitted myself of the commission with which you honoured me when last in America, by delivering your letters with my own hands at Paris to the persons to whom they were addressed."

He also wrote Franklin and Mr Ross. Both of these letters have interest.

"Amsterdam, December 27, 1789.

"Dear Sir,—I beg leave to refer you to Doctor Franklin or to General St Clair for an explanation of my reasons for having left Russia. I have by this opportunity sent to those gentlemen testimonies in French that cannot fail to justify me in the eyes of my friends in America.

"You have no doubt been informed, perhaps by Mr Parish, of the *unhandsome* conduct of Le Conteulex and Co. with regard to the letter of credit you gave me on them when I was last in America for six thousand livres. As I was landed in England instead of France, I went to London to make an arrangement with Dr Bancroft for supplying the expense of my mission to Denmark. He promised to place funds for my use at Amsterdam. I went to Paris, and took a letter of credit from Le Conteulex on Amsterdam *by way of precaution.* On my arrival at Amsterdam I found that Bancroft had not kept his word, nor ever wrote me a line. I then depended on the credit that Le Conteulex had, *without the least difficulty*, given me in an open letter; but his correspondent informed me he had received orders to pay me nothing till more explicit and satisfactory accounts should be received from you! I had then no funds in my hands; and if I had not had the fortune to be immediately relieved from a quarter on which I had no claim, I should have found myself in great distress.

"I should be glad to know the state of the bank, &c., though I at present want no remittance. My address is, *under cover*, to Messrs N. and J. Van-Stophorst and Hubbard, Amsterdam. Present my respectful compliments to Mrs Ross and the young ladies. I may perhaps return to America in the latter end of the summer; and in that case I shall wish to purchase a *little farm*, where I may live in peace. I am always affectionately yours.

"*John Ross, Esq., Philadelphia.*

"*N. B.*—I presume you have received my bust, as Mr Jefferson has forwarded it for you."

"*Paul Jones to Dr Franklin.*

"Amsterdam, December 27, 1789.

"Dear Sir,—The enclosed documents from my friend, the Count de Segur, Minister Plenipotentiary of France at St Petersburgh, will explain to you in some degree my reasons for leaving Russia, and the danger to which I was exposed by the dark intrigues and mean subterfuges of Asiatic jealousy and malice. Your former friendship for me, which I remember with particular satisfaction, and have ever been ambitious to merit, will, I am sure, be exerted in the kind use you will make of the three pieces I now send you, for my justification in the eyes of my friends in America, whose good opinion is dearer to me than any thing else. I wrote to the Empress from Warsaw in the beginning of October, with a copy of my journal, which will show her Majesty how much she has been deceived by the account she had of our maritime operations last campaign. I can easily prove to the world that I have been treated unjustly, but I intend to remain silent at least till I know the fate of my journal.

" I shall remain in Europe till after the opening of the next campaign, and perhaps longer, before I return to America. From the troubles in Brabant, and the measures now pursuing by the King of Prussia, &c., I presume that peace is yet a distant object, and that the Baltic will witness warmer work than it has yet done. On the death of Admiral Greig, I was last year called from the Black Sea by the Empress to command a squadron in the Baltic, &c. This set the invention of all my enemies and rivals at work, and the event has proved that the Empress cannot always do as she pleases. If you do me the favour to write to me, my address is, *under cover*, to Messieurs N. and J. Van Stophorst and Hubbard at Amsterdam.

" I am, with sincere affection, dear Sir, your most obedient and most humble servant.

" *His Excellency B. Franklin, Esq. &c. &c.*
Philadelphia.

" *N. B.*—It is this day ten years since I left the Texel in the Alliance."

To Mr Parish, the well-known Hamburgh merchant, with whom Paul Jones had become acquainted on his journey to Russia, he thus wrote under a vague idea of going to Hamburgh till his fate was determined:—" My departure from Copenhagen was so sudden, that I omitted writing to you, intending to have done it from St Petersburgh. There I found myself in such a round of feasting and business till the moment of my departure for the Black Sea, that I again postponed.

" Had I wrote you after my arrival at Cherson, I have every reason to think my letters would have been intercepted; but, notwithstanding my past silence, I can truly assure you, that I have constantly entertained the most perfect and grateful sense of your friendly and polite behaviour to me at Hamburgh and Copenhagen. I will now thankfully pay to your order the cost of the smoked beef you were so obliging as to send to my friend, Mr Jefferson, at my request. The kind interest you have taken in my concerns, and the great desire to cultivate your esteem and friendship, are my present inducements for troubling you with the enclosed packet for the Chevalier Bourgoing, (the French resident at Hamburgh,) which I leave under a flying seal for your perusal, praying you to shut the exterior cover before you deliver it. I shall make no comments on the documents I send for the Baron de la Houze, but let the simple truth speak for herself. I shall show you, when we meet, things that will surprise you, for you can scarcely have an idea how much our operations have been misrepresented.

"As I am for the present the master of my time, I shall perhaps make you a visit in the spring, and pay my court to some of your kind, rich, old ladies. To be serious, I must stay in Europe till it is seen what changes the present politics will produce, and till I can hear from America; and if you think I can pass my time quietly, agreeably, and at a small expense at Hamburgh, I should prefer it to the fluctuating prospects of other places."

The documents above referred to were copies of the letters of Count Segur for Baron de la Houze, the French minister at Copenhagen: from him they drew a polite and soothing reply:—

"*Baron de la Houze to Paul Jones.*

"Copenhagen, 9th February, 1790.

"It is but a few days since I received, with the letter with which you have honoured me of the 29th December, the copies of that of the Count de Segur, which you have been pleased to communicate to me, and which were accompanied by the article inserted on your account in the Gazette of France, and which I had read. This article, which has been repeated in many foreign gazettes, has entirely destroyed all the venomous effects which calumny had employed to tarnish the distinguished reputation which you have acquired by your talents and valour. In consequence, public opinion still continues to render you justice, and the most noble revenge you can take on your enemies is to gather fresh laurels. The celebrated Athenian general, Themistocles, has said,—'I do not envy the situation of the man who is not envied.'"

Baron Krudner had been actively useful to Paul Jones while in Copenhagen, both in promoting his views in entering the Russian service, and in the affair of the Danish pension. Though we are aware that the Rear-Admiral had property of different descriptions, the state of his finances must, about this time, have been embarrassed by his large disbursements during the Russian campaign, his long journeys, indisposition, and other causes of expenses. In writing from America to a lady in whom he took a strong interest, he represents himself, immediately previous to his last voyage in 1787, as "almost without money, and puzzled to obtain a supply." He wrote, as has been seen, in this emergency to Dr Bancroft,* who afterwards, in London, promised him assistance, but failed to keep his word. He intimates to Mr Parish, that he could wish "to

---

* Dr Bancroft had pecuniary transactions with Paul Jones, and at this time may have owed him money. The Doctor was addicted to gambling in the English funds, and on this account lost the confidence of Congress, and the diplomatic appointment which he held. It is probable that he employed the money of his friends in the same speculations, partly for his own advantage, and partly for theirs.

live at small expense;" and there are other reasons to conclude, that his finances, at least so far as regarded ready money, were not flourishing. This circumstance of actual exigency may, as was formerly hinted, account for the anxiety respecting the Danish pension manifested in this letter to Baron Krudner; it is in other respects curious:—

"*Rear-Admiral Paul Jones to Baron Krudner, Russian Envoy at Copenhagen.*

"Amsterdam, 29th December, 1789.

"My dear Sir,—Though I have not written to your Excellency since I set out on my first journey to St Petersburgh, yet I have constantly retained the most lively sense of your kind behaviour to me at Copenhagen. I must beg to refer you to his Excellency the Baron de la Houze, to whom I now transmit three documents for my justification in the eyes of my friends in Denmark. Notwithstanding the unjust treatment I received in Russia, the warm attachment with which the Empress inspired me at the beginning still remains rooted in my heart. You know, Sir, that her Imperial Majesty thought my sword an object worthy of her attention, sought it with the most flattering eagerness, and treated me the first time I was at her court with unexampled distinction. That sword has been successfully and frequently drawn on critical occasions, to render the most essential services to her empire, and to cover her flag with fresh laurels. For this I have greatly exposed my reputation, and entirely sacrificed my military pride. Yet I have seen the credit of my services bestowed on others, and I am the only officer who made the campaign of the Liman without being advanced. In a letter I wrote the Empress the 17th of May last, I mentioned that her Majesty would soon receive a direct proof from America of the unanimous approbation with which I am honoured by the United States. I alluded to the gold medal which I am to receive, and respecting which you have in your hands a copy of the unanimous act of Congress. That medal is now elegantly executed, and is ready for me at Paris. The United States have ordered an example of my medal to be presented to every sovereign in Europe, Great Britain excepted. When we meet, I shall produce clear proof of all I have said respecting Russia. The only promise I asked from the Empress at the beginning, and, indeed, the only condition I made with her Majesty, was, that '*she should not condemn me without having heard me.*' I need make no remark to a man of your clear understanding. You advised me *to write to the Empress by the post.* I wrote several letters while in the department of the Black Sea to my friend Mr Jefferson, at Paris, containing no detail of our operations, yet they were all intercepted. I have, I think, reason to apprehend that there will be no peace this winter, and that the Baltic will witness *warmer* work than it has yet done.

"You remember that Count B——— (Bernstorf) showed you a paper which he sent, to be delivered to me by the Danish Minister at St Petersburgh. I received that paper without any alteration whatever, either in the '*date*' or otherwise. If I understood you right, it was intended that '*a year's payment would be made in advance*,' but I have not since heard a word in that respect. I wish to be informed how the payment is intended to be made. It cannot surely be in Danish bank-paper. You will do me a great favour if you can obtain an explicit answer, and it would be much more agreeable if the payment could be made here, instead of being made at any other place. I have not yet mentioned this affair to any person whatever, except yourself. You are no stranger to my sentiments. You know the present happy state of America. That nation will soon create a respectable marine. It is now a year since I gave a plan to the court of St Petersburgh, for forming a political and commercial connexion with the United States. The Empress approved this much, and there was question of sending me to America in consequence. But a great man told me, 'que cela enrageroit les Anglais d'avantage contre la Russie, et qu'il falloit auparavant faire la paix avec les Turcs.' Accept my warm congratulations on the well-merited advancement you have received in the Order of St Wolodimer. I hear that your lady* is at Paris. I beg you to assure her of my great respect," &c. &c.

Baron Krudner replied, entirely blinking the memorial touching Russian affairs, but assuring his correspondent of success in obtaining the Danish pension, of which he had spoken to Count Bernstorf, and obtained a promise of immediate payment;—which promise, it is to be inferred, was never meant to be kept,—as it certainly never was.

Paul Jones appears to have gone to England in the spring of this year, (1790,) but did not remain long. The object of his visit does not transpire; and that he had been there only comes out incidentally in his correspondence, especially

---

* The afterwards well-known Madam Krudner, who was still enchanting Parisian circles with her charms and attitudes in the "shawl-dance," not having as yet assumed the part of devotee, or prophetess, in which she afterwards made an equally remarkable figure.

in a letter to M. de Genet,* written in June, when he had reached Paris. In this letter he informs that gentleman, that he had not yet paid his respects to his sister, (Madam Campan,†) but intended doing so, and presenting the lady with

---

* M. Genet remained in St Petersburgh after the return of Count de Segur to France. Both were revolutionists to a moderate extent; and for this they incurred the dislike of the Empress. Genet was removed from Russia, and soon afterwards appointed by the Gironde party, to which he was attached, ambassador to the United States. When the faction of Robespierre obtained the ascendency, he was ordered home, to answer at the bar of the Convention for his malversations in obeying the instructions of the former government. There was in those days but a very short way between the bar of the Convention and the scaffold. He took the wiser part of marrying the daughter of Governor Clinton, and settling in America as a planter.

† M. Genet had several sisters; but as Madam Campan was the best known and most *influential* person of the family, it is taken for granted that this is the sister alluded to here.

his bust, as a mark of personal regard for her father and brother. He continues, "I have shown M. de Simolin proof that, if I have not sought to avenge myself of the unjust and cruel treatment I met with in Russia, my forbearance has been only the result of my delicate attachment towards the Empress. You will oblige me by inquiring at the cabinet, and demanding the appointments due to me for the current year, which ends the 1st of July, agreeably to the promise of the Empress, communicated to me by the Counts de Bruce and Besborodko. I wish to have that money immediately transmitted to me."

While in Amsterdam the Rear-Admiral received letters from Madame Le Mair d'Altigny, a lady who appears to have taken a peculiar interest in his welfare. This lady was probably a widow; but her actual condition as wife or widow we have no means of verifying, and leave it entirely to the penetration of our fair readers.

" Rear-Admiral Paul Jones to Madame Le Mair d'Altigny, at Avignon.

" Amsterdam, 8th Feb. 1790.

" I have received, my dear Madam, the two obliging letters you did me the honour to address to me from Avignon on the 18th and 22d of December. Accept also, I pray you, my sincere acknowledgments for the two letters you had the kindness to send me at Strasburgh. I am infinitely flattered by the interest with which I have the happiness to have inspired you, and your good wishes in my concerns give me true pleasure. I am not come here on account of any thing connected with military operations; and though I think it right to retain my rank, I have always regarded war as the scourge of the human race. I am very happy that you are once more above your difficulties. Past events will enable you to value the blessings of Providence, among which, to a sensible heart, there are none greater than health and independence, enjoyed in the agreeable society of persons of merit. As soon as circumstances permit, I shall feel eager to join the delightful society in which you are. As you have not sent me your address at Avignon, I beg of you to do so, and to be assured of my entire esteem."

The lady, to visit whom the Rear-Admiral was willing to make so long a journey, when circumstances permitted, appears to have replied in the following month; but it was not till December in the same year that she obtained an answer.

"Paris, December 27, 1790.

"My dear Madam,—I have received your charming letter of the 2d March. Having an affair of business to arrange in England, I went from Amsterdam to London at the beginning of May, to settle it. I escaped being murdered on landing.* From London I came hither, and have not had an hour of health since my arrival. I now feel convalescent, otherwise I would not have

* This is undoubtedly meant in jest; Paul Jones was by no means so senseless as to fear assassination in England.

dared to write, for fear of giving pain to your feeling heart. In leaving Holland my plan was to repair to Avignon, in compliance with your obliging invitation. My health formed an invincible obstacle, but I still hope to indemnify myself on the return of the fine weather. I was for a long time very much alarmed by the disturbances which interrupted the peace of your city, and am very glad to see they are ended. I have learned, with lively satisfaction, that they have had no disagreeable consequences so far as regards you. Give me news of yourself, I pray you, and of those interesting persons of whom you speak in your last letter. Accept the assurance of the sincere sentiments which you are formed to inspire.

"My address is, under cover, to M. Dorbery, No 42, Rue Tournon, Paris.

"*N. B.*—Have you not sufficient confidence in my discretion to explain 'the enigma' of the happiness with which you say 'I will be loaded, and which will astonish me so soon as I know it?'"

Of Madame Le Mair d'Altigny we hear nothing more, so that her enigma in all probability remained unexpounded.

It might be presumed that the mind of Jones was now effectually weaned from the service of the country where he had been so "unjustly and cruelly treated;" but such was not the fact. At intervals, during the last ten years of his life, he had been subject to severe attacks of indisposition, and about this time he was labouring under that illness which, with brief intermission, never again left him; yet was his mind as ardently occupied as ever with hopes of serving in Russia. He addressed Prince Potemkin, he addressed the Empress:—his mind on this subject appears to have been possessed; his very eagerness must have tended to defeat his anxious wishes. These letters from Paris, together with one other document, conclude the history of his unfortunate connexion with Russia,—a connexion which one cannot help regarding as the cause of his premature death. The generous reader must be pained to see a man of unquestioned bravery, and of very considerable talent and professional skill, who, in his own adopted country of America, might have lived to old age in peace and honour, fighting her battles in the senate, as he had already done on the ocean, clinging thus in hopeless pertinacity to the delusion which had undone him.

" *To his Highness the Prince-Marshal Potemkin.*

" Paris, 24th July, 1790.

" My Lord,—I do not think it becomes me to let pass the occasion of the return of your aide-de-camp, to congratulate you on the brilliant success of your operations since I had the honour to serve under your orders, and to express to you, in all the sincerity of my heart, the regret I feel in not being fortunate enough to contribute thereto. After the campaign of Liman, when I had leave, according to the special desire of her Imperial Majesty, to return to the department of the Northern Seas, your Highness did me the favour to grant me a letter of recommendation to the Empress, and to speak to me these words, 'Rely upon my attachment. I am disposed to grant you the most solid proofs of my friendship for the present and for the future.' Do you recollect them? This disclosure was too flattering for me to forget it, and I hope you will permit me to remind you of it. Circumstances and the high rank of my enemies have deprived me of the benefits which I had dared to hope from the esteem which you had expressed for me, and which I had endeavoured to merit by my services. You know the disagreeable situation in which I was placed; but if, as I dared to believe, I have preserved your good opinion, I may still hope to see it followed by advantages, which it will be my glory to owe to you. M. de Simolin can testify to you that my attachment to Russia, and to the great Princess who is its sovereign, has always been constant and durable; I attended to my duties, and not to my fortune. I have been wrong, and I avow it with a frankness which carries with it its own excuse—1st, That I did not request of you a carte-blanche, and the absolute command of all the forces of the Liman. 2d, To have written to your Highness under feelings highly excited, on the $\frac{14}{3}$th October, 1788. These are my faults. If my enemies have wished to impute others to me, I swear before God that they are a calumny. It only rests with me, my Lord, to unmask the villany of my enemies, by publishing my journal of the operations of the campaign of Liman, with the proofs, clear as the day, and which I have in my hands. It only rests with me to prove that I directed, under your orders, all the useful operations against the Capitan Pacha; that it was I who beat him on the 7th June; that it was I and the brave men I commanded who conquered him on the 17th June, and who chased into the sands two of his largest galleys, before our flotilla was ready to fire a single shot, and during the time a very considerable part of the force of the enemy remained at anchor immediately in rear of my squadron; that it was I who gave to General Suwarrow, (he had the nobleness to declare it at court before me, to the most respectable witnesses,) the first project to establish the battery and breast-works on the isthmus of Kinbourn, and which were of such great utility on the night of the 17—18th June; that it was I, in person, who towed, with my sloops and other vessels, the batteries which were the nearest to the place, the 1st July, and who took the Turkish galleys by boarding, very much in advance of our line, whilst some gentlemen, who have been too highly rewarded in consequence of it, were content to remain in the rear of the struggles of our line, if I may be allowed to use the expression, sheltered from danger. You have seen, yourself, my Lord, that I never valued my person on any occasion where I had the good fortune to act under your eye. The whole of Europe acknowledges my veracity, and grants me some military talents, which it would give me pleasure to employ in the service of Russia, under your orders. The time will arrive, my Lord, when you will know the exact truth of what I have told you. Time is a sovereign master. It will teach you to appreciate the man, who, loaded with your benefits, departed from the court of Russia with a memorial prepared by other hands and the enemies of your glory, and of which memorial he made no use, because your brilliant success at the taking of Oczakow, which he learned on his arrival in White Russia, gave the lie to all the horrors which had been brought forward to enrage the Empress against you. You know it was the echo of another intriguer at the court of Vienna. In fine, time will teach you, my Lord, that I am neither a mountebank nor a swindler, but a man true and loyal. I rely upon the attachment and friendship which you promised me. I rely on it, because I feel myself worthy of it. I reclaim your promise, because you are just, and I know you are a lover of truth. I commanded, and was the only responsible person in the campaign of the Liman, the others being only of inferior rank, or simple volunteers; and I am, however, the only one who has not been promoted or rewarded. I am extremely thankful for the order of St Anne which you procured for me, according to your letter of thanks, *for my conduct in the affair of the 7th June*, which was not decisive. The 17th June I gained over the Capitan Pacha a complete victory, which saved Cherson and Kinbourn, the terror of which caused the enemy to lose nine vessels of war in their precipitate flight on the following night, under the cannon of the battery and breast-work which I had caused to be erected in the isthmus of Kinbourn. On this occasion I had the honour again to receive a *letter of thanks*; but my enemies and rivals have found means to abuse your confidence, since they have been exclusively rewarded. They merited rather to have been punished for having burnt nine armed prizes, with their crews, which were absolutely in our power, having previously ran aground under our guns.

"I have been informed that, according to the institution of the order of St George, I have the right to claim its decorations in the second class for the victory of the 17th June, but I rely upon your justice and generosity. I regret that a secret project, which I addressed to the Count de Besborodko the 6th of June of the last year, has not been adopted. I communicated this project to the Baron de Beichler, who has promised me to speak to you of it. I was detained in St Petersburgh until the end of August, in order to hinder me, as I have heard, from proceeding into the service of Sweden. My poor enemies, how I pity them! But for this circumstance my intention was to have presented myself at your head-quarters in the hope to be of some utility; and the Baron de Beichler, in departing from St Petersburgh in order to join you, promised me to assure you of my devotion for the service of your department, and that I should hold myself ready to return to you the instant I was called. My conduct has not since changed, although I hold in my hand a parole for two years, and I regard eighteen months of this parole, in a time of war, more as a punishment than as a favour. I hope that your Highness will succeed in concluding peace this year with the Turks; but, in a contrary case, if it should please you to recall me to take command of the fleet in the ensuing campaign, I would ask permission to bring with me the French officer concerning whom I spoke to you, with one or two others, who are good tacticians, and who have some knowledge of war. On my return here I received a gold medal, granted me by the *unanimous* voice of Congress, at the moment I received a parole from this honourable body. The United States have decreed me this honour, in order to perpetuate the remembrance of the services which I rendered to America eight years previous, and have ordered a copy to be presented to all the sovereigns and all the academies of Europe, with the exception of Great Britain. There is reason to believe that your Highness will be numbered among the sovereigns of Europe, in consequence of the treaty of peace which you are about to conclude with the Turks; but in any case, if a copy of my medal will be acceptable to you as a mark of my attachment for your person, it will do me an honour to offer it to you. "PAUL JONES."

The Rear-Admiral suffered much bodily illness during the interval which elapsed between the despatch of this letter and the period when he sent off his forlorn hope, the subjoined epistle, in the spring of the following year:—

"*To her Imperial Majesty of all the Russias.*

"Paris, $\frac{\text{25th Feb.}}{\text{8th March,}}$ 1791.

"MADAM,—If I could imagine that the letter which I had the honour to write to your Majesty from Warsaw, the 25th September,

1789, had come to hand, it would be without doubt indiscreet in me to beg you to cast your eyes on the documents enclosed, which *accuse no person*,* and the only intent of which is, to let you see that in the important campaign of Liman, the part which I played was not either that of a *zero* or of a *harlequin*, who required to be made a colonel at the *tail* of his regiment. I have in my hands the means to prove, incontestably, that I directed all the useful operations against the Capitan Pacha. The task which was given to me at this critical conjuncture was very difficult. I was obliged to sacrifice my own opinion and risk my military reputation for the benefit of your empire. But I hope you will be satisfied with the manner in which I conducted myself, and also of the subsequent arrangements, of which I am persuaded you have not been ac-

---

* In a letter from Warsaw to Mr Littlepage, he says, the Count de B——, (we know not whether de Bruce or de Besborodko, though it is probably the latter,) had intercepted his despatch to the Empress till orders could be got from Potemkin.

quainted until this moment. The gracious counsel which your Majesty has often done me the honour to repeat to me before my departure for the Black Sea, and in the letter which you deigned to write to me afterwards, has since been the rule of my conduct; and the faithful attachment with which you had inspired me for your person, was the only reason which hindered me from requesting my dismissal when I wrote to you from Warsaw; for I confess that I was extremely afflicted, and even offended, at having received a parole for two years in time of war,—a parole which it has never entered into my mind to wish for, and still less to ask, and of which I have not profited to go to America, or even to Denmark, where I had important business; for I had always hoped to be usefully employed in your service, before the expiration of this parole, which has done me so much injury; and although in public I would not have failed to have spoken to you at the last audience which you granted me, yet I was unfortunately led to believe the repeated promises made me, that I should have a private audience in order to lay before you my military projects, and to speak of them in detail.

"I hope that the brilliant success with which Providence has blessed your arms will enable you to grant peace to your enemies without shedding more of human blood; but in a contrary case your Majesty can be well instructed from my project, No 12, of the last year.

"As I have my enemies, and as the term of my parole is about to expire, I await the orders of your Majesty, and should be flattered, if it is your pleasure for me to come and render you an account in person. Mr ——, who has the goodness to charge himself with this packet, which I have addressed to him, sealed with my arms, will also undertake to forward me your orders; I therefore pray you to withdraw me as soon as possible from the cruel uncertainty in which I am placed. Should you deign, Madam, to inform me that you are pleased with the services which I have had the happiness to render you, I will console myself for the misfortunes which I have suffered, as I drew my sword for you from personal attachment and ambition, but not for interest. My fortune, as you know, is not very considerable; but as I am philosopher enough to confine myself to my means, I shall be always rich.

"I have the honour to be,
Madam,
Of your Imperial Majesty
The most faithful and
Obedient servant,
PAUL JONES."

So late as the month of July of the same year, we find Paul Jones still in Paris, and now in very bad health, but even yet occupied with Russia. His next and final letter is addressed to Baron Grimm, the literary correspondent of the Empress, who, a dozen years before, had celebrated his praises.* His former attempts having

* In the original correspondence of Grimm we find the following passage, which does not appear in the much-abridged edition of his voluminous works published in this country. This passage, which we had not seen till after the first volume of the Memoir

been so utterly unsuccessful, he discovers considerable address in trying his fortune in a new

---

was printed, shows that both Mr Sherburne and the present editor are mistaken in supposing that the bust of Paul Jones was originally taken at his own suggestion. The letter of Baron Grimm bears date January, 1780, at which time he says Paul Jones had been some weeks in Paris. This cannot be correct, as it was among the very last days of December when he escaped from the Texel; the only error, however, is of a few weeks. "The intrepid Paul Jones," says the Baron, "has been here for some weeks. He has had the honour to be presented to the King. He has been applauded with transport at all the public places where he has shown himself, and particularly at the opera. It is a singularity worthy of remark, that this brave Corsair, who has given multiplied proofs of possessing a soul the most firm, and courage the most determined, is at the same time the most feeling and mild man in the world, and that he has made a great many verses full of elegance and softness, the sort of poetry which appears most congenial to his taste being the elegy and the pastoral. The Lodge of the Nine Sisters, of which he is a member, have employed M. Houdon to take his bust. This resemblance is a new masterpiece worthy of the chisel which appears tack. The Empress, it may be premised, had long shown herself ambitious of being considered the munificent patroness of science and of scientific men, in whatever regarded the improvement of her country, and particularly of her navy.

" *Rear-Admiral Paul Jones to Baron Grimm.*

" Paris, 9th July, 1791.

" SIR,—M. Houdon has sent to your house the bust which you have done me the honour to accept.* Mademoiselle Marchais has told me

---

destined to consecrate to immortality illustrious men of all kinds."

* His own bust, " now decorated," he says, " with the order of St Anne, on the American uniform, one reason why I wish to be authorised by the American States to wear that order." This is said in a letter to Mr Jefferson, written soon after his final epistle to the Empress, and when he had formed the design of again entering the French fleet of evolution, if bodily indisposition, and the worse sickness of hope deferred, left him power to form any considerate or consistent plan of future conduct.

all the obliging things you have said regarding me.

"As it is my duty to interest myself in objects that may be useful to Russia, I must inform you that I have met with a man here, whom I have known for fifteen years, who has invented a new construction of ships of war, which has small resemblance, either externally or internally, to our present war-ships, and which will, he says, possess the following advantages over them :—

"I. The crew will be better sheltered during an engagement.

"II. The lodging-room of the crew will be more spacious; every individual may have a bed

---

There were five orders of knighthood in Russia, three of which were instituted by Peter the Great, and two, that of St George and St Vladimir, by the Empress Catharine the Second. The order of St Anne was a Holstein, and not a Russian order. The Empress never conferred this order herself. She left it to the Grand Duke Paul, as Duke of Holstein, and from him Paul Jones received it. It was accordingly less valued than those of her own institution bestowed by herself.

or a hammock, and there may be as much air as is wished for, night and day, in the sleeping apartments.

"III. There will be less smoke during an engagement."

The enumeration of all the rare qualities of this *beau idéal* of a war-ship might prove tedious; suffice it, that a ship of the new construction, of 54 guns, if well armed and commanded, might have faced one of the old make carrying 100 guns; that it would cost less both in artillery and timber, be a better sailer, go nearer the wind, and possess many other advantages. "For a long time," the Rear-Admiral states, "he had, in conjunction with his friend Dr Franklin, tried to construct a ship combining the advantages of being a fast sailer, not driving to leeward, drawing little water, &c.; but they always encountered great obstacles. From the death of that great philosopher," he continues, "having rather too much time on my hands, (a very gentle hint,) I think I have surmounted the difficulties which baffled us, and stopped our progress. The ship-builder of whom I have spoken has explained nothing to me in detail, and I can form no idea on the subject. He wishes to preserve his invention, and to draw emolument from it; and nothing can be more just, if on experiment his discovery holds. As this is a thing which appears to me to deserve the attention of the Empress, I beg of you to acquaint her Majesty as soon as possible. This person wished to go to England to offer his discovery, where I think it would have been received; but, as I have some influence with him, I have persuaded him to remain here, and wait your reply. If he receive any encouragement, he will communicate his ideas more fully to me. But in every case I dedicate to the Empress, without any stipulation, all that my feeble genius has accomplished in naval architecture." The Rear-Admiral then relates his own supposed discovery, and, like a skilful orator, winds up, by pressing hard the main point of his argument. "Will not this, presuming it correct, be of great advantage to the infant marine of the Black Sea, and consequently to the prosperity of the Russian empire?"

It appears that Baron Grimm received an

answer from the Empress in relation to this first application, though it can scarcely be called a satisfactory one. She says there was a prospect of a speedy peace; but if peace did not take place, she would let M. Paul Jones know her intentions respecting himself: and she tacitly reproves Grimm's interference by saying, that she would not choose him as the medium of her communications with Paul Jones.

CHAPTER V.

The voluminous papers left by Paul Jones afford very scanty materials for his domestic history. From boyhood his place in society was completely isolated. His extensive correspondence, as it came into the hands of his relatives, is chiefly that of business, or of the ceremonial connected with business, and with the courtesies of acquaintanceship. His intercourse with society amounted to little more than the exchange of the customary offices of kindness and civility. He was early separated, by insurmountable circumstances, from his own relatives; he never afterwards found a fixed home, nor does his correspondence afford any trace of the kindly, genial, unbending, and cordial familiarity of confidential friendship. His letters consequently want the charm of a particular or individual interest. Few of them contain a single observation on men or manners, or even the expression of an opinion not merely professional. His journals, in like manner, are strictly confined to professional affairs, and contain little that can either extend the range of knowledge or gratify a liberal curiosity. With the fields of observation, whether in America, France, and Russia, that were presented to a mind so active and acute, this is much to be regretted. As it is, the interest of this memoir must rest wholly on the public life of its subject. The few of his private confidential letters which exist, do, however, unfold his character in a very amiable way. Those to his relations in Scotland, written in the latter years of his life, display the most affectionate solicitude for the happiness of those who could but little add to his, and much good sense in his endeavours to promote it.

According to his London or American biographer, Paul Jones was " as chivalrous in love as in war." This is assumed, it is probable, on the principle that every seaman is bound to be so, as a point of professional duty,—from Nelson of the Nile down to Jack or

Ben just paid off at Portsmouth. "Paul Jones," we are gravely told, "was always seriously in love," and, what is more singular, "often with women he had never seen." This contradicts all ordinary experience, and even goes beyond romantic tradition. Though seamen are not remarkable for tedious or roundabout modes of courtship, they are seldom so far spiritualized as not to require at least one passing glance of the fair objects that kindle the sudden flame. That among all existing unknown beauties, Paul Jones should have singled out Lady Selkirk as the object of his romantic and passionate admiration, appears, at least on this, the frigid side of the Atlantic, too absurd for serious refutation. His gallantry of disposition, and the disagreeable and derogatory imputations to which his descent on St Mary's Isle was liable, sufficiently account for the address to Lady Selkirk of a man who had so quick a sense of dishonour, and so tenacious a regard for reputation, as Paul Jones evinced in every transaction of his life. It is therefore quite unnecessary to account for his conduct in this memorable affair, by raising the ridiculous hypothesis of his having fallen in love with a married lady of high rank, whom he had never seen, and whose eldest son was at that time of an age to have acted as his lieutenant. It is indeed just possible, that, while Paul Jones was still a lad, sailing to the port of Kirkcudbright, he might have seen the lady of St Mary's Isle, though even then it would be preposterous to imagine such long-lived and romantic consequences from this transient vision, however fair and captivating.

Paul Jones was by no means so great a fool as his historian, no doubt to do him honour, would insinuate. A man "in the singular situation of being in love with every woman in Paris," and "often with women he had never seen," was evidently in no imminent peril from the attractions of any individual charmer, however powerful these might be. In the present case this seems to have been the fact. The true, and, it may be said, the only mistress to whom Paul Jones was ever devoted with all the powers of his heart and mind was—GLORY, in pursuit of whom he made no scruple at any time to set his foot on the neck of "the gentle Cupid," or, if need were, to use that "soft integument" as a stepping-stone in his mounting path.

It is said that John Paul Jones, soon after entering the navy, formed an ardent attachment to an American lady. Their affection was mutual, but circumstances forbade their union; and from this period he formed the resolution of never marrying. There is, however, much to intervene between the cradle and the grave of the passions; and when a man expresses resolutions of this kind, his friends generally know with what proper degree of credit or allowance to receive them. He sent a message to his sisters, by Mr Kennedy,—the French teacher of Dumfries, who waited on him with letters from his relations, about the year 1784,—purporting that he would never marry; yet shortly after this we find him expressing a very tender and anxious interest for a French lady (Madame T———,) with whom he was in correspondence.

The most brilliant period of the *bonnes for-*

tunes of Paul Jones was during his residence at Paris and Versailles in 1780, and immediately after his escape from the Texel; the period commemorated by Baron Grimm, the era of his court favour, military order, and gold sword. He at this time engaged in various *flirtations*, of the kind and complexion which no man of his age and profession, moving in gay society in Paris, could have avoided, if he wished to live in the odour of gallantry. His acquaintance with the lady who assumes, or who received the poetical appellation of Delia, must have commenced about this time, as the hottest fire of her love-letters appears to have fallen upon the Chevalier at L'Orient during the existence of Landais' mutiny.

The conduct of the Chevalier at this time was, it is to be feared, more creditable to his general spirit of gallantry than to his fidelity to the fair and devoted Delia. Among the ladies whom he met most frequently in the society he frequented at Versailles was the Countess of Lavendal, a married woman, (and marriage in Paris at this time made an indispensable ingredient in the attractions of a mistress,) young, beautiful, witty, and withal a little intriguing. To the good graces of this lady the Chevalier Paul Jones anxiously and assiduously recommended himself. There is, however, reason to surmise, that the gentleman might have been somewhat of a self-seeker even in his admiration of the beautiful Countess. It is undeniable, that he owed all the distinction he had just obtained solely to court-favour,—to the French ministry he owed nothing. "La belle Comtesse," indeed, appeared to have looked to him as the medium of advancement or employment for her husband, without affecting to possess court-patronage herself; but there was no limiting the influence of a clever and beautiful woman at the Court of Versailles, where, although the reigning sovereign was unassailable, there were always so many open channels, through ministers and favourites, high and low, male and female. When the lady, whose object was to obtain employment for her husband, in conjunction with the American hero, but who had no objection to the by-play of a little harmless coquetry, thought it prudent to draw back, after a course of very promising encouragement, her admirer appears to have borne his disappointment with great philosophy; and to have turned the tables upon the fickle charmer, and extricated himself from the affair with a cool dexterity that might command the applause of Chesterfield himself.

This Parisian "course of true love" is fully elucidated by the following extracts of published letters, attributed to a young English lady, a Miss Edes, residing at the time in Versailles. They were written early in June and July, 1780. Coupling the fact of their immediate publication in England, with the staple of their composition, if left to our own instincts, and not positively assured that they were originally the private letters of a young lady, we would be inclined to attribute them to some of the gentlemen of the press who flourished fifty years ago; and who then exported the scandal of Paris to London, in a somewhat clumsier way than the same business is still managed, but exactly in the same spirit.

"The famous Paul Jones dines and sups here

often," says Miss Edes; "he is a smart man of thirty-six, speaks but little French, appears to be an extraordinary genius, a poet as well as a hero; a few days ago he wrote some verses extempore, of which I send you a copy. He is greatly admired here, especially by the ladies, who are all wild for love of him, as he for them; but he adores Lady ——, (the Countess Lavendal,) who has honoured him with every mark of politeness and distinction."

"*Verses addressed to the Ladies who have done me the Honour of their polite Attention!" Presented by Paul Jones to Mademoiselle G——.**

"Insulted Freedom bled,—I felt her cause,
And drew my sword to vindicate her laws,
From principle, and not from vain applause.
I've done my best; self-interest far apart,
And self-reproach a stranger to my heart;

* This is supposed to be one of the daughters of M. Genet, but could not have been his eldest daughter, who was by this time married to M. Campan, and a woman of the bedchamber to the Queen.

My zeal still prompts, ambitious to pursue
The foe, ye fair! of liberty and you:
Grateful for praise, spontaneous and unbought,
A generous people's love not meanly sought;
To merit this, and bend the knee to beauty,
Shall be my earliest and my latest duty."

In this, and other effusions fully more creditable to his muse, Paul Jones, we presume, makes no worse figure than other clever men have done, when, departing from their true character, they choose to engage in the solemn fooleries or trifling puerilities of a part for which neither nature, education, nor habit, has fitted them.*

---

* In vindication of the critical opinions of Grimm, who praises the "grace and softness" of the verses of Paul Jones, we subjoin what is considered a tolerably fair specimen of his poetical vein. It is no disparagement of our own great naval hero to say, that the verses of Paul Jones are far superior to those of Nelson. Indeed, of all such effusions the opinion of Byron ought to be adopted as quite canonical—they are so good, that—"bad were better." The only use of the verses of Paul Jones is the evidence they afford, that their author could not have been the

The same young lady, supposed to be the Miss Edes, sometimes noticed in the correspondence of

---

brutal, ignorant, and ferocious pirate he is frequently described. In this view they are invaluable to truth and to his honest fame :—

" *Verses written on Board the Alliance off Ushant, the 1st Day of January, 1780, immediately after escaping out of the Texel from the Blockade of the British Fleet; being in Answer to a Piece written and sent to the Texel by a young Lady at the Hague.*

TO MISS DUMAS.

I.

" Were I, Paul Jones, dear maid, the 'King of Sea,'
I find such merit in thy virgin song,
A coral crown with bays I'd give to thee,
A car which on the waves should smoothly glide along;
The Nereïds all about thy side should wait,
And gladly sing in triumph of thy state,
'Vivat, vivat' the happy virgin muse!
Of Liberty the friend, whom tyrant power pursues!

II.

" Or, happier lot! were fair Columbia free
From British tyranny, and youth still mine,

the Chevalier with the Genet family, on another occasion, and after further acquaintance, writes thus:—

"Since my last, Paul Jones drank tea and supped here. If I am in love with him, for love I may die; I have as many rivals as there are

---

I'd tell a tender tale to one like thee
With artless looks, and breast as pure as thine.
If she approved my flame, distrust apart,
Like faithful turtles, we'd have but one heart;
Together then we'd tune the silver lyre,
As Love or sacred Freedom should our lays inspire.

III.

"But since, alas! the rage of war prevails,
And cruel Britons desolate our land,
For Freedom still I spread my willing sails,
My unsheath'd sword my injured country shall command.
Go on, bright maid, the Muses all attend
Genius like thine, and wish to be its friend.
Trust me, although convey'd through this poor shift,
My new-year's thoughts are grateful for thy virgin gift."*

* This gallant effusion was despatched from Corogne, where Jones put in for a short time on his way to Groix. The lady was the daughter of M. Dumas, the American agent at Amsterdam.

ladies, but the most formidable is still Lady ——, (the Countess Lavendal,) who possesses all his heart. This lady is of high rank and virtue, very sensible, good-natured, and affable. Besides this, she is possessed of youth, beauty, and wit, and every other female accomplishment. He is gone, I suppose, for America. They correspond, and his letters are replete with elegance, sentiment, and delicacy. She drew his picture, (a striking likeness,) and wrote some lines under it, which are much admired, and presented it to him, who, since he received it, is, he says, like a second Narcissus, in love with his own resemblance; to be sure he is the most agreeable sea-wolf one would wish to meet with. As to his verses you may do with them what you please. The King had given him a magnificent gold sword, which, lest it should fall into the hands of the enemy, he has begged leave to commit it to the care of her ladyship,—a piece of gallantry which is here highly applauded. If any further account of this singular genius should reach my hands, you shall have it."

We believe that even the most finished French

coquet would feel rather startled at the eclat of an appearance like the above in an English periodical published within the month. The Countess must have been alarmed, and she took her measures accordingly.

When Jones was compelled to return to L'Orient, and in the prospect of an immediate departure for America, he took courage to speak more plainly to this condescending Countess. Though, as has been noticed, he found it afterwards expedient to give the affair another turn, his first letter, which follows, cannot be mistaken:—

" I am deeply concerned," he says, " in all that respects your happiness; I therefore have been and am much affected at some words that fell *in private* conversation from Miss Edes the evening I left Versailles. I am afraid that you are less happy than I wish, and am sure you deserve to be. I am composing a cipher for a key to our future correspondence, so that you will be able to write me very freely, and without risk. It is a small dictionary of particular words, with a number annexed to each of them. In our letters we will write sometimes the corresponding number instead of the word, so that the meaning can never be understood until the corresponding words are interlined over the numbers.

"I beseech you to accept the within lock. I am sorry that it is now eighteen inches shorter than it was three months ago. If I could send you my heart itself, or any thing else that could afford you pleasure, it would be my happiness to do it. *Before* I had the honour of seeing you, I wished to comply with the invitation of my lodge,* and I need not add that I have *since* found *stronger* reasons that have compelled me to seek the means of returning to France again as soon as possible."

There was a manifest want of *retenue* in this epistle. The lady, it is said, kept the trophies, namely, the cipher, the letter, and the lock of hair, but wrote to Jones, expressing her astonishment at his audacity, and her conjecture that his packet had been *misdirected* when sent to herself. She begged, at the same time, to introduce

* Probably the lodge of the *Neuf Sœurs*, of which he was a member.

to him the Count her husband, who was to pass through L'Orient. "She should be obliged to the Chevalier to show him every civility." This he did, and afterwards wrote the Countess:—

"L'Orient, July 14, 1780.

"MADAM,—Since I had the honour to receive your packet from Versailles, I have carefully examined the copy of my letter from Nantes, but am still at a loss, and cannot conceive, what part of the letter itself could have occasioned your imagining I had mistaken the address. As for the little packet it contained, perhaps it might better have been omitted: if so, it is easily destroyed. If my letter has given you even a moment's uneasiness, I can assure you, that to think so would be as severe a punishment as could be inflicted upon me. However I may have been mistaken, my intention could never have been to give you the most distant offence. I was greatly honoured by the visit of the Count, your husband, and am so well convinced of his superior understanding, that I am glad to believe Miss Edes was mistaken. I admire him so much, that I should esteem myself very happy indeed to have a joint expedition with him by sea and land, though I am certain that his laurels would far exceed mine. I mention this, because M. de Genet has both spoken and written to me on the subject as from the Count himself.

"I had the honour to lay a project before the King's ministers in the month of May, for future combined expeditions under the flag of America, and had the satisfaction to find that my ideas were approved by them. If the Count, your husband, will do me the honour to concert with M. de Genet, that the court may send with me to America the application that was intended to be made to Congress, conformable to the proposal I made, it would afford me a pleasing opportunity of showing my gratitude to the King, to his ministers, and to this generous-minded nation. I should be greatly proud to owe my success to your own good offices; and would gladly share with your husband the honour that might result from our operations. I have within these few days had the honour to receive from his Majesty the cross of Military Merit, with a sword that is worthy the royal giver, and a letter which I ardently wish to deserve. I hold the sword in too high estimation to risk its being taken by the enemy; and therefore propose to deposit it in the care of a friend. None can be more worthy of that sacred deposite than you, Madam; and if you will do me the honour to be its guardian, I shall esteem myself under an additional obligation to deserve your ribbon, and to prove myself worthy of the title of your knight. I promised to send you a particular account of my late expedition; but the late extraordinary events that have taken place, with respect to the frigate Alliance, make me wish to postpone that relation until after a court-martial in America shall have furnished evidence for many circumstances that would, from a simple assertion, appear romance and founded on vanity. The only reason for the revolt on board the Alliance was, because the men were not paid either wages or prize-money; and because one or two envious persons persuaded them that I had concurred with M. de Chaumont to defraud them, and to keep them in Europe during the war, which, God knows, was not true.

For I was bound directly for America; and far from concurring with M. de Chaumont, I had not even written or spoken to him, but had highly resented his mean endeavours to keep the poor men out of their just rights, which was the only business that brought me to court in April.

"If I am to have the honour of writing you from beyond sea, you will find that the cipher I had the honour to send you may be necessary; because I would not wish all my informations to be understood, in case my letters should fall into the hands of the enemy. I shall communicate no idea in cipher that will offend even such great delicacy as yours; but as you are a philosopher, and as friendship has nothing to do with sex, pray what harm is there in wishing to have the picture of a friend? Present, I pray, my best respects to the Count. If we are hereafter to be concerned together in war, I hope my conduct will give him satisfaction; at any rate I hope for the honour of his friendship. Be assured that I shall ever preserve for you the most profound esteem and the most grateful respect.

"PAUL JONES."

The lady waived the honour of being constituted guardian of the gold sword; and whatever her influence with the Chevalier might have been, it now declined rapidly. From the Road of Groix Jones wrote to her in the following well-considered and measured terms; and, from his next letters, it appears that the correspondence henceforth languished on his side:—

"*Paul Jones to the Countess de Lavendal.*

"Ariel, Road of Groix, September 21, 1780.

"MADAM,—I was honoured with the very polite letter that your Ladyship condescended to write me on the 5th of last month. I am sorry that you have found it necessary to refuse me the honour of accepting the deposite mentioned in my last, but am determined to follow your advice, and be myself its guardian. I have been detained in this open road by contrary and stormy winds since the 4th of this month. There is this moment an appearance of a fair opportunity, and I will eagerly embrace it. I have received a letter from the first minister, very favourable to the project I mentioned to you, and you may depend on my utmost interest with Congress to bring the matter to issue. I am sure that assembly will with pleasure say all yourself or the Count could wish respecting the Count, if my scheme is adopted.

"I have the satisfaction to inform you, that, by the testimony of all the persons just arrived in four ships at L'Orient from Philadelphia, the Congress and all America appeared to be warmly my friends; and my heart, conscious of its own uprightness, tells me I shall be well received. Deeply and gratefully impressed with a sense of what I owe to you and your husband's attentions and good wishes, and ardently desiring to merit your friendship and the love of this nation by my whole conduct through life,

"I remain, Madam, &c. &c.

"P. S.—I will not fail to write whenever I have any thing worth your reading; at the same time, may I hope to be honoured now and then with a letter from you, directed to Philadelphia. I was selfish in begging you to write me in French, because your letters would serve me as an exercise. Your English is correct, and even elegant."*

Long afterwards his correspondence with the Countess is thus ceremoniously resumed:—

Captain Paul Jones to M. de Genet, enclosing Letters to the Countess de Lavendal and the Marquis de Castries.

"Triomphant, Porto la Bello,
February 28, 1783.

"DEAR SIR,—I had the honour to receive your favour of the 16th May, 1781, only a few days before I launched the America at Portsmouth. Perhaps Colonel Lawrence, (who is no more,) in the warmth of his public zeal, had forgot my letter, and carried it with him to the fate of Corn-

* The above letter is addressed, in the copy before us, to the Countess de Bourbon. It is, however, obviously intended for the Countess de Lavendal. Paul Jones could not have been in correspondence with two different ladies to whom he would have wished to intrust "the deposite."

wallis. My mind was so much on the stretch from receiving your letter till I reached Boston, that you will, I hope, excuse my silence. I expected to have written by the Iris; but the stormy weather after leaving Boston rendered it impossible to put letters on board, and I had not a moment's time before we left the port. I leave the seal of my letter to the Marquis de Castries open, that you may read it yourself, and show it to the Countess de Lavendal before you seal and deliver it. She will there see that invincible obstacles have defeated my projects, which I have pursued with unremitting attention. I am happy that my little present was accepted by Miss Sophy* with so much favour, and that it was taken in good part by her family and intended husband. I am not surprised that your son-in-law is a worthy man. It could not be otherwise, since he has your approbation, and is the choice of the young lady. From the complexion of the King of England's speech of the 5th December the war ought now to be at an end. I hope and

---

* A daughter of M. Genet.

sincerely wish it, for humanity has need of peace. But if the war should continue, it is not impossible that I may command again before it is finished. Returning my respectful compliments to all your family, and to Miss Edes; and still hoping to revisit France, I am,

"Dear Sir, &c. &c.

"M. de Genet, Versailles."

"Captain Paul Jones to the Countess de Lavendal, enclosed in the above.

"Triomphant, Porto Cabello,
February, 28, 1783.

"I RECEIVED, Madam, a short time before I left North America, from M. Genet, a letter, dated Versailles, 18th May, 1781, containing a message from your Ladyship respecting the military projects I had in contemplation in connexion with the Count when I left Versailles. As nothing could add more to my disappointment than a supposition on your part that I had not pursued these objects with constant zeal, I have desired M. Genet to put into your hands, before it is delivered to the person for whom it is directed, a letter, by which you will see that invincible obstacles alone have prevented the full operation of my schemes, which, till very lately, have always been supported by hope. I now think the war at an end; but if it should continue, I shall not voluntarily remain out of the busy scene, and I am still of opinion my former projects might be adopted with public utility. I can, however, promise nothing, but that my principles are invariably the same. I hope to return to France, and am persuaded you will rather feel compassion for my disappointment than withdraw from me any part of your esteem.—I am,

Madam, with sentiments of the most profound respect, &c. &c.

" *To the Countess de Lavendal.*"

In reference to her husband, this lady had evidently formed expectations from Paul Jones which he never possessed the power to realize; and which, it is to be presumed, arose rather from the strength of her own wishes, than from false hopes held out by her admirer. How he could have proposed to connect himself with a man of no professional eminence, whom, when the idea was formed, he had never seen, and, from Miss Edes' report, supposed a fool, must be left to the sagacity of the reader, and will, perhaps, require his indulgence.

The letter sent for the perusal of the Countess does not appear much in point, nor could it have proved very satisfactory to her.

" *Captain Paul Jones to the Marquis de Castries, enclosed to M. Genet, for the perusal of the Countess de Lavendal.*

" Triomphant, Porto Cabello,
28th February, 1783.

" My Lord Marquis,—You have no doubt been officially informed of the act of Congress presenting the America to his Majesty, to replace the Magnifique, when that ship was lost at Boston. Perhaps you may have also heard, that soon after my return from France to Philadelphia, in the Ariel, I was unanimously elected by Congress to command the America. It was proposed by his Excellency, Mr Morris, Minister of Marine, to arm the America *en flute*, and send her to Brest in December, 1781, with a cargo of large masts, fit for ships of the line, to be armed for war, &c. But when I arrived at Portsmouth, I found the ship not half built, and all the materials were wanting to finish the construction. Instead of commanding a fine ship, and being attended by frigates belonging to the continent, the inspection of the construction fell entirely upon me, almost without money or materials to carry it on. I had been thus employed for sixteen months before the act of Congress presenting the America to the King deprived me of that command. It was thought that act of Congress must give me pain, but those who were of that opinion did not well know my character. It was a sacrifice I made with pleasure, to testify my grateful regard for his Majesty, and my invariable attention and zeal to promote the common cause. I continued my inspection till the America was launched, and having then delivered her to M. de Martigne, appointed by his Excellency the Marquis de Vaudreuil, I set out for Philadelphia. A project was then in contemplation between Mr Morris and the Chevalier de la Luzerne, for employing me immediately with a command of some frigates; but not being able to get the South Carolina frigate out of the hands of Mr Gillan, their project did not succeed. Thus disappointed, I applied to Congress to send me back to Boston to make a campaign for my instruction on board his Majesty's fleet. Congress having passed an act for that purpose, I returned to Boston the day before the fleet sailed, with letters from the Minister of Marine, and the Chevalier de la Luzerne, to his Excellency the Marquis de Vaudreuil, who kindly received me as a volunteer on board of his ship. I have been so handsomely treated, both by him and the officers, both of the fleet and army, that they leave me nothing more to wish for from them. I am directed to return to Philadelphia when the campaign is ended, unless, in the meantime, I should receive orders to the contrary. I beseech you to assure his Majesty, that I will eagerly embrace every opportunity to testify by my conduct the high sense I have of the honourable marks conferred on me of his favour and esteem, and that I feel a superior obligation for the many marks of his bounty.—I am,

"My Lord Marquis,

with profound respect, &c.

"*To his Excellency the Marquis de Castries,*" *&c.*

Of the Countess de Lavendal we learn no more; nor would the affair have been worth notice, were it not already before the public. The motives which led to the earlier part of this correspondence cannot be mistaken; nor is the address displayed in the attempt to give the affair a turn much to be commended, unless, as seems extremely probable, the coquetry of the lady, and her retention of the gifts she disclaims in words, justify the affected astonishment of an admirer whose vanity was to all appearance more interested than his serious affections. If the apology be offered for this correspondence, that Paul Jones did not understand French manners, this will more strongly justify the lady than her admirer; and it is to be feared that another aggravation is, its being simultaneous with that of the devoted Delia, the anonymous lady mentioned at page 261, vol. I.

Delia has so dexterously preserved her incognita, that it is scarce possible, even if it were important, to ascertain her real condition. Her letters which are preserved appear to have been written to Jones while at L'Orient, and when he was supposed on the eve of sailing for America. These epistles, which are warmly passionate, breathe the eloquence of deep and genuine feeling, and display the boundless generosity of a devoted if not very discreet attachment; but they, at the same time, discover a larger experience in "affairs of the heart" than was likely to be possessed or acknowledged by a very young woman, and habits of life which intimate more independence and freedom than custom permitted to any unmarried French girl, if above the very lowest rank. Delia appears to have received the visits of gentlemen,—a privilege enjoyed only by married women or widows; and she alludes to her income of eight thousand livres (no small fortune in those days) as if it were under her sole and uncontrolled command. She alleges her liberality of disposition as the cause of her narrow fortune, and thus warrants the conclusion, that her conduct was perfectly independent of control. Her extreme apprehension lest her letters or her portrait should be seen, which is repeatedly expressed, is but a natural and becoming female feeling, from which nothing can be surmised of her real character and condition. It was a duty that her lover owed to her memory, or, if she survived him, to the memory of their attachment, to have placed this warm and animated correspondence beyond the power of either misrepresentation or derision.

In the American Memoir of Paul Jones republished in London, it is said, "the Commodore grew alarmed when the lady proposed to follow him to America." Her original letters, which Paul Jones has preserved with a care he was not likely to have bestowed on those of a person to whom he was indifferent, bear no trace of any proposition so indecorous. In the most fervid of her eloquent compositions, with an abundant lack of discretion, there is no symptom of indelicacy. Her distress, her agonies at parting with her lover, are very frankly proclaimed, but she contemplates no such termination of her misery as an elopement. "Heaven," she says, "will reunite us, and watch over the fate of two beings who love faithfully, and whose upright hearts deserve to be happy. I incessantly address myself to Heaven for your safe arrival in America. If you are satisfied with that government you will continue in its service; if not, resign, and rejoin your faithful friend. The whole world besides may forsake you, but her heart is eternally yours. You inquire how you can render me happy?—take care of yourself, love me, study the means of enabling us to pass our lives together, and never forget that my life is bound up in yours." Delia makes her lover repeated offers of such assistance as she had the power of affording during the exigency of his affairs at L'Orient:—"She had trinkets, she had effects," and with the most disinterested spirit she is willing to sacrifice them all. These offers are made with grace and delicacy, but it does not appear that they were accepted; and, from a

M 2

passage in one of her letters, it would seem that Paul Jones had given her assistance of a pecuniary nature.

It is said by the poet,—

> "Those who greatly love must greatly fear;"—

the love of Delia was extreme, and her fears corresponded to its excess. The letters of Jones were tolerably frequent for a man engaged in quelling a mutiny, and corresponding with a coquetish Countess. They appear to have soothed the fears of Delia, and filled her with rapturous delight for the moment. She alludes to his responding tears, sighs, and verses; envies her own portrait in his possession, but as regularly relapses into a state of distracting doubt if his silence exceeded the period she had fixed for receiving a letter.

We can perceive no reason for believing "Delia a young and high lady of the court;" but her early letters possess those indelible marks of sincerity, and of warmth and generosity of feeling, which could not fail to interest, were it possible to ascertain who the writer really was. Her memory, nevertheless, possesses some claim with that class of readers pre-eminently called "gentle;" nor is it possible to look on the tear-stains that blot those crooked characters, traced by a hand then trembling with youthful passion, and over which the grave must long since have closed, without a feeling of pity and kindness for the fair writer, so devoted, so eloquent, and probably so unfortunate.

Of the "irresistible love-letters" of Paul Jones, commemorated by Miss Edes and the London editor, we subjoin one specimen, as they have given none. It, we fear, does not lessen the suspicion, that, in the case of Delia, the attachment at this time was strongest on the wrong side. It is written on Christmas-day,—a season for which lovers seldom wait, though parted friends often choose on it to make quittance of neglected correspondence.

Paul Jones to Delia.

"December 25th, 1781.

"I wrote, my lovely Delia, various letters from Philadelphia, the last of which was dated the 20th of June. On the 26th of that month I was unanimously elected by Congress to command the America of 74 guns, on the stocks at Portsmouth, New Hampshire. I superintended the building, which I find so much more backward than I expected, that a plan of operations which I had in view is entirely defeated. I expected to have been at sea this winter, but the building does not go on with the vigour I could wish. Since I came here I have not had a single good opportunity to write to Europe. This situation is doubly irksome to me, my lovely friend, as it stops my pursuit of honour as well as love. It is now more than twelve months since I left France, yet I have not received a single letter from thee in all that time, except the one written in answer to my letter at taking leave. That one is a tender letter indeed, and does honour to thy matchless heart. I read often, and always with transport, the many charming things that are expressed in thy letters, but especially the last. Thy adieu has in it all the finer feelings blended with the noblest sentiments of the heart. Providence, all just and good, has given thee a soul worthy to animate nature's fairest work. I rest, therefore, assured, that absence will not diminish but refine the pure and spotless friendship that binds our souls together, and will ever impress each to merit the affection of the other. Remember and believe my letter at parting; it was but a faint picture of my heart. I will find opportunities to write, and be every thing thou canst wish. My address is under cover to the Hon. Robert Morris, Esq., Minister of Finance, Philadelphia.

"I have not since heard of your relation I left behind, but suppose he is with the army."

We cannot tell whether Delia profited or not by this address; but three years afterwards, when the Chevalier arrived in Paris as agent for prize-money, we find her still alive and faithful. Paul Jones has preserved her first note, and in his own handwriting affixed the date to it:—"From her apartments in the Boulevard," &c. &c. He had some reason to be proud of her fidelity:—this was Paris in 1783. Delia's note is exceedingly characteristic of her country, though we like its tone much less than that of the earlier effusions of its author :—" Is it possible that you are then so near me, and that I am deprived of the sight of a mortal who has constituted the misery of my life for four years ?—O ! most amiable and most ungrateful of men, come to your best friend, who burns with the desire of seeing you. You ought to know that it is but eight days since your Delia was at the brink of the grave. Come, in the name of Heaven !"

It is probable that the Chevalier obeyed this summons, since he thought it worth while to preserve the billet in which it is conveyed.

Delia now disappears from the scene as abruptly as the " beautiful Countess," unless we are able to identify her with Madame T———, a lady for whom, about this time, the Chevalier evinces a warm interest. The supposition, that Madame T———, a widow, it may be presumed, from her friendless and unprotected state, and Delia, are the same individual, is feasible in itself, creditable to both parties, and readily accounts for all the ambiguities in the letters, and still more in the situation of Delia. With Madame T———

Jones corresponded after his return to America in 1786. Her letters to him were sent to the care of the American minister, as those of Delia had formerly been. The reader has the advantage of being introduced to this lady by Paul Jones himself in the following letter to Mr Jefferson:—

"I am much obliged to you for the letter from Madame T——, which you forwarded by the June packet. I now take the liberty to enclose a letter for that worthy lady; and, as I had not the happiness to introduce you to her, (because I wished her fortune to have been previously established,) I shall now tell you *in confidence*, that she is the daughter of the late King and of a lady of quality, on whom his Majesty bestowed a very large fortune on his daughter's account. Unfortunately the father died while the daughter (his great favourite) was very young, and the mother has never since shown her either justice or natural affection. She was long the silent victim of that injustice; but I had the pleasure to be instrumental in putting her in a fair way to obtain redress. His present Majesty received her last year with great kindness. He gave her afterwards several particular audiences, and said ‘he charged himself with her fortune.’ Some things were, as I have understood, fixed on, that depended solely on the King, and he said he would dictate the justice to be rendered by the mother. But the letter you sent me left the feeling author all in tears! Her friend, her protectress, her introductress to the King, was suddenly dead! She was in despair! She lost more than a mother! A loss, indeed, that nothing can repair; for fortune and favour are never to be compared to tried friendship. I hope, however, she has gone to visit the King in July, agreeably to his appointment given her in the month of March. I am persuaded that he would receive her with additional kindness, and that her loss would, in his mind, be a new claim to his protection, especially as he well knows, and has acknowledged, her superior merit and just pretensions. As I feel the greatest concern for the situation of this worthy lady, you will render me a great favour by writing her a note, requesting her to call on you, as you have something to communicate from me. When she comes, be so good as to deliver the within letter, and show her this, that she may see both my confidence in you and my advice to her."

Living so long in Paris or Versailles, it is scarcely possible that Paul Jones could have been deceived in the character or pretensions of Madame T——, though such is not the way in which the daughters "of Louis XV., by ladies of quality," were usually treated. It might also be supposed, that some trace of this daughter would be found in the numerous memoirs, letters, and secret histories of the Court of France. We are not aware that any such evidence does exist. It would, however, be high presumption to limit the number of the illegitimate children of so patriarchal a monarch as Louis XV. Madame T—— was therefore, in all probability, one of his numerous descendants, the only inexplicable circumstance being, that a daughter, "his great favourite," should not otherwise be ever heard of; and that, "very young" when her father died, (in 1774,) we should find in her either the Delia of 1780, or the Madame T——, a widow unknown or unfriended, of 1786. The lady, her protectress, to whom Paul Jones alludes, was, we are incidentally informed, the Marchioness de Marssan, to whom he introduced her. This lady we should presume to be her of the same name, governess to the grand-daughters of Louis XV. and sisters of his unfortunate successor. There is, in short, something inexplicable to us in the history of Madame T——: The sentiments entertained for her by Paul Jones are, however, abundantly clear; they breathe a far more anxious interest than that of friendship. The subjoined letter is a copy of that enclosed to Madame T—— in the letter to Mr Jefferson; the other letter was written to her shortly afterwards.

" *Paul Jones to Madame T——.*

" New York, September 4th, 1787.

" No language can convey to my fair mourner the tender sorrow I feel on her account! The loss of our worthy friend is indeed a fatal stroke! It is an irreparable misfortune which can only be alleviated by this one reflection, that it is the will of God, whose providence has, I hope, other blessings in store for us. She was a tried friend, and more than a mother to you! She would have been a mother to me also had she lived. We have lost her! Let us cherish her memory, and send up grateful thanks to the Almighty that we once had such a friend. I cannot but flatter myself that you have yourself gone to the K—— in July as he had appointed. I am sure your loss will be a new inducement for him to protect you, and render you justice. He will hear you, I am sure; and you may safely unbosom yourself to him, and ask his advice, which cannot but be flattering to him to give you. Tell him you must look on him as your father and protector. If it were necessary, I think, too, that the Count d'A——,* his brother, would, on your personal application, render you good offices by speaking in your favour. I should like it better, however, if you can do without him. Mr Jefferson will show you my letter of this date to

* Count d'Artois, now Charles X.

him. You will see by it how disgracefully I have been detained here by the Board of Treasury. It is impossible for me to stir from this place till I obtain their settlement on the business I have already performed; and as the season is already far advanced, I expect to be ordered to embark directly for the place of my destination in the North. Mr Jefferson will forward me your letters. I am almost without money, and much puzzled to obtain a supply. I have written to Dr B.,* to endeavour to assist me. I mention this with infinite regret, and for no other reason than because it is impossible for me to transmit you a supply under my present circumstances. This is my fifth letter to you since I left Paris. The two last were from France, and I sent them by duplicates. But you say nothing of having received any letters from me! Summon, my dear friend, all your resolution! Exert yourself, and plead your own cause. You cannot fail of success—your cause would move a heart of flint! Present my best re-

* Bancroft.

spects to your sister. You did not mention her in your letter; but I persuade myself she will continue her tender care of her sweet god-son, and that you will cover him all over with kisses from me: they come warm to *you both* from the heart!"

To the same.

"New York, October 24, 1787.

"The last French packet brought no letter to me from the person whose happiness is dearer to me than any thing else. I have been on the rack of fear and apprehension, and am totally unable to account for that silence! My business is done here, and the moment of my return to Europe approaches. My sentiments are unchanged, and my impatience can better be imagined than expressed. I have been honoured here beyond my own expectations.* But your silence makes even honours insipid. I am, however, far from blaming you; want of health, or some other mis-

* See page 305, vol. i.

fortune, must have interposed. If this reaches you, remember me affectionately to your sister and her god-son. May Heaven avert all trouble from you!"

Paul Jones almost immediately followed this letter to Europe. During his short stay in Paris in the winter of 1787, he must in all probability have again seen the lady to whom it was addressed. Both the letters, as well as that sent to Mr Jefferson, bear testimony how deeply his feelings were involved in this attachment, by whatever name it is called, love or friendship. Yet it must have terminated unsatisfactorily, if not unhappily. From the period of his setting out for Denmark and Russia, his correspondence bears no trace of Madame T——; and by the time he reached Amsterdam on his return, this lady must either have been forgotten, or deemed unworthy of remembrance. Whether this arose from his own conduct or fickleness, or the inconstancy of that friend of whose silence while in America he had complained as "making even honours insipid," it is now impossible to determine, though on this occasion we are inclined to decide against the lady, should she even be, as we have surmised, the "eternally devoted" Delia herself.

From a letter written by Paul Jones to two ladies whom he numbered among his friends, and who had pointedly alluded to the supposed state of his affections, and his engagements in Paris, there is reason to suppose that he may, in addition to baffled professional hopes, have suffered disappointment of a more tender kind.

"*Paul Jones to Mesdames Le Grande and Rinsby, à Trevoux, près de Lion.*

"Paris, Feb. 25, 1791.

"Dear and amiable Ladies,—Madame Clement has read me part of a letter from you, in which you conclude that I prefer love to friendship, and Paris to Trevoux. As to the first part you may be right, for love frequently communicates divine qualities, and in that light may be considered as the cordial that Providence has bestowed on mortals, to help them to digest the nauseous draught of life. Friendship, they say, has more solid qualities than love. This is a question I shall not attempt to resolve; but sad experience generally shows that where we expect to find a friend we have only been treacherously deluded by false appearances, and that the goddess herself very seldom confers her charms on any of the human race. As to the second, I am too much a philosopher to prefer noise to tranquillity: if this does not determine the preference between Paris and Trevoux, I will add, that I have had very bad health almost ever since your departure, and that other circumstances have conspired to detain me here, which have nothing to do either with love or friendship. My health is now recovering, and as what is retarded is not always lost, I hope soon to have the happiness of paying you my personal homage, and of renewing the assurance of that undiminished attachment which women of such distinguished worth and talents naturally inspire. I am, in the mean time, dear and amiable Ladies,

"Your most obedient and most humble servant,

"Paul Jones."

The lady's answer merits to be preserved. It displays the true kindness of female friendship, and the frank politeness of a Frenchwoman.

"Trevoux, 6th March, 1791.

"SIR,—I had given up the hope of receiving any intelligence of your Excellency, and I acknowledge it cost me much before I could believe that the promise of a great man was no more to be relied on than that of the herd of mankind. The letter with which you have honoured me convinces me that my heart knew you better than my head; for though my reason whispered that you had quite forgotten us, I was unwilling to believe it.

"Madame Wolfe, as well as myself, is much concerned for the bad state of your health. I am sorry that, like myself, your Excellency is taught the value of health by sickness. Come to us, Sir; if you do not find here the pleasures you enjoy in Paris, you will find a good air, frugal meals, freedom, and hearts that can appreciate you.

“ I am concerned to perceive that your Excellency is an unbeliever in friendship. Alas, if you want friends, who shall pretend to possess them ! I hope you will recover from this error, and be convinced that friendship is something more than a chimera of Plato.

“ Do me the favour to acquaint me with the time we may expect the honour of seeing you. I must be absent for some days, and I would not for any thing in the world that I should not be here on your arrival. If I knew the time, I would send my little carriage to meet the stage-coach, as I suppose you will take that conveyance.

“ Madame Wolfe expects the moment of your arrival with as much eagerness as myself, (she says ;) but as I best know my own feelings, I am certain I go beyond her. Of this I am certain, that we shall both count the day till we have the happiness of seeing you. Come quickly then, I pray you.

“ I beg you, Sir, to receive the assurance of the respectful consideration with which I have the honour to be your Excellency's most humble and obedient servant."

The letters of Paul Jones to his sisters in Scotland are those in which his private character is most truly and advantageously seen. With them he had no part to act, no interests to pursue. His fraternal feelings were warm and steady, and the advice he conveyed to his discordant family, who acquainted him with their dissensions, as a person to whom both parties were disposed to appeal, does equal credit to his head and heart. That these letters should display any traits of the affectionate, confidential cordiality which render the familiar letters of near relatives so delightful, is not to be expected. With his sisters he had enjoyed no domestic intercourse from boyhood, and he could little know of them by an unfrequent interchange of letters. Though not alienated from his affections, they were strangers to his tastes, his habits, his friends, and modes of life, and it is therefore of their own interests and affairs only that he chooses to speak to them.

"Paul Jones to his Sister, Mrs Taylor.

"Amsterdam, March 26, 1790.

"I WROTE you, my dear friend, from Paris, by Mr Kennedy, who delivered me the kind letter you wrote me by him. Circumstances obliged me to return soon afterwards to America, and on my arrival at New York, Mr Thomson delivered me a letter that had been intrusted to his care by Mrs Loudon. It would be superfluous to mention the great satisfaction I received in hearing from two persons I so much love and esteem, and whose worthy conduct as wives and mothers is so respectable in my eyes. Since my return to Europe, a train of circumstances and changes of residence have combined to keep me silent. This has given me more pain than I can express; for I have a tender regard for you both, and nothing can be indifferent to me that regards your happiness and the welfare of your children. I wish for a particular detail of their age, respective talents, characters, and education. I do not desire this information merely from curiosity.

It would afford me real satisfaction to be useful to their establishment in life. We must study the genius and inclination of the boys, and try to fit them, by a suitable education, for the pursuits we may be able to adopt for their advantage. When their education shall be advanced to a proper stage, at the school of Dumfries for instance, it must then be determined whether it may be most economical and advantageous for them to go to Edinburgh or France to finish their studies. All this is supposing them to have great natural genius and goodness of disposition; for without these they can never become eminent. For the females, they require an education suited to the delicacy of character that is becoming in their sex. I wish I had a fortune to offer to each of them; but though this is not the case, I may yet be useful to them. And I desire particularly to be useful to the two young women, who have a double claim to my regard, as they have lost their father. Present my kind compliments to Mrs Loudon, to her husband, to Mr Taylor, and your two families, and depend on my affectionate attachment.

"Write me without delay, and having sealed and directed your letter as you did the one you sent me by Mr Kennedy, let it be enclosed in a cover, and direct the cover thus, 'To Messieurs Stophorst and Hubbard, Amsterdam.' You will inquire if it be necessary to pay a part of the postage, in order that the letter may be sent to Holland in the packet. I should be glad if the two Miss Youngs* would do me the favour to write me each a paragraph in your letter, or to write me, if they prefer it, each a separate letter, and I should be glad to find that they understand and can write the French."

This letter, like all those to his own family, has no signature.

In the end of this year (1790) we find another of his letters, from which, with very great pleasure, we give the following extract. The sisters of the Rear-Admiral, who were probably both in the wrong, had, it appears, appealed to him in their disputes. It is to be hoped they profited by his admonitions.

---

* His orphan nieces alluded to above.

" Paris, December 27, 1790.

" I duly received, my dear Mrs Taylor, your letter of the 16th August, but ever since that time I have been unable to answer it, not having been capable to go out of my chamber, and having been for the most part obliged to keep my bed. I have now no doubt but that I am in a fair way of a perfect recovery, though it will require time and patience.

" I shall not conceal from you that your family discord aggravates infinitely all my pains. My grief is inexpressible, that two sisters, whose happiness is so interesting to me, do not live together in that *mutual tenderness and affection* which would do so much honour to themselves and to the memory of their worthy relations. Permit me to recommend to your serious *study* and *application* Pope's Universal Prayer. You will find more morality in that little piece than in many volumes that have been written by great divines—

‘ Teach me to *feel* another's wo,
To hide the fault I see ;
That mercy I to others show,
Such mercy show to me !’

“ This is not the language of a weak superstitious mind, but the spontaneous offspring of true religion, springing from a heart sincerely inspired by *charity*, and deeply impressed with a sense of the calamities and *frailties* of human nature. If the sphere in which Providence has placed us as members of society requires the exercise of brotherly kindness and charity towards our neighbour in general, how much more is this our duty with respect to individuals with whom we are connected by the *near* and *tender* ties of nature as well as moral obligation. Every lesser virtue may pass away, but *charity* comes from Heaven, and is immortal. Though I wish to be the instrument of making family-peace, which I flatter myself would tend to promote the happiness of you all, yet I by no means desire you to do violence to your own feelings, by taking any step that is contrary to your own judgment and inclination. Your reconciliation must come free from your heart, otherwise it will not last, and therefore it will be better not to attempt it. Should a reconciliation take place, I recommend it of all things, that you never mention past grievances, nor show, by *word*, *look*, or *action*, that you have not forgot them."

From this time Paul Jones never quitted Paris. His continual bad health, and the state of France, and of the capital, torn by faction,—the threatening shadow of those evil days, which were so soon to follow, already lowering over it,—alike enjoined retirement from society. It does not appear to what political party he was attached, though it is probable that of the Girondists, which was the legitimate offspring of the American revolution, had his good wishes, tempered by strong feelings of personal attachment and gratitude towards the amiable Prince who had shown him such distinguished marks of favour. He had never appeared at Court from the time of his return from Russia; and if he appeared at all, it was only once, which must have been a very few months before his death.

The scroll of a letter, dated December 7th, 1791, to the Marquis of La Fayette, remains among his papers, and explains his situation and his loyal and grateful feelings, and proves that, as this crisis drew near, he took the generous part. The Marquis at this time, from his official situation, was constantly in the Palace.

"*Rear-Admiral Paul Jones to the Marquis de la Fayette.*

"Paris, December 7th, 1791.

"DEAR GENERAL,—My ill health for some time past has prevented me from the pleasure of paying you my personal respects, but I hope shortly to indulge myself with that satisfaction.

"I hope you approve the quality of the fur-linings I brought from Russia for the King and yourself. I flatter myself that his Majesty will accept from your hand that little mark of the sincere attachment I feel for his person; and be assured, that I shall be always ready to draw the sword with which he honoured me for the service of the virtuous and illustrious 'PRO-

TECTOR OF THE RIGHTS OF HUMAN NATURE.'

"When my health shall be re-established, M. Simolin will do me the honour to present me to his Majesty as a Russian admiral. Afterwards it will be my duty, as an American officer, to wait on his Majesty with the letter* which I am directed to present to him from the United States.

"I am, dear General,
"With sincere friendship,
"Your affectionate and
"Most humble servant."

From the mutilated fragment of an angry but very energetic letter, addressed to the Minister of Marine, we gather that the claims of Paul Jones on the French government still remained unsettled, which was indeed the case at his death, and that he had been treated with indignity as well as denied justice. The following

---

* That given at page 305, vol. I.

letter, which introduces this warm statement of injuries, has peculiar interest, as it is presumed to be the last effusion of his pen. It does not appear to whom this letter was addressed, though it might probably be to the Minister of Marine for the time. It proves that, however sunk in health and hope, the writer retained the same keenness of temper and acuteness of mind which distinguished him at all periods.

"*Rear-Admiral Paul Jones to the Minister of the French Marine.*

"Paris, March, 1792.

Sir,—In the beginning of the administration of your predecessor, I informed him, that this government, not having paid the salary due to a part of the crew of the Bon Homme Richard at the time when they were discharged from the service, they had been paid on their arrival at Boston ; and having myself been sent back here after the war, under a special commission from the United States, to settle the claims of my crews, I presented a memorial, reclaiming that part of the salary that had never been reimbursed. The Minister held me in suspense for about five months, and then, to my great surprise, instead of satisfying my just demand, he addressed me in a very uncivil letter, treating me, as I conceive, like a schoolboy, and permitting himself to cast unjust and uncivil reflections on my past conduct. My health did not permit me to answer him immediately; but I had prepared a letter, and was just going to send it, when I learned that he had resigned his place as the Minister of the Marine, and that you were named as his successor.

"I request the favour, Sir, that you may read his letter and my answer; after which I persuade myself you will do justice to my first demand, which is merely official. As to my personal pretensions, I never should have set up a claim on that score under circumstances less affecting to my sensibility. Of this I need offer no other proof than my silence in that respect for twelve years past. My losses and unavoidable expenses during my long connexion with this nation amount to a large sum, and have greatly lessened my fortune. I have given solemn proofs of my great attachment towards France, and that attachment still remains undiminished. I persuade myself that I may with full assurance repose my interests through your ministry on the national justice.

"I have the honour to be," &c. &c.

The beginning of the letter referred to above is wanting, as well as the letter of the minister which drew forth the following pithy reply. What of it remains entire commences with the "risks" of the writer in the Texel "for three months together, blocked," he says, "within by the fleet of Holland, and without by the fleets of England, while my head was rendered a prize to excite private treachery and avarice. My fortitude and self-denial alone dragged Holland into the war,—a service of the greatest importance to this nation; for without that great event no calculation can ascertain when the war would have ended.

"Would you suppose, Sir, that my prisoners, 600 in number, were treacherously taken out of my hands in the Texel, with two of my prizes, a new ship of war, pierced for 56 guns, and a frigate of 24 guns in one battery?—Would you suppose that I was driven out of the Texel in a single frigate belonging to the United States, in the face of 42 English ships, and vessels posted to cut off my retreat?—My prisoners were disposed of without my consent, and contrary to my intention. My prizes were all wrested out of my hands, and some of them, particularly the ship of 56 guns, degraded and cut to pieces before my eyes, and in contempt of my authority, though that ship, by the laws of the American flag, was the exclusive property of the captors.

"You appear, Sir, to treat me like a schoolboy, when you say,—'*J'ai l'honneur de vous observer, monsieur, qu'il est toujours d'usage de payer directement aux marins le décompte des salaires qui leur reviennent au désarmement de bâtimens.*' I could not have supposed, Sir, that you had thought me so ignorant as to need that information seventeen years after I was first honoured with the rank of captain in the navy.

* * * * * * * .

" Though my crews were almost naked, and I had no money to administer to their wants, yet my constant application to Court for two months produced no relief, no payment whatever, either for salary or prize-money. I was on the point of sailing back to America, without any appearance of obtaining justice,—without the least acknowledgment, direct or indirect, that the Court was satisfied with my services!—Under these circumstances, in a moment of despair, I came to Court to demand satisfaction.

" The Minister of the United States accompanied me to M. Sartine, who gave us a reception as cold as ice, did not say to me a single word, nor ask me if my health had not suffered from my wounds and the uncommon fatigue I had undergone. The public did me more justice than the minister; and I owe to the King *alone* the flattering marks of distinction with which I was honoured,—a gold sword, and the Order of Military Merit.

" But I solicited in vain for salary and prize-money; and the Minister of Marine detained me so long at Court, that the crew of the American frigate I had left at L'Orient, despairing to obtain redress, revolted, and carried that frigate back to America. * * * *

"It is true, the Marquis de Castries pretended for a long time that I should give him security for the prize-money; but I at last made him recede from the absurdity of that demand. I was detained in Europe four years; and having in that time spent sixty thousand livres of my own money, I received for my share of all the prizes, as commander of the Bon Homme, thirteen thousand livres! * * * * Permit me, by way of comparison, just to mention the treatment the French officers received who served in the American army. The war had been carried on for several years by the Americans alone, and there is no instance where the United States *invited* a French officer to enter into their service. Such as presented themselves and were accepted, have all of them bettered their situation by that connexion. At the end of the war they received a gratification of five years' pay, the Order of Cincinnatus, and a lot of land; and they now enjoy grades far superior to what they could have attained under other circumstances. If we except the Marquis de la Fayette, none of them were rich when they went to America. They are all now in easy circumstances. In short, they have been treated much better than the Americans themselves, who served from the beginning to the end of the Revolution.

"I hope and desire, Sir, that you may lay this letter before the King. It contains many things out of the general rule of delicacy which marks my proceedings, and which, on any occasion less affecting to my sensibility, would never have escaped from my tongue or pen."

From about this time the health of Paul Jones sunk rapidly. Symptoms of jaundice appeared, —a disease which not unfrequently follows mental chagrin and disappointment. It does not, however, appear that he was long confined. About the beginning of July dropsical symptoms supervened on his other disorders, and he expired on the evening of the 18th of that month. Though far from those on whose affection he had a natural claim, his dying hours were not unsolaced by the constant and tender offices of friendship.

Many idle rumours connected with his death have been circulated, as if his latter days had been spent in extreme poverty, chilling neglect, and entire abandonment. These are of a piece with the other calumnies and marks of obloquy with which his memory and character have been loaded. The subjoined letters and documents afford a simple and an ample refutation of charges and assumptions made, probably, as much in ignorance as malice.

"*Letter of M. Beaupoil to either Mrs Taylor or Mrs Loudon, Sisters of Paul Jones, Esq. Admiral in the Russian Service.*

"MADAM,—I am sorry to acquaint you that your brother, Admiral Paul Jones, my friend, paid, yesterday, the debt we all owe to nature. He has made a will, which is deposited in the hands of Mr Badinier, notary, St Servin Street, Paris. The will was drawn in English, by Mr Governor Morris, Minister of the UNITED

STATES, and translated faithfully by the French notary aforesaid. The Admiral leaves his property, real and personal, to his two sisters and their children. They are named in the will as being married, one to William Taylor, and the other to ——— Loudon, of Dumfries. The executor is Mr Robert Morris of Philadelphia. If I could be of any service to you in this business, out of the friendship I bore your brother, I'll do it with pleasure. I am a Frenchman and an officer. I am sincerely yours,

"BEAUPOIL.

"Paris, July 19, 1792, No 7, Hôtel Anglais,
Passage des Petits Pères."

"The English will is signed by Colonels Swan, Blackden, and myself. The schedule of his property lying in Denmark, Russia, France, America, and elsewhere, is signed by Mr Morris, and deposited by me in his bureau, with the original will. Every thing is sealed up at his lodgings, Tournon Street, No 42, Paris.

"You may depend also on the good services of Colonel Blackden, who was an intimate friend of the Admiral's. That gentleman is setting out for London, where you may hear of him at No 18, Great Tichfield Street, London."

On receiving this letter, Mrs Taylor wrote to Colonel Blackden in London, and obtained a reply in course of post.

"Colonel Blackden to Mrs Taylor of Dumfries, eldest Sister of Admiral Paul Jones.

"Great Tichfield Street,
London, Aug. 9th.

"MADAM,—I had the honour of receiving your letter of the 3d instant, and shall answer you most readily. Your brother, Admiral Jones, was not in good health for about a year, but had not been so unwell as to keep house. For two months past he began to lose his appetite, to grow yellow, and show signs of the jaundice; for this he took medicine, and seemed to grow better; but about ten days before his death his legs began to swell, which increased upwards, so that two days before his exit he could not button his waistcoat, and had great difficulty of breathing.

" I visited him every day, and, beginning to be apprehensive of his danger, desired him to settle his affairs; but this he put off till the afternoon of his death, when he was prevailed on to send for a *notaire*, and made his will. Mr Beaupoil and myself witnessed it at about eight o'clock in the evening, and left him sitting in a chair. A few minutes after we retired he walked into his chamber, and laid himself upon his face, on the bed-side, with his feet on the floor; after the Queen's physician arrived, they went into the room, and found him in that position, and upon taking him up, they found he had expired.

" His disorder had terminated in dropsy of the breast. His body was put into a leaden coffin on the twentieth, that in case the United States, whom he had so essentially served, and with so much honour to himself, should claim his remains, they might be more easily removed. This is all, Madam, that I can say concerning his illness and death.

" I most sincerely condole with you, Madam, upon the loss of my dear and respectable friend, for whom I entertained the greatest affection, and as a proof of it, you may command the utmost exertion of my feeble abilities, which shall be rendered with cheerfulness.

"I have the honour to be,

"Madam,

"Your most obedient humble servant,

"S. Blackden."

The American Ambassador, Governor Morris, did not think it necessary to claim the remains of Admiral Jones, nor did the United States. As a protestant and heretic, it was still, we believe, necessary to obtain liberty of burial in consecrated ground, and this was probably done. The National Assembly paid his memory the honour of sending a deputation of twelve of their body to attend the funeral. He was buried at Paris on the 20th July, and the following funeral discourse was pronounced over his grave by Mr Marron, a protestant clergyman of Paris; busy faction at this period seizing this and every other occasion to promote its own interests:—

(Translation.)

" *Discourse pronounced by Mr Marron, officiating Protestant Clergyman, at the Funeral of Admiral Paul Jones, July 20, 1792, in Paris.*

" Legislators! citizens! soldiers! friends! brethren! and Frenchmen! we have just returned to the earth the remains of an illustrious stranger, one of the first champions of the liberty of America, of that liberty which so gloriously ushered in our own. The Semiramis of the north had drawn him under her standard, but Paul Jones could not long breathe the pestilential air of despotism; he preferred the sweets of a private life in France, now free, to the eclat of titles and of honours, which, from an *usurped throne*, were lavished upon him by Catharine. The fame of the brave outlives him, his portion is immortality. What more flattering homage could we pay to the manes of Paul Jones, than to swear on his tomb to live or to die free? It is the vow, it is the watch-word of every Frenchman.

"Let never tyrants, nor their satellites, pollute this sacred earth! May the ashes of the great man, too soon lost to humanity, and eager to be free, enjoy here an undisturbed repose! Let his example teach posterity the efforts which noble souls are capable of making, when stimulated by hatred to oppression. Friends and brethren, a noble emulation brightens in your looks; your time is precious, *the country is in danger!* Who amongst us would not shed the last drop of their blood to save it? Associate yourselves to the glory of Paul Jones, in imitating him in his contempt of dangers, in his devotedness to his country, in his noble heroism, which, after having astonished the present age, will continue to be the imperishable object of the veneration of future generations!"

(Translated from the French.)

"*Testament of Paul Jones, 18th July,* 1792.

"Before the undersigned notaries, at Paris, appeared Mr John Paul Jones, citizen of the United States of America, resident at present in Paris, lodged in the street of Tournon, No 42, at the house of Mr Dorberque, *huissier audiancier* of the tribunal of the third *arrondissement*, found in a parlour in the first storey above the floor, lighted by two windows opening on the said street of Tournon, sitting in an arm-chair, sick of body, but sound of mind, memory, and understanding, as it appeared to the undersigned notaries by his discourse and conversation,—

" Who, in view of death, has made, dictated, and worded, to the undersigned notaries, his testament as follows:—

" I give and bequeath all the goods, as well moveable as heritable, and all, generally, whatever may appertain to me at my decease, in whatever country they may be situated, to my two sisters, Janet, spouse to William Taylor, and Mary, wife to Mr Loudon, and to the children of my said sisters, to divide them into as many portions as my said sisters and their children shall make up individuals, and to be enjoyed by them in the following manner:—

" My sisters, and those of their children, who on the day of my death shall have reached the age of twenty-one, will enjoy their share in full property from the date of decease. As for those of my nephews and nieces who at that period of time may not reach the age of twenty-one years, their mothers will enjoy their shares till such time as they attain that said age, with charge to them to provide for their food, maintenance, and education; and as soon as any of my nephews or nieces will have reached the age of twenty-one years, the same will enjoy his share in full property.

"If one or more of my nephews and nieces should happen to die without children before having reached the age of twenty-one, the share of those of them who may have deceased shall be divided betwixt my said sisters and my other nephews and nieces by equal portions.

"I name the honourable Robert Morris, Esq. of Philadelphia, my only testamentary executor.

"I revoke all other testaments or codicils which I may have made before the present, which alone I stand by as containing my last will.

"So made, dictated, and worded, by said testator, to the said notaries undersigned, and afterwards read, and read over again to him by one of them, the other being present, which he well understood, and persevered in, at Paris, the year 1792, the 18th July, about five o'clock afternoon, in the room heretofore described, and the said testator signed the original of the present, unregistrated, at Paris the 25th September, 1792, by Defrance, who received one livre, provisionally, save to determine definitively the right after the declaration of the revenue of the testator. The original remained with Mr Pottier, one of the notaries at Paris, undersigned, who delivered these presents this day, 26th September, 1792, first of the French Republic.

" Pottier.

" (Signed) L'Avernier."

(Copy)

" *Schedule of the Property of Admiral John Paul Jones, as stated by him to me this 18th of July,* 1792.

" 1st, Bank stock in the Bank of North America, at Philadelphia, 6000 dollars, with sundry dividends.

" 2d, Loan-Office certificate left with my friend,

John Ross of Philadelphia, for 2000 dollars at par, with great arrearages of interest, being for ten or twelve years.

" 3d, Such balance as may be in the hands of my said friend, John Ross, belonging to me, and sundry effects left in his care.

" 4th, My lands in the State of Vermont.

" 5th, Shares in the Ohio Company.

" 6th, Shares in the Indiana Company.

" 7th, About L.1800 sterling due to me from Edward Bancroft, unless paid by him to Sir Robert Herries, and is then in his hands.

" 8th, Upwards of four years of my pension due from Denmark, to be asked from the Count de Bernstorf.

" 9th, Arrearages of my pay from the Empress of Russia, and all my prize-money.

" 10th, The balance due to me by the United States of America, and sundry claims in Europe, which will appear from my papers.

" This is taken from his mouth.

(Signed) " GOVR. MORRIS,

" Ambassador from the United States to the Court of France."

The manners and moral character of Paul Jones have been the frequent subject of discussion and of very contradictory statements. His professional talents and personal appearance are less the topics of dispute. It is agreed that he was about the middle size, slightly made, but active and agile, and in youth capable of considerable exertion and fatigue. In advancing life, though he continued equally hardy and active in his habits, it was the vehement, fiery spirit that o'erinformed its shattered tenement; and after almost every journey we find him suffering from cold and fatigue, or having serious illnesses. He was of the complexion usually united with dark hair and eyes, which his were; but his skin had become embrowned by exposure from boyhood to all varieties of weather and of climate. His physiognomical expression indicated that promptitude and decision in action which were striking characteristics of his mind. His bust is said to be a good likeness; his portrait, painted in America, and probably a very indifferent resemblance, exhibits a rather precise-looking little man. The style of the highly-powdered hair, or wig, would, however, convert Achilles himself into a pedant or a *petit-maître*.

In manners Paul Jones has been described by one party as stiff, finical, and conceited; by another as arrogant, brutal, and quarrelsome. The first statement may have some colour of truth, the last is impossible. He had reached manhood before he could have had much intercourse with polite society; and manners, formed so late in life on the fashionable models of Paris and Versailles, may have sat somewhat stiffly on the Anglo-American, who, in giving up his own republican simplicity, and professional openness and freedom, might not have acquired all the ease and grace, even if he did attain the elegance and polish of French manners; but his appearance and manners must have been those of a gentleman. *Mauvais ton*, to a certain degree, might have been tolerated in a seaman and a foreigner; but "rudeness, arrogance, and brutality," must have proved an effectual barrier of exclusion from those polite and courtly circles where Paul Jones was not only received but welcomed; and into which he made his own way, and maintained his place, long after he had lost the gloss and resistless attraction of novelty. The letter of Madame Rinsby, and other published documents, prove the footing he held in respectable French female society to his death, and are quite conclusive as to the propriety of his manners. He has again been described as "grossly ignorant." No one who pursues his career, or peruses his letters, can for a moment believe a charge so absurd. From his first appearance as a ship-boy he must have been set down as a very clever and promising lad; and if not a prodigy of learning, which was an impossibility, he had far more literature than was at all usual in his day, even in the very highest ranks of his profession. His verses are far from despicable. Baron Grimm, we think, overrates them, yet he was an admirable critic. They were found amusing and agreeable in polished society, which is the very best test and use of occasional verse, namely, of all such verse as the public can well spare, and his muse was humanizing to his own mind. We like his prose better than his verse. It is often admirable if struck off at one hit, particularly when the writer gets warm, and gives way to his feelings of indignation. It is said, that a minister, in reading the despatches of Lord Collingwood, who went to sea at twelve years of age, used to ask, "Where has Collingwood got his style ?—He writes better than any of us." With fully more propriety many of the members of Congress, so far as regarded their own compositions and *resolves*, might have put a similar question in relation to Paul Jones. He is allowed to have been kind and attentive to his crews, and generous and liberal in all pecuniary transactions of a private nature; though his correspondence shows that he was commendably tenacious of his pecuniary claims on states and public bodies. His memoirs afford some pleasing instances of his kindness to his prisoners, and of his desire to rescue them from the fangs of agents and commissaries. So far as discipline *descends*, Paul Jones was a rigid and strict disciplinarian. In his own person he appears to have been so impatient of all control and check as to be unfit for any regularly-organized service, though admirably adapted to the singular crisis at which he appeared. To his dress he was, or at least latterly became, so attentive as to have it remarked. It was a better trait that his ship was at all times remarkable for cleanliness and neatness, and for the same good order and arrangement which pervaded all his private affairs. He is said to have been fond of music, and to have performed himself.

The acute understanding of Paul Jones perpetually conflicting with his natural keenness and warmth of temper, gave at times the appearance of vacillation to his conduct, and the unpleasant and unwise alternation of bold defiance with undue submission. This is painfully conspicuous in his unhappy and heartbreaking connexion with Potemkin. On other occasions, as on the sailing of Landais in the mutiny, he showed a remarkable degree of self-command and forbearance. On many occasions he betrays the jealousy and dislike of England, which mark the half-conscious renegade. Franklin confines his vituperation to the Sovereign; Paul Jones extends it to the whole nation. The extravagant self-eulogium which so frequently obtrudes itself in his writing, and which must be very offensive to English readers, was, it should be recollected, generally called forth by peculiar circumstances. A man has every right to bring forward his services, when those who should remember appear disposed to forget them. Besides, what is here concentrated into two small volumes, was in reality diffused over the correspondence of twenty years of an active life. Boasting, for some reason which we leave to philosophy to investigate, appears an inherent quality in great naval commanders. Nelson, Rodney, Drake, were all, in one sense, arrant braggarts.

It is a less amiable trait in the character of Paul Jones, that we find him very frequently quarrelling with rival and associate commanders, and never once bestowing hearty cordial praise on any one of them. His avarice of fame, like the same vice of a more sordid kind, not only gave him the insatiable desire of accumulation, but tempted him, if not to defraud, at least to trench on the rights of others; and his hostility, though open, was often far from generous: yet his squabbles were wholly professional. In private life there appears to have been no reason to fasten on him the odious imputation of being quarrelsome, which some have attempted. He was fonder, not of glory alone, but of its trappings and badges, than quite became the champion of a republic, and the pupil of Franklin; but this is a mere subject of opinion. He may have considered these symbols as the seals with which Fame ratifies her bonds.

The moral character of Paul Jones, at all stages of his career, has been in this country the subject of violent abuse and of gross misrepresentation. If this has been done by Englishmen from a mistaken love of their country, they dishonour their country and themselves. If it is, as we hope, to be attributed to ignorance of facts, such statements should henceforth cease. The writer of this sketch by no means looks on the career of Paul Jones with Transatlantic eyes, nor views his character or attainments through the medium of Transatlantic partiality, as will be obvious to any one who pursues the course of this narrative. His political sins have been in no shape extenuated; and to the full extent of the evidence afforded by his papers—the best and only evidence now to be obtained—his moral delinquencies have been fairly unfolded. Judging by the ordinary averages of human conduct, they shrink into very small compass. His failings were precisely such as he must have been a moral monster to have escaped; they arose from his natural character and from his profession:—it is the utmost malice could say, and more than is warranted by truth, that he was

> "Jealous in honour; sudden and quick in quarrel:
> ——Seeking the bubble reputation
> Even in the cannon's mouth."

APPENDIX.*

B.

" *Particulars of the Engagement between the Bon Homme Richard and the Serapis, by Richard Dale, First Lieutenant of the Bon Homme Richard.*

" On the 23d of September, 1779, being below, was roused by an unusual noise upon deck. This induced me to go upon deck, when I found the men were swaying up the royal yards, preparatory to making sail for a large fleet under our lee. I asked the coasting pilot what fleet it was? He answered, ' The Baltic Fleet, under convoy of the Serapis of forty-four guns, and the Countess of Scarborough of twenty guns.' A general chase then commenced of the Bon Homme Richard, the Vengeance, the Pallas, and

* The charges against Landais (A.) have been omitted in the Appendix, as their substance is given in the text.

the Alliance—the latter ship being then in sight, after a separation from the squadron of nearly three weeks; but which ship, as usual, disregarded the signals of the Commodore. At this time our fleet headed to the northward with a light breeze, Flamborough-head being about two leagues distant. At seven *p. m.* it was evident the Baltic fleet perceived we were in chase, from the signal of the Serapis to the merchantmen to stand in shore. At the same time, the Serapis and Countess of Scarborough tacked ship and stood off shore, with the intention of drawing off our attention from the convoy. When these ships had separated from the convoy about two miles, they again tacked and stood in shore after the merchantmen. At about eight, being within hail, the Serapis demanded, 'What ship is that?' He was answered, 'I can't hear what you say.' Immediately after the Serapis hailed again, 'What ship is that? Answer immediately, or I shall be under the necessity of firing into you.' At this moment I received orders from Commodore Jones to commence the action with a broadside, which indeed appeared to be simultaneous on board both ships. Our position being to windward of the Serapis, we passed ahead of her, and the Serapis coming up on our larboard quarter, the action commenced abreast of each other. The Serapis soon passed ahead of the Bon Homme

Richard, and when he thought he had gained a distance sufficient to go down athwart the fore-foot to rake us, found he had not enough distance, and that the Bon Homme Richard would be aboard him, put his helm alee, which brought the two ships on a line; and the Bon Homme Richard having head-way, ran her bows into the stern of the Serapis. We had remained in this situation but a few minutes, when we were again hailed by the Serapis, 'Has your ship struck?' To which Captain Jones answered, 'I have not yet begun to fight.' As we were unable to bring a single gun to bear upon the Serapis, our top-sails were backed, while those of the Serapis being filled, the ships separated. The Serapis wore short round upon her heels, and her jib-boom ran into the mizen-rigging of the Bon Homme Richard; in this situation the ships were made fast together with a hawser, the bowsprit of the Serapis to the mizen-mast of the Bon Homme Richard, and the action recommenced from the starboard sides of the two ships. With a view of separating the ships, the Serapis let go her anchor, which manœuvre brought her head and the stern of the Bon Homme Richard to the wind, while the ships lay closely pressed against each other. A novelty in naval combats was now presented to many witnesses, but to few admirers. The rammers were run into the respective ships to enable the men to load, after the lower part of the Serapis had been blown away, to make room for running out their guns, and in this situation the ships remained until between ten and eleven o'clock *p. m.*, when the engagement terminated by the surrender of the Serapis.

"From the commencement to the termination of the action there was not a man on board of the Bon Homme Richard ignorant of the superiority of the Serapis, both in weight of metal and in the qualities of the crews. The crew of that ship were picked seamen, and the ship itself had been only a few months off the stocks; whereas the crew of the Bon Homme Richard consisted of part American, English, and French, and a part of Maltese, Portuguese, and Malays; these latter contributing, by their want of naval skill and knowledge of the English language, to depress rather than elevate a just hope of success in a combat under such circumstances. Neither the consideration of the relative force of the ships, the fact of the blowing up of the gun-deck above them, by the bursting of two of the eighteen-pounders, nor the alarm that the ship was sinking, could depress the ardour or change the determination of the brave Captain Jones, his officers and men. Neither the repeated broadsides of the Alliance, given with the view of sinking or disabling the Bon Homme Richard, the frequent necessity of suspending the combat to extinguish the flames, which several times were within a few inches of the magazine, nor the liberation, by the master-at-arms, of nearly 500 prisoners, could change or weaken the purpose of the American commander. At the moment of the liberation of the prisoners, one of them, a commander of a twenty-gun ship, taken a few days before, passed through the ports on board the Serapis, and informed Captain Pearson that if he would hold out only a little while longer, the ship along-side would either strike or sink, and that all the prisoners had been released to save their lives; the combat was accordingly continued with renewed ardour by the Serapis. The fire from the tops of the Bon Homme Richard was conducted with so much skill and effect as to destroy ultimately every man who appeared upon the quarter-deck of the Serapis, and induced her commander to order the survivors to go below. Nor even under shelter of the decks were they more secure. The powder-monkeys of the Serapis finding no officer to receive the eighteen-pound cartridges brought from the magazines, threw them on the main-deck, and went for more. These cartridges being scattered along the deck, and numbers of them broken, it so happened that some of the hand-grenades thrown from the main-yard of the Bon Homme Richard, which was direct over the main-hatch of the Serapis, fell upon this powder, and produced a most awful explosion. The effect was tremendous; more than twenty of the enemy were blown to pieces, and many stood with only the collars of their shirts upon their bodies. In less than an hour afterwards the flag of England, which had been nailed to the mast of the Serapis, was struck by Captain Pearson's own hand, as none of his people would venture aloft on this duty; and this too when more than 1500 persons were witnessing the conflict and the humiliating termination of it from Scarborough and Flamborough-head.

"Upon finding that the flag of the Serapis had been struck, I went to Captain Jones, and asked whether I might board the Serapis? to which he consented; and, jumping upon the gunwale, I seized the main-brace pennant, and swung myself upon her quarter-deck. Midshipman Mayant followed with a party of men, and was immediately run through the thigh with a boarding-pike by some of the enemy stationed in the waist, who were not informed of the surrender of the ship. I found Captain Pearson standing on the leeward side of the quarter-deck, and addressing myself to him, said,—'Sir, I have orders to send you on board the ship along-side.' The first lieutenant of the Serapis coming up at this moment, inquired of Captain Pearson whether the ship along-side had struck to him? To which I replied, 'No, Sir, the contrary; he has struck to us.' The lieutenant renewing his inquiry, 'Have you struck, Sir?' was answered, 'Yes, I have.' The lieutenant replied, 'I have nothing more to say;' and was about to return below, when I informed him he must accompany Captain Pearson on board the ship along-side. He said, 'If you will permit me to go below, I will silence the firing of the lower-deck guns.' This request was refused, and with Captain Pearson he was passed over to the deck of the Bon Homme Richard. Orders being sent below to cease firing, the engagement terminated, after a most obstinate contest of three hours and a half.

"Upon receiving Captain Pearson on board the Bon Homme Richard, Captain Jones gave orders to cut loose the lashings, and directed me to follow him with the Serapis. Perceiving the Bon Homme Richard leaving the Serapis, I sent one of the quarter-masters to ascertain whether the wheel-ropes were cut away, supposing something extraordinary must be the matter, as the ship would not pay off, although the head-sails were aback, and no after-sail; the quarter-master returning, reported that the wheel-ropes were all well, and the helm hard a-port. Excited by this extraordinary circumstance, I jumped off the binnacle, where I had been sitting, and, falling upon the deck, found, to my astonishment, I had the use of only one of my legs; a splinter of one of the guns had struck, and badly wounded my leg, without my perceiving the injury until this moment. I was replaced upon the binnacle, when the sailing-master of the Serapis, coming up to me, observed, that from my orders he judged I must be ignorant of the ship being at anchor. Noticing the second lieutenant of the Bon Homme Richard, I directed him to go below and cut away the cable, and follow the Bon Homme Richard with the Serapis. I was then carried on board the Bon Homme Richard to have my wound dressed."

C.

"FROM THE LONDON GAZETTE.

"*Manifesto.*

"GEORGE R.

"Through the whole course of our reign, our conduct towards the States General of the United Provinces has been that of a sincere friend and faithful ally. Had they adhered to those wise principles which used to govern the republic, they must have shown themselves equally solicitous to maintain the friendship which has so long subsisted between the two nations, and which is essential to the interests of both.—From the prevalence of a faction devoted to France, and following the dictates of that court, a very different policy has prevailed. The return made to our friendship, for some time past, has been an open contempt of the most solemn engagements, and a repeated violation of public faith.

" On the commencement of the defensive war, in which we found ourselves engaged by the aggression of France, we showed a tender regard for the interest of the States General, and a desire of securing to their subjects every advantage of trade, consistent with the great and just principle of our own defence. Our ambassador was instructed to offer a friendly negotiation, to obviate every thing that might lead to a disagreeable discussion; and to this offer, solemnly made by him to the States General, the 2d of November, 1778, no attention was paid.

" After the number of our enemies increased by the aggression of Spain, equally unprovoked with that of France, we found it necessary to call upon the States General for the performance of their engagements. The fifth article of the perpetual defensive alliance between our crown and the States General, concluded at Westminster the 3d of March, 1678, besides the general engagements for succours, expressly stipulates, ' That that party of the two allies that is not attacked shall be obliged to break with the aggressor in two months after the party attacked shall require it.' Yet two years have passed without the least assistance given to us,—without a single syllable in answer to our repeated demands.

" So totally regardless have the States been of their treaty with us, that they readily promised our enemies to observe a neutrality, in direct contradiction to those engagements; and whilst they have withheld from us the succours they were bound to furnish, every secret assistance has been given the enemy; and inland duties have been taken off, for the sole purpose of facilitating the carriage of naval stores to France.

" In direct and open violation of treaty, they suffered an American pirate to remain several weeks in one of their ports, and even permitted a part of his crew to mount guard in a fort in the Texel.

" In the East Indies the subjects of the States General, in concert with France, have endeavoured to raise up enemies against us.

" In the West Indies, particularly at St Eustatius, every protection and assistance has been given to our rebellious subjects. Three privateers* are openly received into the Dutch harbours, allowed to refit there, supplied with arms and ammunition, their crews recruited, their prizes brought in and sold; and all this in direct violation of as clear and solemn stipulations as can be made.

"This conduct, so inconsistent with all good faith, so repugnant to the sense of the wisest part of the Dutch nation, is chiefly to be ascribed to the prevalence of the leading magistrates of Amsterdam, whose secret correspondence with our rebellious subjects was suspected long before it was made known, by the fortunate discovery of a treaty, the first article of which is,—

"'There shall be a firm, inviolable, and universal peace, and sincere friendship, between their High Mightinesses the estates of the Seven United Provinces of Holland and the United States of North America, and the subjects and people of the said parties, and between the countries, islands, cities, and towns, situate under the jurisdiction of the said United States of Holland and the said United States of America, and the people and inhabitants thereof, of every degree, without exception of persons or places.'

"This treaty was signed in September, 1778,

* Paul Jones's squadron.

by the express order of the Pensionary of Amsterdam, and other principal magistrates of that city. They now not only avow the whole transaction, but glory in it, and expressly say, even to the States General, that what they did 'was what their indispensable duty required.'

"In the mean time the States General declined to give any answer to the memorial presented by our ambassador, and this refusal was aggravated by their proceeding upon other business, nay, upon the consideration of this very subject to internal purposes; and while they found it impossible to approve the conduct of their subjects, they still industriously avoided to give us the satisfaction so manifestly due.

"We had every right to expect that such a discovery would have roused them to a just indignation at the insult offered to us and to themselves, and that they would have been eager to give us full and ample satisfaction for the offence, and to inflict the severest punishment upon the offenders. The urgency of the business made an instant answer essential to the honour and safety of this country. The demand was accordingly pressed by our ambassador in repeated conferences with the ministers, and in a second memorial: it was pressed with all the sense of recent injuries, and the answer now given to a memorial on such a subject, delivered about five weeks ago, is, *That the States have taken it ad referendum.* Such an answer, upon such an occasion, could only be dictated by the fixed purpose of hostility meditated, and already resolved by the States, induced by the offensive councils of Amsterdam, thus to countenance the hostile aggression which the magistrates of that city have made in the name of the republic.

"There is an end of the faith of all the treaties with them, if Amsterdam may usurp the sovereign power, may violate those treaties with impunity, by pledging the States to engagements directly contrary, and leaguing the republic with the rebels of a sovereign to whom she is bound by the closest ties. An infraction of the law of nations by the meanest member of any country gives the injured State a right to demand satisfaction and punishment: how much more so, when the injury complained of is a flagrant violation of public faith, committed by leading and predominant members of the State? Since, then, the satisfaction we have demanded is not given, we must, though most reluctantly, do ourselves that justice which we cannot otherwise obtain; we must consider the States General as parties in the injury which they will not repair, as sharers in the aggression which they refuse to punish, and must act accordingly. We have, therefore, ordered our ambassador to withdraw from the Hague, and shall immediately pursue such vigorous measures as the occasion fully justifies, and our dignity and the essential interests of our people require.

"From a regard to the Dutch nation at large, we wish it were possible to direct those measures wholly against Amsterdam; but this cannot be, unless the States General will immediately declare that Amsterdam shall, upon this occasion, receive no assistance from them, but be left to abide the consequences of its aggression.

"Whilst Amsterdam is suffered to prevail in the general councils, and is backed by the strength of the state, it is impossible to resist the aggression of so considerable a part, without contending with the whole. But we are too sensible of the common interests of both countries, not to remember, in the midst of such a contest, that the only point to be aimed at by us, is to raise a disposition in the councils of the republic to return to our ancient union, by giving us that satisfaction for the past, and security for the future, which we shall be as ready to receive as they can be to offer, and to the attainment of which we shall direct all our operations. We mean only to provide for our own security, by defeating the dangerous designs that have been formed against us. We shall ever be disposed to return to friendship with the States General, when they sincerely revert to that system which the wisdom of their ancestors formed, and which has now been subverted by a powerful faction, conspiring with France against the true interests of the republic, no less than against those of Great Britain.

(Signed) " G. R.

" St James's, December 20, 1780."

THE END.

ERRATA.

Vol. I. p. 31, line 7 from bottom, for *Duncan* read *Dunmore*.
II. p. 30, line 10, and p. 95, line 5, for *Saporoses*, read *Zaporavians*.

Oliver & Boyd, Printers.